Linnæus Cumming

Electricity treated experimentally

For the use of schools and students

Linnæus Cumming

Electricity treated experimentally

For the use of schools and students

ISBN/EAN: 9783337214821

Printed in Europe, USA, Canada, Australia, Japan

Cover: Foto ©Paul-Georg Meister /pixelio.de

More available books at **www.hansebooks.com**

ELECTRICITY

TREATED EXPERIMENTALLY

FOR THE USE OF SCHOOLS AND STUDENTS

LINNÆUS CUMMING, M.A.
LATE SCHOLAR OF TRIN. COLL. CAMBRIDGE
ASSISTANT MASTER IN RUGBY SCHOOL

RIVINGTONS
WATERLOO PLACE, LONDON
MDCCCLXXXVI

PREFACE

THE author has endeavoured in this work to give the substance of experimental lectures delivered to some of the senior boys in Rugby School.

The course lasts for one school year, consisting of about seventy lessons, each of one hour. Of these about ten are devoted to testing the progress of the boys.

These lessons are educational, not technical; accordingly, ample explanation and numerous experiments are devoted to the principles of the science, while many applications claim but the briefest notice.

In every part of the subject quantitative measurement has been kept in view, and attention has been directed to the absolute system of measurement.

To understand certain instruments it is necessary to assume results obtained from theory. Articles in which such assumptions are made are marked with an asterisk (*), and may be passed over at the teacher's discretion. It is probably wiser, where possible, to defer them till the learner has gained some acquaintance with the theory, such as is afforded by the present author's *Introduction to the Theory of Electricity*.

It is assumed that, in teaching the subject, the apparatus is before the student, and not a mere diagram.

Articles referring to a few rather expensive pieces of apparatus have been marked with an asterisk, to suggest that they may be passed over in the absence of the apparatus.

Every experiment described has been performed by the author before his class with the apparatus shown, except in cases where reference is made to an historical experiment, not suited for class demonstration, or requiring instruments of higher power than those commonly in use.

The author wishes to record his thanks to his wife, and to G. C. Richards, Esq., of Balliol College, Oxford, who have made drawings, from the apparatus actually in use, for the woodcuts. His thanks are also due to his colleague, G. Stallard, Esq., who has read the whole of the proof-sheets and the MSS. of the portions referring to Chemical Science, making many valuable corrections and suggestions.

The numerical data are chiefly taken from S. Lupton's *Numerical Tables and Constants*, a most valuable small work of reference.

L. CUMMING.

RUGBY, 1886.

CONTENTS

BOOK I.—MAGNETISM.

CHAPTER I.—MAGNETS.

[*Pages* 1-12.]

Definition of Magnetism—Magnet Poles—North and South Poles of a Magnet—Action of Magnetic Poles on each other—Magnetism induced in Soft Iron—Induction by Induced Magnetism—Steel under Induction—Hypothesis of Magnetized Molecules—Magnetic Substance.—(SECT. 1 to 9.)

CHAPTER II.—FIELD OF MAGNETIC FORCE.

[*Pages* 13-32.]

Definition of a Field of Magnetic Force—Magnetic Force on a Pole at a Point—Lines of Force—Strength of Magnetic Field of a Single Pole, by Coulomb's Balance—Strength of Field by the Method of Oscillations—Strength of Magnetic Field by Method of Deviations—Comparison of Strength of two Magnet Poles—*Meaning of an Absolute System of Measurement—*Absolute Unit of Magnetism—Theories suggested by Experiment.—(SECT. 10 to 19.)

CHAPTER III.—METHODS OF MAGNETIZATION.

[*Pages* 33-37.]

Quality and Temper of Steel—Method of Single Touch—Method of Divided Touch—Method of Double Touch—Magnetic Battery—Magnetic Saturation—Retention of Magnetism.—(SECT. 20 to 26.)

CHAPTER IV.—TERRESTRIAL MAGNETISM.

[*Pages* 38–65.]

Field of Terrestrial Magnetic Force—Magnetic Elements of a Place—The Declinometer—The Dipping Needle—The Intensity—*Gauss' Method for Finding Intensity—*Magnetic Moment of a Maguet in Absolute Measure—Magnetic Elements of Greenwich—Changes in Elements—Relation to Aurora Borealis and to Solar Phenomena—Other Variations—Magnetic Charts—Isoclinal Chart—Isodynamic Chart—Isogonic Chart—Hypotheses of one or two Maguets — The Mariner's Compass—Effect of iron masses in Ships — Semicircular Variation — Quadrantal Variation — Magnetism of Steel-plated Ships—Questions on Book I.—(SECT. 27 to 48.)

BOOK II.—FRICTIONAL ELECTRICITY.

CHAPTER I.—ELECTRIFICATION.

[*Pages* 67–80.]

Definition of Electricity—Means of detecting Electricity—Action of Electrified Bodies on each other—Vitreous and Resinous Electricity—Conductors and Non-Conductors—Effect of Damp or Dry Atmosphere — Gold-Leaf Electroscope—Development of the two Electricities, simultaneous and in equal quantities—The Electrical Series—Electrification by Pressure and Cleavage — Pyro-Electricity.—(SECT. 49 to 59.)

CHAPTER II.—THE FIELD OF ELECTRIC FORCE.

[*Pages* 81–97.]

The Electric Field—Coulomb's Torsion Balance—Law of Action at different Distances—Law of Action with different Quantities—*Absolute Measure of Electricity—Use of Proof-Plane—No Electricity within a hollow Conductor—Electrical Density—Electrical

Contents.   ix

Potential—Capacity of a Conductor—Potential Experiments with the Gold-Leaf Electroscope—Electrical Force requires varying Potential.—(SECT. 60 to 71.)

CHAPTER III.—ELECTRICAL INDUCTION.

[*Pages* 98–121.]

Electrification induced on an Insulated Conductor—Induction on a Body connected with the Earth—Electroscope charged by Induction—Faraday's Ice-pail Experiment—The Earth our Zero of Potential—*Potential in Absolute Measure—*Absolute Measure of Potential at a Point in the Field—*Equipotential Surfaces—*Application to a Sphere—Electrification of two Parallel Plates, one initially charged—The Leyden Jar—Volta's Condensing Electroscope—*Discharge by Alternate Contacts—Specific Inductive Capacity—Condition of the Dielectric in a Leyden Jar—Faraday's Theory of Induction.—(SECT. 72 to 87.)

CHAPTER IV.—ELECTRICAL MACHINES.

[*Pages* 122–149.]

The Cylinder Machine—The Plate Machine—The Electrophorus—The Voss or Wimshurst Machine—*The Holtz Machine—Experiments with the Electrical Machine—Experiments with a Leyden Jar Battery—Chemical Decompositions by the Machine discharge.—(SECT. 88 to 95.)

CHAPTER V.—ABSOLUTE MEASURE OF ELECTRICITY.

[*Pages* 150–169.]

The Unit Jar, and Experiments with it—*Theory of Thomson's Electrometers—*The Absolute Electrometer—*The Portable Electrometer—*The Quadrant Electrometer—*The Gauge—*The Replenisher—*Uses of Quadrant Electrometer—Questions on Book II,—(SECT. 96 to 103).

BOOK III.—VOLTAIC ELECTRICITY.

CHAPTER I.—THE BATTERY.

[*Pages* 171–189.]

Electrical Conditions of a Zinc-Copper Couple—Chemical Conditions of the Cell—Thermal Condition of the Cell—Source of Energy of the Current—Local Action—Action of Evolved Hydrogen—Smee's Cell—The Bichromate Cell—Daniell's Cell—Grove's and Bunsen's Cells—Leclanché's Cell—Marie Davy's Cell—Becquerel's Cell—Electromotive Force—Battery arranged in Simple Circuit—Battery arranged in Compound Circuit—Frictional Electricity obtained from a Battery—Comparison of Frictional with Voltaic Electricity—Dry Piles.—(SECT. 104 to 122.)

CHAPTER II.—ELECTROLYSIS.

[*Pages* 190–214.]

Phenomena of the Current—Direction of the Current—Electrolysis of Potassium Iodide—Electrolysis of Water—Electrolysis of Hydrogen Chloride—Secondary action in Decomposition of Sulphates, etc.—Potassium set free by Electrolysis—Faraday's Terminology for Electrolysis—Quantity of Ions separated by the same current—Electro-Chemical Equivalents—Battery obeys the Laws of Electrolysis—E.M.F. necessary for Electrolysis—*E.M.F. measured thermally—Hypothesis of Molecular Electrification—Grotthüs' Hypothesis—Polarisation of Electrodes—Grove's Gas Battery, and Ritter's Secondary Pile—Polarisation the test of an Electrolyte—Planté's and Faure's Cells—Electro-metallurgy—Nobili's Rings—The Lead Tree.—(SECT. 123 to 144.)

CHAPTER III.—OHM'S LAW.

[*Pages* 215–250.]

Ohm's Law—Measurement of Resistance—*Potential Gradient—Oersted's Experiment: Galvanometers—The Tangent Galvanometer—Sine Galvanometer—Astatic Galvanometer—The Mirror

Galvanometer—Magnetic action of a Current in a Liquid—Units employed in Voltaic Electricity—Illustrations of Ohm's Law—Experimental Determination of Battery Resistance—Resistance of the Galvanometer—To find the Resistance of a given Wire Coil—Relation of Resistance to Dimensions of Conductor: Specific Resistance—Application of Ohm's Law to Simple Circuit—Application of Ohm's Law to a Compound Circuit—Application of Ohm's Law to a Mixed Circuit—*Arrangement of Battery for the Greatest Current—Method of changing rapidly the Battery arrangement—Measurement of E.M.F. by Galvanometer—Laws of Divided Currents—Galvanometer Shunts—Thermal Effects of a Current in the Conductor—*Measure of Heating Effect.—(SECT. 145 to 169.)

CHAPTER IV.—WHEATSTONE'S BRIDGE.

[*Pages* 251-258.]

Theory of the Bridge—*Use of the Bridge to find the Resistance of a Coil—*Method of Finding Galvanometer Resistance—*Method of Finding Battery Resistance—*Method of Comparing the E.M.F. of Cells.—(SECT. 170 to 174.)

CHAPTER V.—ELECTRO-MAGNETISM AND ELECTRO-DYNAMICS.

[*Pages* 259-318.]

Bertins' Commutator—Magnetic Field of a Straight Current—Rotation of a Magnet Pole round a Current—Rotation of a Current round a Magnet Pole — Movement of Current in a Magnetic Field—Methods of Suspending Currents—Effects of Terrestrial Magnetism on Moveable Currents—Magnetic Properties of a Closed Circuit carrying a Current—*Distinction between a Voltaic Circuit and a Magnetic Shell—*Absolute Electro-magnetic Units—Attractions and Repulsions of Parallel and Inclined Currents (Electro-Dynamics)—Action of an Infinite Current on another wholly on one side—Equivalence of a Sinuous and Straight Current—*The

Magnetic Field inside a Solenoid—Electro-Magnets—Paramagnetic and Diamagnetic Substances—Electro-magnetic Toys—Electromotors—The Electric Bell—The Electric Telegraph—The Line for Land or Marine Telegraph—The Battery—The Single Needle Telegraph Communicator—The Single Needle Indicator—Arrangement of Apparatus at Telegraph Station—Codes of Telegraph Signals—*The Morse Key—*The Morse Indicator—*The Morse Relay—*The Morse Sounder—*Electrostatic Induction in Cables—*Thomson's Marine Galvanometer—*Thomson's Syphon Recorder—*Step by Step, or ABC Telegraph—*Ampère's Theory of Magnetism—Reiss's Telephone.—(SECT. 175 to 210.)

CHAPTER VI.—CURRENT INDUCTION.

[*Pages* 319-365.]

Work done in the Electro-magnetic Field at Expense of the Current—*Theoretical Explanation of foregoing Experiment—Induced Currents—Current induced in a Coil by a Moving Pole—Reversal of Barlow's Wheel—Currents induced by Terrestrial Magnetism—Current induced by Moving Parallel Conductors—Currents induced by Changes in Strength of the Magnetic Field—Currents induced in Electromotors—The extra Current, or Galvanic Spark—Lenz's Law—Currents induced in Solid Conductors moved in the Magnetic Field—Clark's Magneto-electric Machine, or Dynamo—Siemens' Armature—The Gramme Machine—The Incandescent Electric Lamp—The Arc Lamp—Source of the Voltaic Arc—Arrangement of Arc Lamps—Jablokoff Candle—Induction Coils—Experiments with the Induction Coil—Discharge through Rarefied Gas—Graham Bell's Telephone—The Microphone—Questions on Book III.—(SECT. 211 to 235.)

BOOK IV.—THERMO-ELECTRICITY.

[*Pages* 367-379.]

Definition of Thermo-Electricity — Elementary Experiments — The Thermopile—Thermo-electric Power and Diagram—E.M.F. of

Thermo-electric Currents—Thermo-electric Diagrams for Higher Temperatures—Thermo-electric Currents in Circuits of one Metal —*The Peltier Effect—*Theoretical Measure of the E.M.F. of a Thermo-electric Couple—*The Thomson Effect—Thermo-electric Batteries—Questions on Book IV.—(SECT. 236 to 246.)

APPENDIX I.—ABSOLUTE UNITS IN C.S.G. SYSTEM.

[*Pages* 381–388.]

Units and Measures—Fundamental Units—Mechanical Units.—(SECT. 247 to 249.)

APPENDIX II.

[*Page* 389.]

Table of Natural Sines and Tangents of Angles for each Degree.

xii

BOOK I.
MAGNETISM.

CHAPTER I.
MAGNETS.

1. Definition of Magnetism.—Magnetism is defined as the property of attracting small masses of iron, possessed by various compounds of iron which are called Magnets. The ancients were acquainted with this property in a certain iron ore obtained from Magnesia, in Asia Minor, whence the name Magnetism is derived. This magnetic iron ore, or Magnetite (denoted by the chemical formula Fe_3O_4), occurs very widely disseminated through the earth, and in various parts, as in Sweden, forms massive beds, which are a very valuable source of iron. Though always acted on powerfully by other magnets, it does not itself always possess magnetic power. The most powerful native magnets are obtained from Siberia and from the Hartz Mountains. These magnets are usually called *natural*, to distinguish them from *artificial* magnets, which are made of tempered steel, magnetised either by rubbing with a natural magnet, or by one of a variety of methods described hereafter. These are in the form of straight, rectangular or lozenge-shaped bars, or else of bars bent into a horse-shoe form.

A

2. Magnet Poles.—If a natural magnet be sprinkled with iron filings, the filings are observed to cling more abundantly on two opposite faces than elsewhere. In the case

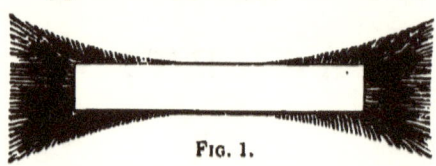

FIG. 1.

of a bar magnet, as in the figure, the iron filings remain clinging only to the ends, and to parts very near to the ends. The ends of the bar, in which the magnetic power seems to be concentrated, are spoken of as the *poles* of the magnet. The straight line drawn from pole to pole is the axis of the magnet, and the plane which bisects the axis at right angles is its equatorial plane, or equator.

3. North and South Poles of a Magnet.—If either a natural or artificial magnet be poised on a point, or suspended by a silk fibre in a paper stirrup (Fig. 2), so as to be free to move in a horizontal plane, it will be observed always to come to rest with its axis in a certain definite direction.[1] Except in very high latitudes, one (and always the same) pole will point more or less towards the north, and the other towards the south. This property leads us to a convenient mode of distinguishing the two poles of a magnet, calling that which is directed towards the north the *north* (or better, the *north-*

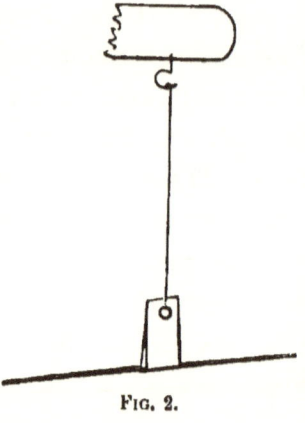

FIG. 2.

[1] This direction is called the Magnetic Meridian.

seeking) pole and the opposite, the *south* or *south-seeking* pole. They are also sometimes distinguished as blue and red poles, or as positive and negative poles. This constancy of direction in a freely-suspended magnet has led to its use in Europe since the twelfth century, and from much earlier times by the Chinese, for directing the course in navigation. On this account the magnet is called the loadstone (more correctly spelt lodestone), from an Anglo-Saxon word denoting to lead. The poles in bar magnets are distinguished by engraving either a line or the letter "N" near the north pole (Fig. 3).

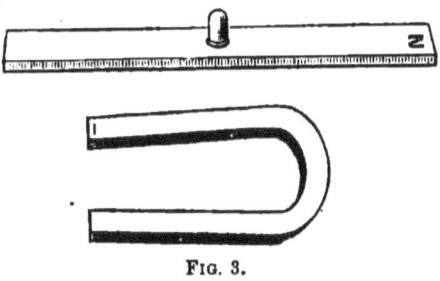

FIG. 3.

4. Action of Magnetic Poles on each other.—We have seen that the poles of a magnet differ from each other in their behaviour under the action of the earth. We now naturally inquire what is the action of the poles of two different magnets on each other. Suspend one magnet freely, having marked its poles; approach towards its poles (Fig. 4) in succession one (say the north) pole of another magnet.. When the north pole is presented towards the north pole of the suspended magnet it will be repelled, and if presented towards the south pole it will be attracted. If, on the other hand, the south pole be presented to the north pole of the suspended magnet it will be attracted, and if the south pole be presented to the south pole it will be repelled. Hence we learn that while both poles have the same power of attracting soft iron, they behave in opposite ways towards the poles of another magnet—like poles repelling, but unlike poles attract-

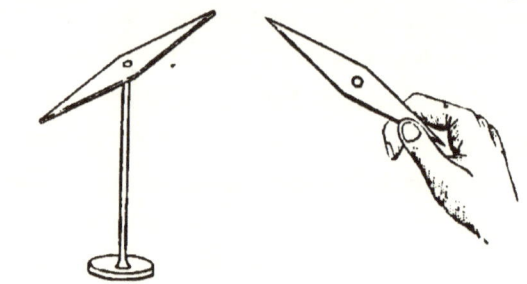

Fig. 4.

ing each other. This property affords a delicate means of detecting feeble magnetization. A long light magnet, supported in a paper stirrup and suspended by a few fibres of cocoon silk (see Fig. 2), is easily deflected from its normal direction. If on presenting the same part of a body to the alternate ends we find one pole attracted and the other repelled, we may conclude that the body is magnetized, the magnet's behaviour towards it showing the name of the pole used.

5. Magnetism induced in Soft Iron.—If we take a bar of annealed or soft iron and present it to the pole of a

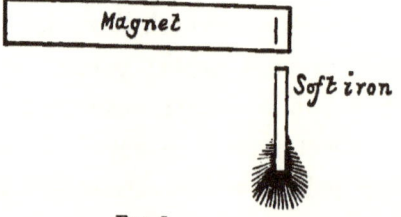

Fig. 5.

magnet, the magnet, if sufficiently powerful, will pick it up and support its weight. If while one end adheres to a pole of the magnet the other end be dipped in iron filings, they will be found to cling to it, just as if it were a magnet (Fig. 5). On removing the magnet the iron filings will nearly all instantly fall off. This magnetism, which exists temporarily in soft iron when in contact with a magnet, is called induced magnetism, the magnet on whose influence it depends being called the inducing magnet. It will be found that actual contact is not necessary, as magnetism is induced in the iron when the magnet is not in actual contact, but at a considerable distance from the bar. The distribution of induced magnetism is easily seen to be exactly similar to that of ordinary magnetism in the magnet; for if the iron under induction of a magnet pole, at a small distance from one of its

FIG. 6.

ends, be sprinkled with iron filings and be lifted up, the iron filings will cling near the ends and fall off near the middle (Fig. 6). It might easily be inferred from the attraction of the magnet pole for the iron bar, that the pole nearest to the inducing pole is of opposite name and the more remote pole of the same name. That this is the case may be shown (Fig. 7) by presenting one end of a long bar of soft iron (A) to the north pole of a suspended magnet (B), placed at such a distance as to produce merely a slight attractive deflection from MM', the Magnetic Meridian. On presenting the north pole of a magnet (C) to the more remote end of the iron bar, the former attraction becomes a strong repulsion. This might apparently be due to the repulsive action of the north pole (C) itself, but on removing the iron bar (A), keeping the magnet

(*C*) in position, the suspended magnet will fall back almost into its normal position. The large magnet (*D*) is placed to steady the movements of the suspended needle in the experiment. These two experiments prove that, under induction of a magnet pole, the part of a soft iron bar nearest to the inducing pole acquires polarity of opposite name, while the part farthest away acquires polarity of the same name. This

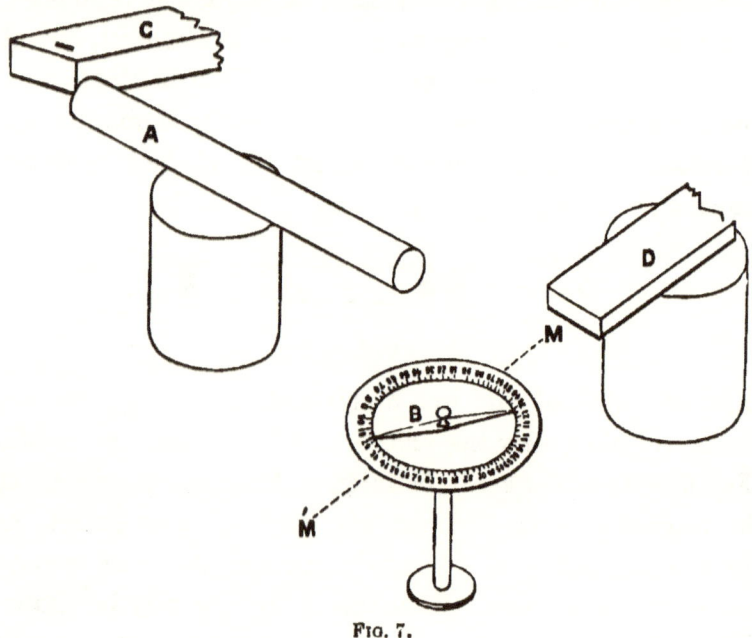

FIG. 7.

can be illustrated by observing the behaviour, under induction, of pieces of iron of various shapes, with one or more magnet poles variously disposed round them. If, for example, a north magnet pole be presented to the middle of a bar, the central part becomes a south pole, and each of the ends a north pole (Fig. 8). If presented to the base of a piece of iron shaped like the letter Y, the extremities of the fork become north poles. If presented to the centre of a star-shaped piece of metal (Fig. 9), each point becomes a north pole. The disposition of the poles is at once seen on dipping

Fig. 8.   Fig. 9.

the body under induction into iron filings and lifting it out, when the filings will be found clinging at each of the various poles.

6. Induction by Induced Magnetism.—It is easy to show that induced magnetic poles have the power of inducing magnetism in other iron bars brought under their influence. If a series of iron bars be arranged end to end, in contact or with space between them (Fig. 10), and a strong magnet pole

Fig. 10.

be brought near one end, the opposite end will be found to be magnetic, having the power of picking up iron filings, and of exerting attraction or repulsion on other poles. If a magnet be drawn slowly through a number of short pieces of iron wire or carpenter's brads (Fig. 11), they will be found to arrange themselves in strings, end to end, each in turn being a magnet, and inducing magnetism in the brad immediately next to it. Of course the length of the string of brads drawn after the pole depends on the strength of the inducing pole. The same explanation applies to the brush-like appearance of the filaments of iron filings round the poles of a magnet, each filing being a magnet and inducing magnetism in the one next it, the terminal pole of each filament being of the same name, and therefore repelling all the other terminal poles around it, thus preventing the neighbouring filaments from falling together.

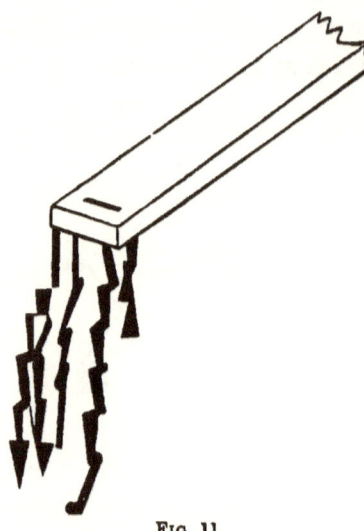

FIG. 11.

7. Steel under Induction.—If, instead of a piece of soft iron we take a piece of unannealed iron, or better, a piece of tempered steel, we notice a remarkable difference in its susceptibility to magnetic induction. Choose, for example, a piece of soft iron wire, and a knitting-needle of about the same dimensions; on dipping them alternately in iron filings, and presenting the pole of a magnet to the opposite end, the mass of iron filings lifted by the iron wire will be found to be many times greater than the mass lifted by the knitting-needle; but on removing the inducing magnet all the filings will fall away from the iron, while most of them will be retained by the knitting-needle. Further, if the knitting-needle be brought down on to the magnet pole with a smart tap, or hammered when under induction, its magnetic power will be very much increased, and will be almost wholly retained when removed from the inducing magnet. This property of tempered steel is usually expressed by saying that steel possesses a *coercive* force which is absent in soft iron, in virtue of which steel cannot at once take up the magnetic condition when placed under magnetic induction, but having once taken it up retains it for ever. Soft iron on the other hand, owing to the absence of coercive force, takes up the magnetic condition at once, and loses it as rapidly when the inducing magnet is removed. It should be borne in mind that there is no such thing in natural or artificial products as soft iron or hard steel which strictly obeys the laws as stated above, all the varieties of iron and steel being intermediate in their behaviour between those two ideal limits—all soft iron retaining a fraction of the magnetism induced in it, and all hard steel being to some extent susceptible of temporary magnetization under induction.

This explains the observation that the pole of a strong magnet attracts either pole of a weak magnet when brought sufficiently near to it. The strong magnet here acts by induction on the weak, and the induced magnetism of opposite name to the inducing pole overpowers the like permanent magnetism, and converts repulsion into attraction. Hence in experiments on weak magnetism, it is necessary to observe the *first* movement of the suspended magnet, as the feeble pole approaches it. The same explanation applies to the use of *armatures* or *keepers*, that is bars of soft iron which are made to lie across between opposite poles when magnets are packed away (Fig. 12). Each armature becomes by induction a magnet, and acts back by induction on the magnet poles to which it owes its magnetic character, tending to prevent their magnetism from dissipating under accidental jars or the induction of neighbouring magnets. It is even possible to increase considerably the magnetism in a weakened horse-shoe magnet by simply drawing the armature several times gently across the poles, removing it at each stroke.

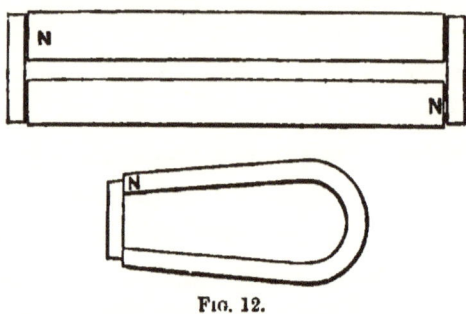

Fig. 12.

8. Hypothesis of Magnetized Molecules.—We will now inquire whether the two magnetisms developed at and near the ends of a magnet are wholly confined to those parts. To answer this question we will break a magnet in halves. The knitting-needle magnetized in a previous experiment will answer well, and can be at once snapped in two when held in a pair of pincers. On performing the experiment, we find

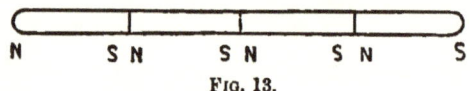

Fig. 13.

that each half has all the properties of a complete magnet; two new poles of opposite name having been developed on opposite sides of the division. This experiment may be repeated to an indefinite extent, and we shall still find the smallest fragments into which a magnet can be divided to be magnetic in the same direction as the original magnet (Fig. 13). We infer that even the smallest molecules into which the magnet can be divided will be magnetic also, and that a bar magnet is an assemblage of such molecules, each of which is a magnet endowed with its opposite poles; the poles of the molecular magnet being arranged as in Fig 14, and the magnetic properties of the magnet being due to the resultant of such a system of magnetic forces.

$$N\{\overline{\underline{= = = = = = = = = = = =}}\}S$$
$$\overline{NS}\ \overline{NS}\overline{NS}\ \overline{NS}\ \overline{NS}\ \overline{NS}\ \ \overline{NS}\ \overline{NS}\ \overline{NS}\ \overline{NS}\ \overline{NS}\ \overline{NS}$$

Fig. 14.

If we have two altogether equal magnets, and place their opposite poles in contact, such an arrangement is exactly equivalent to a magnet of double the length of either magnet; the two opposite poles when placed in contact each neutralising the other's effect on all external magnetism. If we apply this principle to the molecular magnets of Fig. 14, all of which we suppose for a moment, of exactly equal magnetic strength, we shall have equal and opposite poles in contact along the whole length of the magnet mutually neutralising each other, and *free* magnetism confined to the ends of the magnet.[1]

If we next assume that the magnetic strength of the successive molecules falls off as we get near the ends of the magnet, we have the free magnetism distributed along the magnet to some distance from the ends; and that appears to be at any rate a fair mental picture of the actual distribution of magnetism in a magnet. If we would form a picture of the state of the magnet before magnetization, we may assume either that the molecules are without magnetism till brought under induction, or that the molecules already magnetized

---

[1] By *free*, we mean magnetism not neutralised by opposite magnetism in adjacent molecules, and therefore free to act on other magnetism at a distance from it.

have their magnetic axes directed in all sorts of directions (see Fig. 15), so as to neutralise each other's action. The

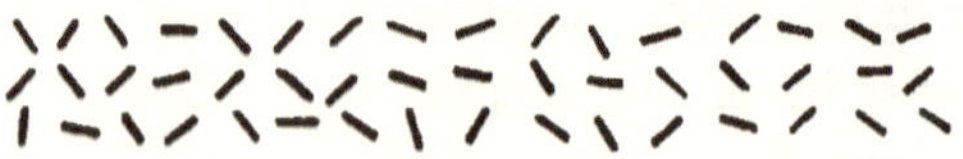

FIG. 15.

process of magnetization then consists in giving the molecules a twist, which brings all their magnetic axes into the same direction, namely that of magnetization. In the case of soft iron this magnetic twist is brought about at once on applying the Inducing Magnet; but in the case of steel there is a greater molecular rigidity, which can only be overcome by the magnetic force when the molecules are in a state of vibration among themselves. This may be illustrated by a glass tube containing iron or steel filings. If the pole of a magnet be drawn along the tube always in the same direction, several times, it will be found to have become a magnet, showing polarity like a feeble bar magnet. On shaking up the filings all trace of magnetism disappears.

These considerations however, belong to hypotheses incapable of direct verification by experiment, whose further consideration had better be deferred till the student has gained a more complete knowledge of experimental details.

9. Magnetic Substance.—It has been shown by Faraday, with the help of very powerful magnets, that almost all substances are susceptible of magnetic influence, but the only substances besides the various compounds of iron, which show magnetic properties under the action of our ordinary magnets, are the metals nickel and cobalt.

CHAPTER II.

FIELD OF MAGNETIC FORCE.

10. Definition of a Field of Magnetic Force.—We have seen that any body possessing induced or permanent magnetism, when brought into the neighbourhood of a bar magnet or any distribution of magnets, experiences mechanical force. It is usual therefore to refer to the space surrounding any distribution of magnetism as a Field of Magnetic Force.

We have also seen that every magnet has two kinds of magnetism developed, each nearly concentrated in a pole. The forces experienced by any magnetized body (suppose for simplicity a thin bar magnet) will therefore usually consist of two forces acting at its two ends, which may be combined into a single resultant force and couple, on ordinary mechanical principles. Before we can find this resultant we must know the action on each pole, at its own place in the magnetic field. To do this might seem impossible, as we cannot separate the north pole from the south, and experiment with each separately. We are able in effect to do exactly this, owing to the fact that the force falls off rapidly as the distance increases, so as to become almost or quite insensible at very moderate distances. If then we choose a long magnet for exploring the field, we can place its more remote pole in such a position that the whole observed force is sensibly, though not accurately, that due to the nearer pole. For we cannot observe with absolute accuracy, and we can easily make the error produced by the distant pole less than that inseparable from our rough methods of observation.

11. Magnetic Force on a Pole at a Point.—Guided by this principle, we proceed now to consider the force experienced by a magnetic pole placed in a given position in a magnetic field. To define a force we require to know three things—the point of application, the direction of action, and the magnitude.

1. *The Point of Application.*—Since in any actual magnet the free magnetism is distributed over a finite portion of the magnet, it might seem that there was no *point* of application of the magnetic force. If, however, we choose a thin and evenly magnetized needle, there will be a certain centre of magnetism very near to the actual end of the magnet, such that the action of the field on the total magnetism is appreciably the same as if it were all concentrated at that point. This centre of magnetism should of course be defined as the physical pole of the magnet. It is scarcely necessary to point out its analogy to the centre of gravity of a material body. We shall in future consider the force on a pole as acting on the total quantity of magnetism concentrated in the pole.

2. *The Direction.*—At each point in the field there will be a certain direction in which a pole will be urged when placed there, the directions being exactly opposite for a north and south pole. These directions are spoken of as the Line of Force through the point in the field, and we may conceive the field mapped out into lines of force; the direction of the line at each point showing the direction in which a magnet pole, if placed at that point, would be urged. It is also clear that two of these lines of force can never intersect (except in a

pole), since we should have in that case two directions in which the force would urge the pole, and this we know to be mechanically impossible. We may further define the positive direction of a line of force as that in which a north (or +) pole would be urged, and the negative direction as that in which a south (or −) pole would be urged.

3. *The Magnitude.*—To determine this we must measure the force with which a certain pole, which we choose as our standard, is urged along the line of force. This may of course be measured, like a statical force in pounds, grains or grams, according to the system of weights and measures we choose to employ. This force, when measured in suitable units, is generally called the strength of the field at the given point.

12. **Lines of Force.**—To exhibit the lines of force due to a system of magnetic poles in one plane, the best method is to lay a sheet of paper or thin card-board over the poles and sprinkle it with iron filings from a sieve. On gently tapping the paper or card the filings arrange themselves along lines of force. Each separate filing becomes, under induction, a magnet, and as the paper is tapped, it settles down with its north pole in the + direction and its south pole in the − direction. These poles exercise their attractions on other filings near them, and we have at last continuous strings of filaments, giving us a vivid picture of the lines of force. These pictures may be made permanent by pouring over them a weak solution of gum, by which each filing is held in its place; or by a solution of potassium cyanide, which causes under each iron filament a deposit of Prussian blue. For this purpose the paper should be laid on a sheet of glass.

We may experiment with a single pole for magnetic system

by placing a long magnet vertical, using only its upper pole. We then notice that the lines of force are in the form of straight lines radiating from a point (Fig. 16).

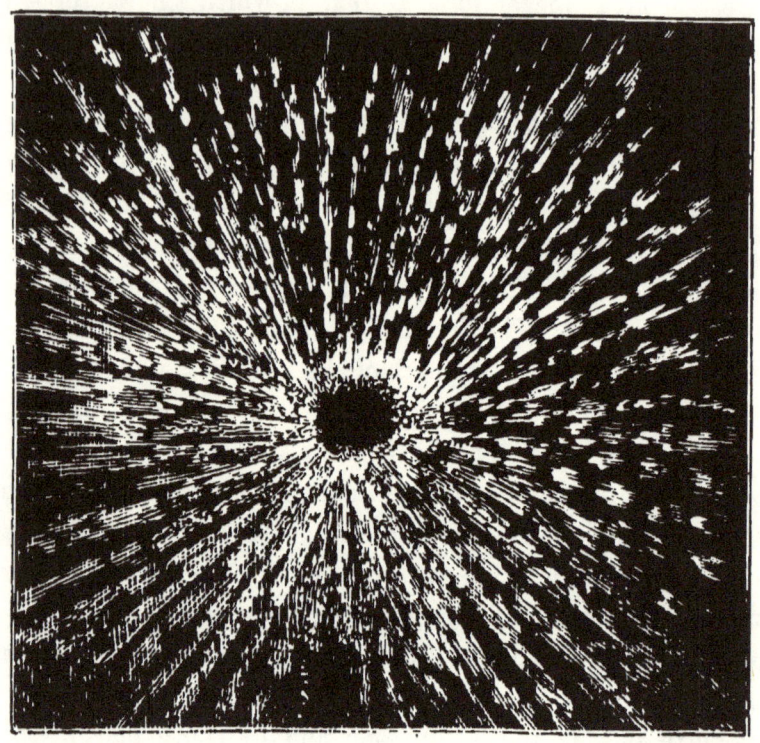

Fig. 16.

In an ordinary bar magnet, laid horizontally under the paper, the lines of force emanate chiefly from the poles (Fig. 17), forming oval curves between them. Theoretically, in a simple bar magnet we should expect all the lines of force to go from one pole to the other, but in an ordinary magnet the free magnetism along the edges causes some of the lines not to proceed directly from the poles, but always from north-polar to south-polar magnetism, as may be seen on examining the figure.

In the system consisting of two poles of like name, the lines emanate from each pole but do not intersect, all approaching towards the equatorial plane of the system without meeting it—this plane being, in mathematical language, an asymptote to the system of lines.

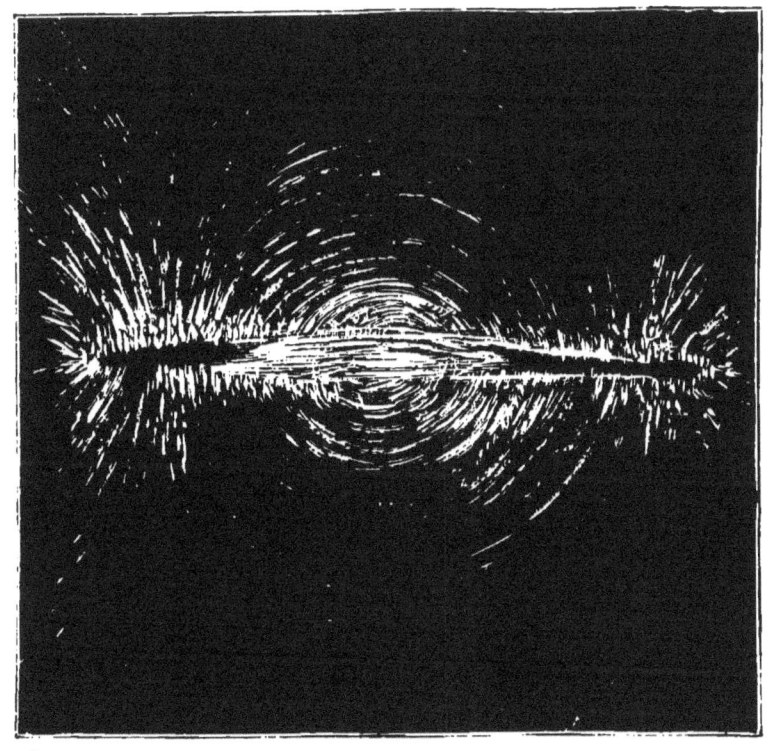

Fig. 17.

In like manner can also be shown the polarity of an iron bar under induction of two opposite or like poles near its ends. Fig. 19 shows the lines of force in a system consisting of two opposite magnet poles and a bar of iron between them.

If, as sometimes happens in a magnet, intermediate poles

by intention or accident have been developed, these are at once shown by the behaviour of the iron filings.

It is instructive to notice that in all these cases the direction of the line of force is the direction of the resultant of a system of forces acting from each pole of the system. Thus

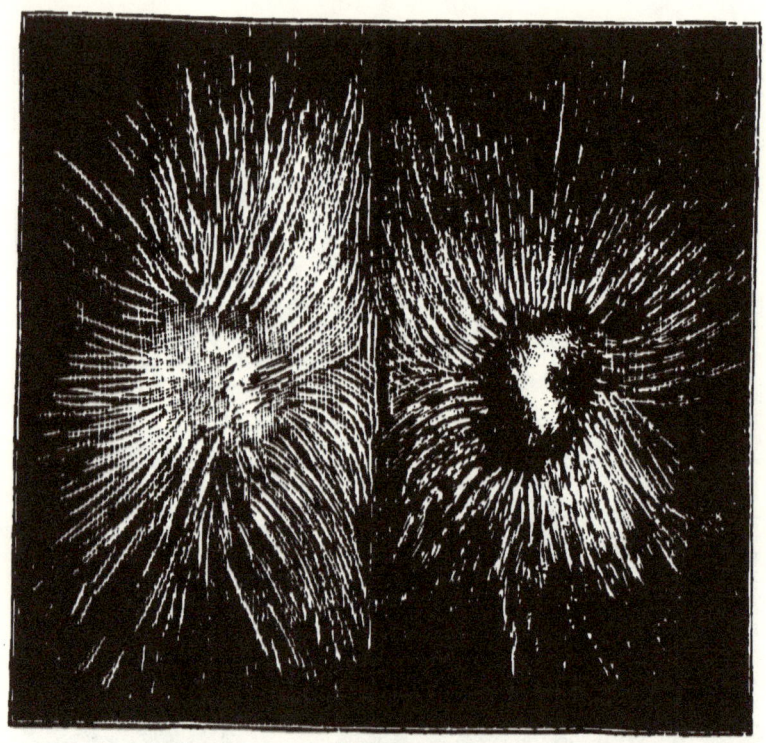

FIG. 18.

in a single bar magnet, AB in Fig. 20, the line of force PF at P will be found by compounding forces in the directions AP and PB, directed respectively from the north and towards the south poles.

13. Strength of Magnetic Field of a Single Pole, by Coulomb's Balance.—We are now in a position to

Chap. II.] *Field of Magnetic Force.* 19

compare the strength of the magnetic field at different points in it. This was originally done by Coulomb for a single pole,

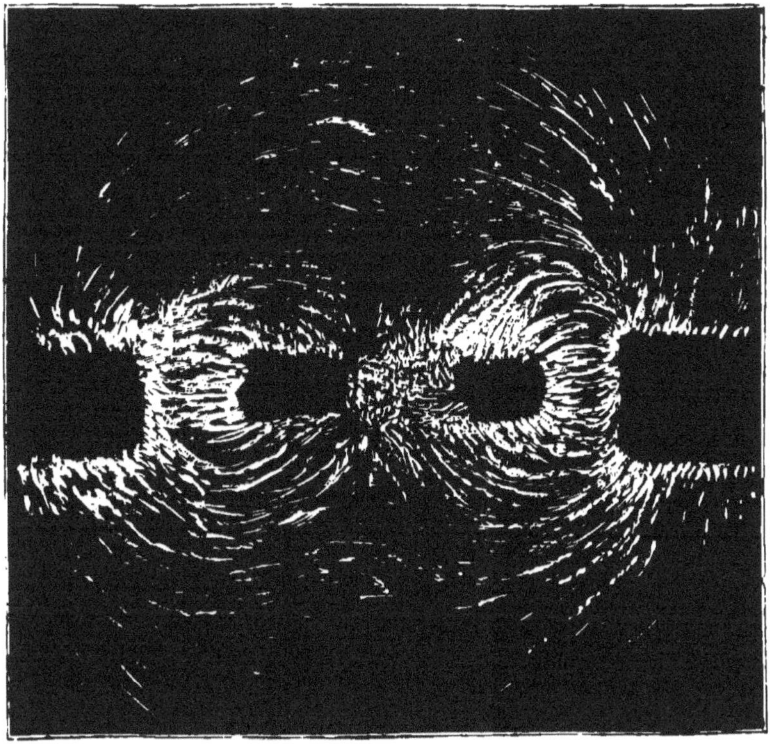

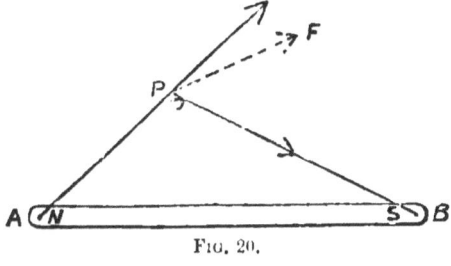

Fig. 19.

Fig. 20.

by means of the Torsion Balance (Fig. 21). It consists essentially of three parts—(1.) A long thin magnetic needle, *A*, evenly magnetized and suspended, so as to swing in a horizontal plane by a fine silver wire, which is attached above to a Torsion Circle, *B*. A square of card is put on one end of the magnet, the resistance of which against the air when swinging tends to bring the needle rapidly to rest. (2.) The torsion

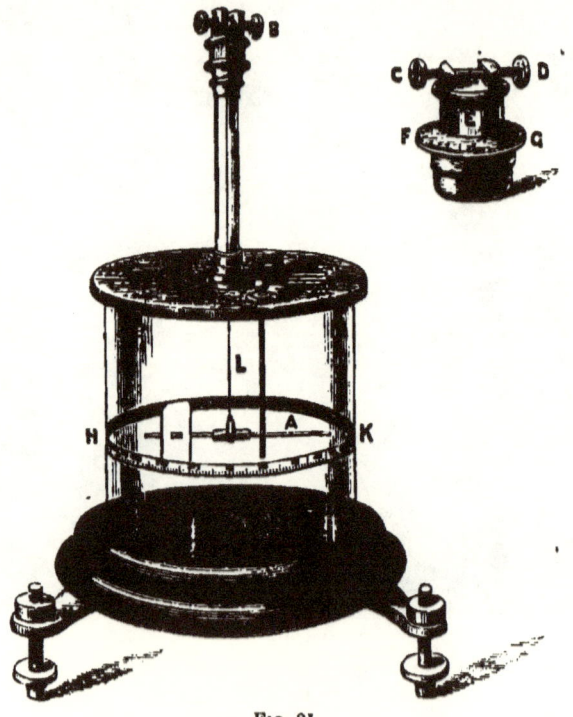

Fig. 21.

circle (shown enlarged on the right of Fig. 21) carries the upper end of the wire coiled on the horizontal arm *CD*, supported on the frame *E*, which can be twisted round the vertical axis, the graduated limb *FG* measuring the twist put on to the wire in performing an experiment. (3.) The needle swings in a glass case (*HK*), graduated on its surface, so as to show the angular movements of the needle. The case is perforated above, so as to allow of the introduction of a magnetic needle (*L*) in a vertical position, whose lower pole creates the magnetic field, whose strength is measured by the pole of the moving needle. The effects of the more distant poles of *L* and *A* are neglected.

We assume at the outset that both the graduated torsion circle (*FG*) has its pointer to zero, and that the needle points to its zero of graduation on the case (*HK*), when the needle is in the magnetic meridian, and the wire has no torsion; also that the magnet pole is introduced immediately opposite the zero of graduation, so as to deflect the needle by its repulsive action, the opposing poles being of like sign. This adjustment is secured in practice by marking the magnetic meridian by means of an independent magnet, and turning the case until the 0° and 180° of graduation are in a line with it; then, replacing the magnetic needle by a copper needle of equal weight, twist the whole torsion circle until the copper needle hangs in the magnetic meridian. On replacing the magnetic needle, it will hang in the magnetic meridian, and the wire will be free from torsion.

On introducing the vertical magnet there will be repulsion, and the needle will take up a position out of the magnetic meridian, in which the repulsion between the two magnet poles is balanced by the combined effect of the earth's directive force on the magnet and the torsion put on to the wire by the deflection of the needle.

The latter of these is simply proportional to the angle through which the wire is twisted, or to the deflection of the needle; and the earth's directive action can also be measured in terms of the twist in the wire. The forces acting on the needle, *PP'*, in Fig. 22, when deflected from the meridian

MM' will be two equal and opposite forces, whose magnitude we will call F, acting parallel to MM'. The effect of such a pair of forces in twisting the magnet round C, back again towards the meridian, will be measured by their moment, or $2.F \times CG$. When the angle of deflection is small, CG is very nearly equal to AP, the arc described by the pole

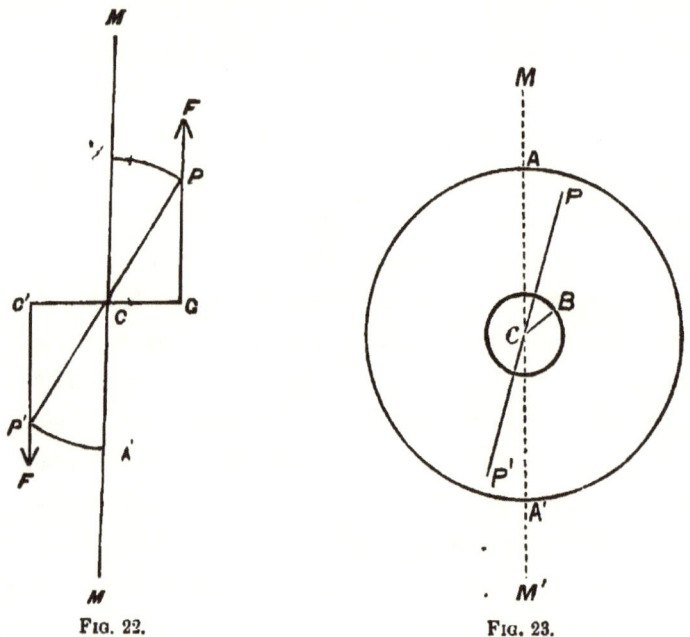

Fig. 22.   Fig. 23.

A in its deflection, and this is proportional simply to the angle of deflection.[1]

To find the action of the earth in terms of the torsion of the wire, we must first find through how many degrees the circle must be turned to give 1° deflection to the needle before the magnet L is introduced. Take a plan of the instrument

---

[1] The moment is really proportional to the sine of the angle of deflection, and the sine for small angles is known to be proportional to the angle.

(Fig. 23) in which the smaller circle represents the torsion circle, and the larger the graduated glass case. Suppose the torsion circle turned from the magnetic meridian, MM', through the angle BCA ($=T°$), and the needle through the angle PCA ($=A°$), the torsion on the wire is $(T-A)°$, and this balances the deflection, $A°$. Hence the torsion per degree of deflection is $\left(\dfrac{T-A}{A}\right)°$, and we may assume that the directive action of the earth for any moderate deflection is found by multiplying the deflection by $\dfrac{T-A}{A}$.

We can now express the force between the magnet poles in any position in terms of the torsion of the wire alone, and this is simply proportional to the angle of torsion in all experiments with the same instrument.

We will now proceed to work out a particular numerical experiment, in which we endeavour to compare the force exerted on the moving by the fixed magnet pole, at two distances whose ratio is as 2 : 1.

(1.) Before introducing the second pole, twist the torsion circle through 35°; the needle is seen to deflect 5°: and therefore 30° of torsion balances the directive action of the earth through 5°; or the earth's directive action is measured by 6° of torsion per degree of deflection.

(2.) Introduce the magnet pole which deflects the needle 40°. Refer to the plan of the instrument (Fig. 24), in which D represents the fixed pole, R the repulsive force which acts in direction DP: the effect in twisting the needle is measured by the moment of R about C, or $CK \times R$. When the angle of deflection is small, CK is nearly equal to CP; and we shall therefore assume that the moment is measured by R, the force itself. Hence R is balanced by 40° torsion, together with the earth's directive action through 40°, which is equal to $40 \times 6°$ of torsion.

∴ R is measured by $(40 + 6 \times 40)° = 280°$ of torsion.

(3.) Twist the torsion circle backwards, as indicated by the arrow, through two complete revolutions, and about 260° in

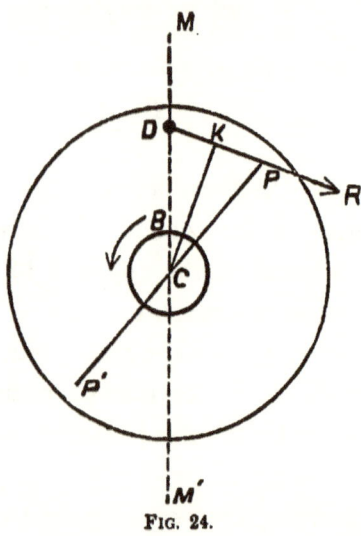

Fig. 24.

addition, and you will find the needle at 20°. If R' denote the repulsion, we have R' balanced by $(2 \times 360 + 260 + 20)° = 1000°$ of torsion and the earth's deflective action, which is equal to $20 \times 6° = 120°$ of torsion.

∴ $R' = (1000 + 120)° = 1120°$ of torsion.

Observing that $1120° = 4 \times 280°$, we conclude that the force is multiplied by 4 when the distance is halved.

By further experiment it will be found that the force, when the reading is $13\frac{1}{3}°$, or one-third of 40°, is $9 \times 280°$, and at 10° it is $16 \times 280°$, and so on. From these observations Coulomb deduced the important law that where the distances of two poles are made in succession proportional to

$$1, 2, 3, 4, \ldots\ldots$$

the forces at these distances are proportional to

$$1, \tfrac{1}{4}, \tfrac{1}{9}, \tfrac{1}{16}, \ldots\ldots$$

which is usually expressed by saying that the forces are inversely as the squares of the distances between the poles.

14. Strength of Field by the Method of Oscillations.—The strength of the field may also be investigated by means of the method of Oscillations. This depends on the well-known dynamical law that a pendulum, when oscillating through a small arc about its position of equilibrium, makes isochronous oscillations—*i.e.* oscillations whose time is independent of the arc (supposed small) through which the pendulum swings—and that the force which is always drawing it back to its position of rest is proportional to the square of the number of oscillations made in a given time.

Now, a magnet, when freely suspended, is a double pendulum, and, when disturbed, oscillates under the same laws as a pendulum; and, since it will continue to oscillate for five or ten minutes, the number of oscillations in that time can be counted within a fraction of a single oscillation.[1]

If we place the south pole of another magnet in the meridian, at a measured distance to the north of the suspended magnet, it will increase the magnetic force on the needle, and make the oscillations more rapid. If the suspended needle be very short, compared with the distance of the magnet pole, the forces on the two poles will be appreciably equal and

[1] For rough experiments, the number of oscillations made in 30 seconds is sufficient.

opposite, and we have the oscillating magnet behaving as a pendulum under the combined action of the earth and magnet pole, whose effects are simply added together.

The experiment is performed by suspending by a single silk fibre a magnetized needle about one centimetre (or half an inch) long, supported in a paper stirrup (Fig. 25). In a particular experiment this needle made 11 oscillations in 30 seconds under the action of the earth alone. If E represents the earth's magnetic force, E is measured by 11^2 or 121.

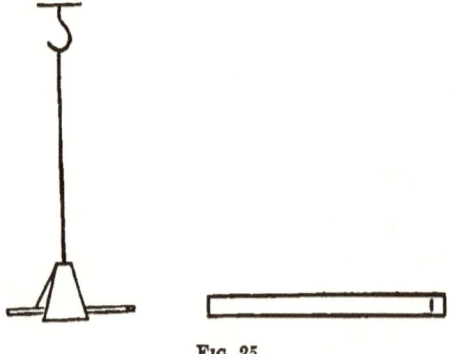

FIG. 25.

On introducing the south pole of a long magnet (about 40 centimetres in length) at a distance of 4 centimetres from the point of suspension, the number of oscillations was 51 in 30 seconds. If then M_4 represent the pull of the magnet at 4 cm., $E + M_4$ is measured by 51^2 or 2601. Hence, M_4 is measured by $2601 - 121 = 2480$. On removing the pole to a distance of 8 centimetres, the number of oscillations was 27. Denoting by M_8 the force of the magnet at 8 cm., we have $E + M_8$ measured by $27^2 = 729$, and therefore M_8 is measured by $729 - 121 = 608$. Hence M_4 has to M_8 the ratio 2480 to 608, or the ratio 4 to 1 within the limit of errors of observation.

The same method employed at other distances will confirm the law of inverse squares, just as in Coulomb's method.

It should be noticed, in this and the following experiments, that it must be the pole as defined in Art. 11, and not the mere end of the magnet, which is to be placed at the given distances from the suspended magnet. A few experiments enable the experimenter to arrive at the true position of the magnet pole, which in an ordinary bar magnet is about ¼ in. from the end.

15. Strength of Magnetic Field by Method of Deviations.—Another method of great use in practical magnetic measurements, is the method of Deviation. In this

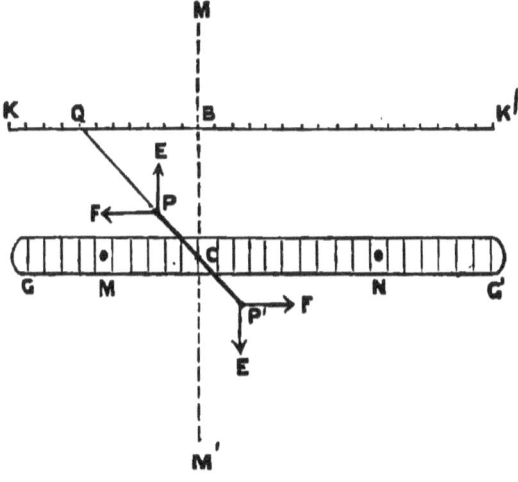

Fig. 26.

method (Fig. 26) we employ a very short magnet PP' (exaggerated in the figure), furnished with a long non-magnetic pointer, by which the deflection of the needle from the magnetic meridian may be measured. The deflecting magnet is placed in a line east or west of the point of suspension of the needle as at M or N. Remembering that the magnet is very short, and considering only one deflecting pole, the forces acting on each pole will be a force along the magnetic meridian (E) due to the earth's action, and a force at right angles to it (F), due to the action of the deflecting pole. The magnet takes up its position along the resultant of these two forces. Let GCG' be a horizontal scale graduated both ways from C; also, let KCK' be a graduated scale placed in a vertical plane, both being east and west of the meridian. If the line CP be produced, either by a pointer or by sights attached to the magnet, and moving with it, so that the distance Q, at which the axis of the magnet cuts the vertical scale is known, the principle of the parallelogram of forces will apply, and we shall have $\frac{F}{E} = \frac{BQ}{BC}$. But BC and E are fixed quantities for all observations, and hence we see that F is measured in each experiment by the distance BQ. If we choose distances for M proportional to 1, 2, 3, . . . we shall find the distances BQ respectively proportional to $1, \frac{1}{4}, \frac{1}{9}, \ldots$, thus giving another proof of the law of inverse squares.

The ratio $\frac{BQ}{BC}$ depends on the angle BCP, and is in fact simply the tangent of that angle. If C be in the centre of a graduated card, the same result may be obtained by observing the angle of deflection, and extracting its tangent from the table given in Appendix II. In performing the experiment, the magnet and its suspension should be placed under a glass case, as otherwise currents of air prevent its remaining at rest in the position of magnetic equilibrium.

16. Comparison of Strength of two Magnet Poles. —To compare two magnetic poles is simply to compare the forces they respectively exert on the same pole when placed at the same distance from it.

This comparison may be made by either of the above methods, simply changing the one pole for the other of two magnets to be tested, keeping the distance from the testing magnet the same, or applying the law of inverse squares to reduce the observations to a constant distance. A better method is to place the two poles as at M and N, on opposite

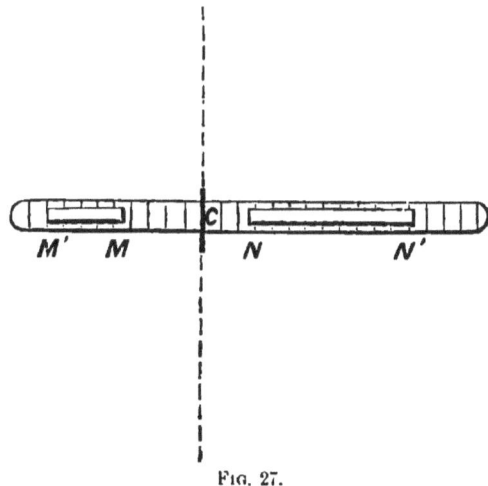

Fig. 27.

sides of the short suspended needle of the last experiment, and move one of them backwards and forwards till the suspended needle remains in the meridian. The strengths of field at C due to M and to N must then be equal, and we shall have strength of pole M at distance CM equal to the pole N at distance CN. Hence their strengths at the same distance would be in the ratio CM^2 to CN^2.

If now m, m' be the strengths of the poles—*i.e.* the forces with which they urge a certain standard pole at unit distance —the strength of the field of m at distance r will be $\dfrac{m}{r^2}$. Assuming this, we can easily correct the last result for the action of the more distant pair of magnet poles. For if we assume MM' and NN' (Fig. 27) to be the two magnets, the force at C due to the magnet MM' will be found by subtracting the force due to M' from that due to M, which gives $\dfrac{m}{CM^2} - \dfrac{m}{CM'^2}$, and that due to NN' will be $\dfrac{m'}{CN^2} - \dfrac{m'}{CN'^2}$; and we have therefore, if the magnet remains undisturbed,

$$m\left(\frac{1}{CM^2} - \frac{1}{CM'^2}\right) = m'\left(\frac{1}{CN^2} - \frac{1}{CN'^2}\right)$$

from which the ratio $m : m'$ is at once determined.

* 17. Meaning of an Absolute System of Measurement.

—In speaking of magnet poles we have frequently referred to a standard pole, but have used in place of it the pole of any needle convenient for the particular experiment we had in hand. No magnet pole can be made to retain its magnetism without change for any length of time; and it is therefore useless to attempt, by means of a single magnet, to compare the strengths of a field or of another pole at any great interval of time.

To enable us to do this we make an absolute system of units in which the strength of our pole must be determined, absolutely at the time of each experiment.

For an account of the absolute system of units employed, the student is referred to Appendix I. We only note here that with three fundamental units (that of length being called the centimetre; of time, the second of our ordinary mean-time clocks; and of mass, the gram) we are able to express every other unit required in physical investigation independently of any new physical quantity. Premising that the absolute unit of force is the *dyne*, we proceed to explain the absolute units used in magnetism.

* 18. **Absolute Unit of Magnetism.**—We know by our experiments that two magnet poles of the same kind repel each other with a force which may be measured in dynes or absolute units of force. We can therefore conceive two equal magnet poles which when a centimetre apart exert a force of exactly one dyne on each other. These two would then be called unit magnet poles, and the quantity of magnetism in each of them a unit of magnetism. We make no assumption here as to the nature of magnetism, referring only to its action in the magnetic field. We should define the strength of any other magnetic pole by the number of units of magnetism it contains, or by the force exerted on a unit pole placed at unit distance. We should also define the strength at any point in a magnetic field, as the force with which a unit of magnetism condensed in a point and placed there would be urged along the line of force.

It follows from this definition, combined with the law of inverse squares of the distance, that if we have a pole of strength M, the strength of the field at a distance D cm. from it will be $\frac{M}{D^2}$: and the force urging a pole of strength M' placed at distance D cm., will be $\frac{MM'}{D^2}$, both expressed in absolute measure.

19. **Theories Suggested by Experiment.**—It will naturally strike the student that by all our methods of experiment, acknowledged everywhere to be rough and ap-

proximate only, we have given an altogether inadequate proof of a law of such precision and generality. We must remind him however that he has in this been only following in the track of the discoverers, both of this and of every other physical law. Such laws have been discovered by something like a happy guess from very rough observations, while the confirmation of the guess depends on methods of greater refinement, which generally depend altogether on a knowledge of the law itself they are intended to prove. As an illustration, we may notice that by help of the law just enunciated we can determine the form of the magnetic curves for a given distribution of poles, and can in many cases trace the theoretical magnetic curves by graphical means, and so compare the curves yielded by theory with those given by experiment.

CHAPTER III.

METHODS OF MAGNETIZATION.

20. Quality and Temper of Steel.—To secure good permanent magnets it is, first of all, necessary to have bars of the best steel evenly tempered. The temper which gives the best results is obtained by cooling the bars when brought to a cherry-red—the same temper as that for the best cutlery.

There are various processes of magnetization, but all depend on overcoming the coercive force of the steel by vibrating its molecules when under powerful external magnetic induction.

21. Method of Single Touch.—The first method, known as *Single Touch*, consists merely in rubbing the bar to be magnetized several times lengthwise, and always in the same direction, across the pole of a strong magnet. In this, as in all cases, the end of the bar at which the magnet pole leaves it becomes of opposite name to the inducing pole. This process is repeated five or six times on both sides of the bar to be magnetized, and gives a fairly strong

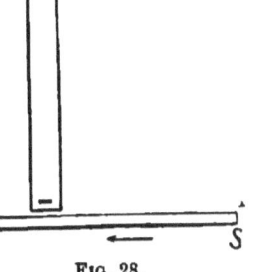

FIG. 28.

magnetism to a short thin bar, such as a piece of watch-spring or small compass needle. The arrow shows the direction in which the bar is rubbed across the pole to communicate the poles shown by the letters *N*, *S*.

22. Divided Touch.—The second method, that of *Divided Touch*, consists in fixing the bar to be magnetized between the opposite poles of two permanent magnets.

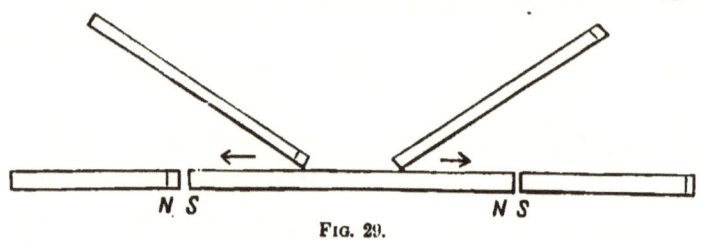

Fig. 29.

While under their induction the bar is stroked, each half with the pole of another magnet of the same name as the corresponding inducing pole, the stroking magnets being held in the hands at an angle of about 30 degrees with the bar; the stroking beginning from the centre of the bar, and the poles being lifted at the ends, in an arch, back again to the centre. The stroking is repeated on the opposite face of the bar. This method gives a strong and even magnetism to moderately thin and long bars.

23. Method of Double Touch.—The third method, called that of *Double Touch*, consists in placing the bar to be magnetized under the induction of two strong poles, as in the last method. The stroking poles are placed at first over

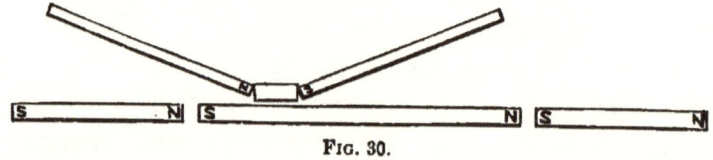

Fig. 30.

the centre of the bar to be magnetized, but separated by a small piece of wood. The stroking magnets, held at an angle of about 15 degrees to the bar, are drawn along the bar steadily from the centre to the end, and back again to the other end, several times, being taken off finally at the centre, after each half has been passed over the same number of times. The bar is turned over, and the same process repeated on the opposite face. This is found to give a strong magnetism to thick bars, but is apt to develop consequent poles, unless the rubbing be performed very steadily.

Some experimentalists prefer the use of a strong horse-shoe magnet, whose two poles are placed on the bar at its centre,

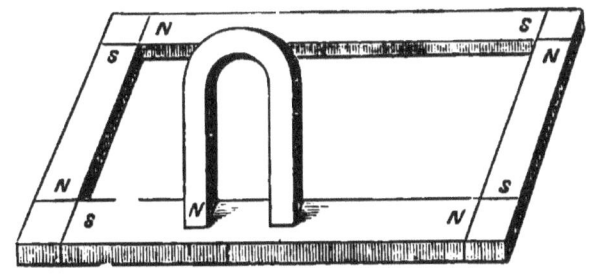

FIG. 31.

and rubbed backwards and forwards, as in the last-named method. When several bars require to be magnetized at once, they are placed with their ends in contact, so as to form a closed circuit, the angular spaces between their ends being filled in with soft iron. The horse-shoe magnet is put down at any part, and simply made to slide round the circuit, always in the same direction, several times, by means of which all the bars are magnetized strongly. Each bar is magnetized in opposite direction to the inducing magnet, and the consecutive ends, acquiring opposite magnetism, increase each other's power by mutual induction.

24. **Magnetic Battery.**—It has been found that thin bars can be magnetized much more strongly than thick ones

in proportion to their weight. In consequence, all large and strong magnets are formed of bars each separately magnetized, and fastened together by screws after magnetization (Fig. 32). In such a magnetic magazine the power of the combination is always less than the sum of the powers of the separate bars, owing to their induction on each other tending to weaken the power of each, and especially of the interior bars.

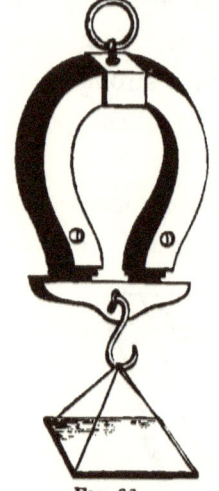

Fig. 32.

This relative weakness of thick bars seems due to the magnetizing power not penetrating far below the surface. This has been proved by soaking magnetized bars in acid, by which the surface is slowly eaten away. During this process the loss of magnetism is found to proceed at a much higher rate than the loss of weight.

25. Magnetic Saturation. — The degree to which a given bar is capable of magnetization depends on the manufacture and temper of the steel, and on the strength of the inducing magnets. For each quality of steel, however, there is a limit, beyond which the magnetism cannot be retained permanently, and in this condition the bar is said to be saturated. In making magnets it is best to magnetize beyond saturation, and then allow the bar to sink back gradually to saturation point, which may sometimes take a considerable length of time. To test these changes in magnetism we have only to place the magnet in the meridian at a constant distance from the same suspended magnet, and count the number of oscillations in a given time. As long as these decrease in number the power of the magnet is diminishing. Another method commonly employed to test the power of a horse-shoe magnet consists in suspending to the armature (Fig. 32) of a fixed magnet a scale-pan, into which weights can be put, and so determine its portative power. The amount the magnet can support can be increased by adding small weights at successive intervals, never allowing the weight to be sufficient to separate the armature from the magnet.

The production of permanent magnets of small size, but great magnetic power, is now a matter of great importance, especially in telephone work, and great improvements have been made in the manufacture of steel for this purpose. In the Paris Exhibition of 1882 there was a magnet which could support seventy-six times its own weight; and the small ordinary magnets now used in Gower-Bell telephones hold up from fifteen to twenty-five times their own weight. (Mr. W. H. Preece, F.R.S., in *Report of Institute of Mech. Engineers*, Jan. 1883.)

26. Retention of Magnetism.—After a magnet has been made, great care must be taken to preserve it from accidental jars, by which the mass is set in vibration, the effect of which, in the absence of strong external induction, is to relax the molecular rigidity on which the magnetism of steel depends. The same effect will be produced by heating the magnet—a red heat not only destroying all traces of magnetism, but making the metal quite indifferent to magnetism.

CHAPTER IV.

TERRESTRIAL MAGNETISM.

27. Field of Terrestrial Magnetic Force.—That the earth, as a whole, is magnetic is proved by its influence on a suspended magnet, which has already (Art. 3) been referred to. Our only source of knowledge as to the nature of the earth's magnetism is by observation of magnetic forces at

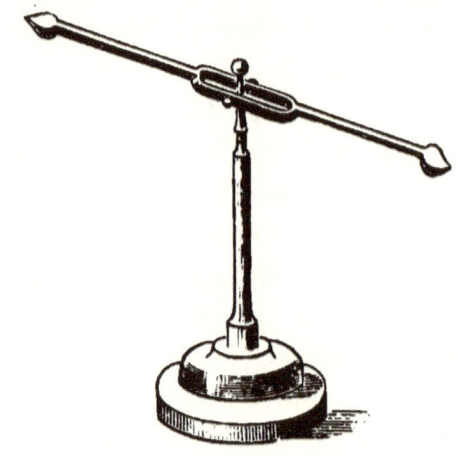

FIG. 33.

points in the earth's field of force. We must, therefore, find for every place on the earth, where possible, the direction of the line of magnetic force, and the strength of the magnetic field. To find the direction of the line of force at a given point, we have only to suspend a bar of steel so as to move freely about its centre of gravity, and after magnetizing it, observe the position it assumes. This may be nearly fulfilled by such a suspension as that of Fig. 33, in which the axis of a needle swinging in a vertical plane is mounted on a pivot, about which it can turn horizontally. Such a needle in England at the present time will always come to rest in a plane inclined 18° to 20° to the west of the astronomical meridian, and will rest in that plane at an angle of 67° to 69° to the horizon. This shows that within any very limited space the lines of force are sensibly a series of straight lines parallel to one another.

That these lines of force should remain straight lines to considerable distances from the earth is very unlikely; but the linear dimensions of the earth are so great, compared with any distances above it at which we can take observations, that we are not likely ever to be able to discover what their true shape is. Their sensible parallelism for moderate distances confirms us in our assumption (Art. 13) that the earth's action on a needle consists of two equal and opposite forces, since we cannot employ a needle so long that the field of force at the two ends of it shows any sensible difference in direction or intensity. This is all that is meant when the earth's action on a needle is said to be directive only; the effect of a couple in mechanics being to twist a body round without altering the position of its centre of gravity, until the two forces constituting the couple are in the same straight line. The needle in our experiment then takes up that position in which the earth's pull consists of two equal and opposite forces on its two ends, directed along it, and therefore maintaining it in equilibrium.

This has been shown experimentally by supporting a magnet on a cork float. In any vessel conveniently small the surface tension of the water will draw the cork to the side, but at a point depending on the position on the surface in which the float is placed, and in no way depending on the direction of the earth's magnetism.

28. Magnetic Elements of a Place.—The definitions of the direction of the line of force and of the strength of the earth's magnetic pull constitute what are called the magnetic elements of the place. They are three in number.

1. *Declination*—is the angle which the vertical plane through the magnetic axis of a freely suspended needle makes with the astronomical meridian of the place. This plane is commonly called the magnetic meridian of the place (see Art. 23), and is the vertical plane which passes through the axis of an ordinary horizontally suspended needle. The declination is counted E. or W. as the north pole of the needle points to the E. or W. of the astronomical meridian or vertical plane which passes due north and south of the place of observation.

2. *Inclination or Dip*—is the angle which the magnetic axis of a magnet, freely suspended about its centre of gravity, makes with the horizon of the place. This may be either north or south according as the north or south end of the needle dips below the horizontal plane.

3. *Intensity*—is the force, expressed in absolute measure, with which the earth's magnetism urges a unit magnet pole at the place.

29. The Declinometer.—To determine each of these elements at any place requires a special piece of apparatus. That for determining the declination is called a Declinometer. This consists (Fig. 34) of a mounted telescope A, swinging on two Y pieces B, B, the axis being levelled by the hanging spirit-level. The Y's are mounted on a framework D, D, having a circular limb which can be turned round in a horizontal plane, and is graduated within. A horizontal magnet needle, E, is pivoted at the centre of the graduations. The zero of these graduations should be in the vertical plane through the optical axis (or, more accurately, through the line of collimation) of the telescope. If this adjustment is made and the telescope is brought into the astronomical meridian, the

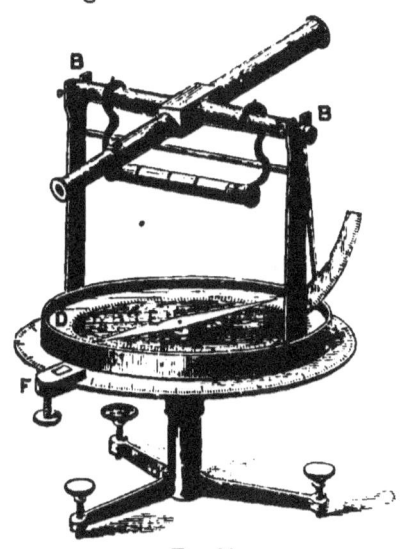

FIG. 34.

reading indicated by the end of the needle is the declination. The framework carries a vernier and clamp F, which slides over a horizontal graduated circle forming part of the fixed base. This enables an observer with the telescope to set it in the astronomical meridian. The base is supported on levelling screws, by which the adjustments in level can be made.

The magnet used for observing is usually a lozenge-shaped magnet, and we read off the graduation corresponding to its pointed extremity. If the poles are not in the geometrical axis of the magnet, this reading will be either too small or too great. To correct this, the faces of the needle are usually reversed, and the reading repeated, since then the declination, which was before too small, will become too great, or *vice versâ;* the mean of the two readings correcting the error. There may be also an error of centering the needle, by which the pivot is thrown out of the centre of the graduations. This is corrected by reading each time both ends of the needle. The mean of the four readings so obtained will give the true declination.

30. **The Dipping Needle.**—The instrument for observing the inclination or dip is called 'the Dipping Needle. It consists essentially of a magnetic needle swinging on a horizontal axis, which passes through its centre of gravity, and is at right angles to its magnetic axis. The needle swings freely in pivots of agate to diminish friction, and the inclination is read off from a graduated limb, BB, which has the axis of the needle at its centre. The whole is usually supported on a horizontal framework movable about a vertical axis. The frame carries a vernier and clamp, C, which slides over a circular graduated limb, fixed to the base of the instrument. Levelling screws and small levels are attached for adjustment. Where great accuracy is required, the positions of the ends of the needle are observed by microscopes carried on an arm whose extremities are made verniers for reading the limb.

To take an observation, it is necessary first to bring the plane of movement of the needle into coincidence with the magnetic meridian. The most convenient method for securing this is to rotate the instrument in azimuth till the needle shows an inclination of 90°, *i.e.* stands vertical. The needle must then be in the plane at right angles to the meridian, for in this position the horizontal component of the earth's pull is balanced by an increased pressure on the south and diminished pressure on the north bearing of the needle, while the vertical component acting alone keeps the needle in a vertical position.

To eliminate the errors of centering, and of want of coincidence between the geometrical and magnetic axes, the hori-

Fig. 35.

zontal circle is read, when each end of the needle points to 90°, and also when the faces of the needle have been reversed, either by turning the instrument through half a revolution or by lifting the needle from its supports and reversing the bearings. The mean of the four readings so obtained, diminished by 90°, will give the plane of the meridian.

When the needle is in the plane of the meridian, it is made to vibrate slightly by bringing a magnet for a moment near to it, and allowed to take up its position of rest after the magnet's removal, when both ends of the needle are read. As it seldom comes to rest twice over in exactly the same position, this method is repeated about ten times.

As before, the faces of the needle are reversed, and the same set of observations repeated.

There is a further error which occurs in the indications of a dipping needle, due to the axis of rotation of the needle not passing through its centre of gravity. If the centre of gravity were ever so little towards the north end of the needle, the weight acting through it would pull down the north end and increase the dip, supposed north. If it were towards the south end, it would pull down the south end, and therefore diminish the dip. This error is neutralised by lifting out the needle and reversing its magnetism, and again repeating the two sets of observations on each end described above. The mean of the eight means so obtained will give the true dip.

We have entered into details of the methods employed in taking observations with the dipping needle, as an illustration of the use of well-directed multiplied observations in using physical instruments, and not because it is likely that such methods could be usefully applied to the rough instruments placed in a student's hands or used in a lecture experiment. The need of such refinements only becomes apparent in instruments brought to the highest perfection in construction, and they would be as much out of place in a rough instrument as a micrometer reading to thousands of an inch on a roughly divided carpenter's rule, or a rider reading thousands of an ounce on the beam of a grocer's balance.

31. **The Intensity.**—To compare the magnetic intensity at various places; we have apparently only to observe the

number of small oscillations made by the same dipping needle in a given time about its position of equilibrium, the intensity being simply proportional to the square of the number of oscillations observed. This method would of course only give us the intensity, referred to an arbitrary standard—say the intensity at some one place—and not in absolute measure. The dipping needle, however, is ill suited to observations on oscillations, the friction on the supports bringing the needle to rest in a comparatively small number of oscillations. For this reason the dipping needle was early abandoned in favour of a horizontal needle suspended by a few fibres of cocoon silk, whose oscillations could be observed continuously for ten or fifteen minutes. By this means the horizontal component only is observed, but know-ing the horizontal component and the dip, the total intensity is at once known (Fig. 36) by the law of the parallelogram of forces.

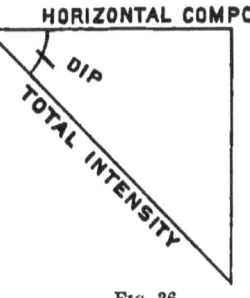

Fig. 36.

The objections to this method will be obvious from what we have stated as to the impossibility of preserving any magnet from change in its magnetic power, or even of ascertaining any law of change. Gauss, however, introduced a method which is independent of any magnetic quantities whatever, and which, from suitable observations, gives us the magnetic intensity in absolute measure. The principle of this very elegant method, stripped of mathematical details, can be made intelligible.

*32. **Gauss's Method for Finding Intensity.**—Let us first consider the forces tending to bring back again a horizontally suspended magnetic needle displaced from the meridian. Using absolute units, assume m to be the magnetic strength of each pole of the magnet, and H the horizontal component of the earth's magnetic intensity. The definition of H is the pull on a unit of magnetism, and since at P there are by supposition m units, the pull at P and P' will be two forces Hm equal and oppositely directed. The moment of this

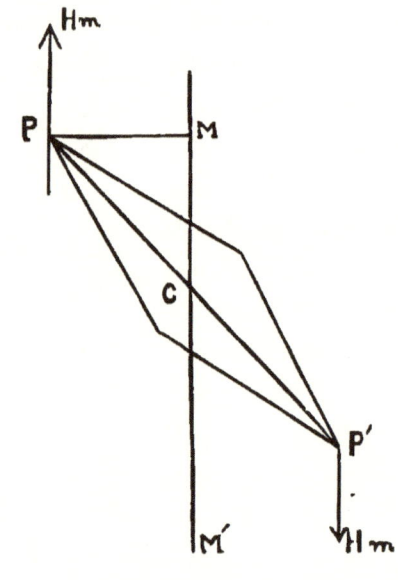

FIG. 37.

couple, tending to twist the magnet back to its position of rest, is $2Hm \times PM$ where PM is the arm of either force. This may be written $Hm.PP' \times \dfrac{PM}{CP}$ when $\dfrac{PM}{CP}$ depends only on the angle PCM, through which the magnet is deflected. The quantity $m \times PP'$ is usually called the *Magnetic Moment* of the magnet, and may be denoted by G.

The pull tending to restore the needle to the meridian is

therefore equal to $HG \times \dfrac{PM}{CP}$. The time of small oscillations is known to be independent of the arc through which the needle vibrates, if that arc be small; and we may therefore infer that it depends, as far as magnetic quantities are concerned, only on the product HG. The non-magnetic quantities on which it depends will be the mass and dimensions of the magnet used, which can be estimated in absolute measure. The observed time of a small oscillation therefore supplies us with an equation from which the product HG can be obtained in absolute measure.

We employ next the Deviation method, using the needle of the foregoing oscillation experiment, PP', to deflect a very short

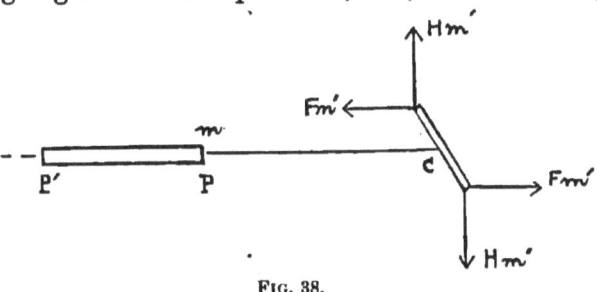

Fig. 38.

needle, the strength of each of whose poles we will call m'. We observe (Art. 15) that the needle takes up its position in the direction of the resultant of two forces, Hm' along the meridian, and Fm' at right angles to it, where F is the strength of field at C due to m at P, and $-m$ at P'. Whence

$$F = \dfrac{m}{CP^2} - \dfrac{m}{CP'^2} = m \cdot \dfrac{(CP' - CP).(CP + CP)}{CP^2 . CP'^2}$$

$$= G \cdot \dfrac{CP' + CP}{CP^2 . CP'^2}; \text{ since } G = m \, (CP' - CP).$$

The position of the needle when in equilibrium furnishes us

(Art. 15) with the ratio $\dfrac{H}{F}$ in terms of non-magnetic quantities, and hence the ratio $\dfrac{H}{G}$ becomes known.

We have thus from the oscillation method,

$HG = A$, a quantity found by observation;

and from the deviation method,

$\dfrac{H}{G} = B$, another quantity found by observation;

whence, by multiplication,

$$H^2 = AB,$$
$$\text{or } H = \sqrt{AB},$$

a result giving us the horizontal component of the earth's magnetism in absolute measure, assuming that all the measurements involved in A and B are expressed in the fundamental units of the absolute system.

*33. **Magnetic Moment of a Magnet in Absolute Measure.**—The method just described may be also used to obtain G. For dividing, in place of multiplying, we have $G^2 = \dfrac{A}{B}$. Hence the same method enables us to express the magnetic moment, and hence the strength of any magnet pole in absolute measure.

34. **Magnetic Elements of Greenwich.**—The magnetic elements found for Greenwich in January 1884, were:—

Declination, .	18° 10′ West.
Dip, . . .	67° 30′.
Intensity, . .	·472.

35. Changes in Elements.

—No sooner had instruments of moderate accuracy been applied to determine these elements, than it appeared that their value was different not only for different parts of the globe, but that their values were undergoing constant change at each place. On account of the universal use of the declination compass, its variations have been more studied than those of the other elements. To register these small variations a specially constructed group of instruments has been invented, which, by means of photography, give a continuous chart of the movements of the magnets employed. The chief variations in the declination needle are the following :—

1. *Secular Variation.*—This is a slow change in the magnetic meridian of the place, which gradually moves in the course of centuries, east and west of the astronomical meridian. The following values of the magnetic declination of London for the years given, will explain this variation :—

Year.	Declination	Year.	Declination.
1580,	11° 15′ E.	1760,	19° 12′ W.
1622,	6° 12′ E.	1796,	24° 0′ W.
1657,	0° 0′	1815,	24° 27′ W.
1700,	9° 40′ W.	1820,	24° 11′ W.

This shows that before 1657 the declination was east. At this date the magnetic and astronomical meridians coincided; after this the declination became west, reaching its maximum west in 1815, since which date it has been slowly decreasing, the present rate of decrease being about 7′ per annum.

2. *Annual Variation.*—From observations at widely different stations it appears certain that there is a variation of small amount (about 1′) depending on the sun's orbital posi-

tion; the north end of the needle pointing to the east of the mean position when the sun is north, and to the west when the sun is south of the equator.

3. *Diurnal Variation.*—The comparison of a series of hourly observations of the declination at Kew, extending over several years, shows that there is a variation in the declination, depending on the sun's position in its daily path.

The needle occupies its mean position when the sun is on the magnetic meridian about 10.30 A.M. Its maximum easterly variation, amounting to 4', occurs three hours earlier, and its maximum westerly, amounting to 6', about three hours later. It again reaches the magnetic meridian about 6.30 P.M., and remains 1' or 2' east of it during the night, moving eastwards again early in the morning.

4. *Perturbations.*—These are irregular movements of the needle, by which its regular advance is broken up into a series of zigzags of greater or less amount. At some periods these perturbations become comparatively very large, the needle continuing to swing rapidly through several minutes of arc on either side of its mean position. These are called Magnetic Storms.

37. Relation to Aurora Borealis and to Solar Phenomena.

—That these are not local disturbances is proved by their occurring simultaneously at stations very widely separated, and it is probable that they have a common cause with the aurora borealis, brilliant displays of which most frequently occur at the same time with the magnetic storms. There is also evidence of a remarkable connection between these magnetic perturbations and changes in the sun's atmosphere. On 1st September 1859 Mr. Carrington, the astronomer, was taking observations on the sun's spots in his Observatory at Redhill, when suddenly, within the area of the largest group of spots, there broke out two patches of intensely bright and white light, which, after increasing for some seconds, gradually died away, the whole duration of the phenomenon being not more than five minutes, during which time the two patches traversed a space on the sun's disc of no less than 35,000 miles. On visiting, a few days afterwards, the magnetic Observatory at Kew, he learned that at the instant he observed this phenomenon the three magnetic elements were disturbed, the declination needle making a movement of 13·2′ to the west.

A further connection between the earth's magnetism and the sun is shown by the apparent coincidence of the periods of greatest frequency of sun-spots with a periodic maximum disturbance of the magnetic needle. It seems pretty well established, by observations extending over 150 years, that there exists a periodic frequency of sun-spots, whose period is from ten to eleven years. Accurate information on magnetic variation extends over a very much shorter period, but there seems to be, at stations widely separated, a marked coincidence between the periods of frequency of sun-spots, of magnetic storms, and of a marked increase in the range of the diurnal variation. These can hardly point to anything else but a very marked influence exercised by the sun on the magnetism of the earth.

38. **Other Variations.**—Such are the chief perturbations in the magnetic elements, their character and amount changing at different places on the earth. That others exist is highly probable, and perturbations with a half-yearly period, and

others depending on the moon, have been pointed out as probable at least. These and many others may yet be detected by careful comparison of the records continually accumulating in the various magnetic observatories of the world.

39. Magnetic Charts.—To get a connected view of the main features of terrestrial magnetism, charts are constructed showing, by lines across the surface of the globe, all places which have one of their magnetic elements the same. Owing to the secular variation in all these elements, the maps constructed for our epoch will require constant correction to bring them up to date. Those given are all for the epoch 1840, and were prepared by Colonel (afterwards General) Edward Sabine, R.A., from all the observations collected during the preceding three years, the lines connecting the stations of observation being supplied by Gauss's mathematical theory of terrestrial magnetism. The lines on the isoclinal map connect all places having the same inclination, on the isodynamic map those which have the same intensity, and on the isogonic map those which have the same declination, the value of the element being denoted by figures above the lines.

40. Isoclinal Chart.—Looking first at the isoclinal chart, we see that the world is divided into two hemispheres, a north magnetic in which the dip of the needle is to the north, and a south magnetic in which the dip of the needle is to the south, the lines of equal dip showing a rough parallelism to the line of no dip, which is often called the Magnetic Equator. This equator, however, is not a circle, and cuts the equator at 2° E. long., and again in 170° W. long.

There are two points, one in the northern hemisphere and one in the southern, at which the dip is 90°, or the magnetic

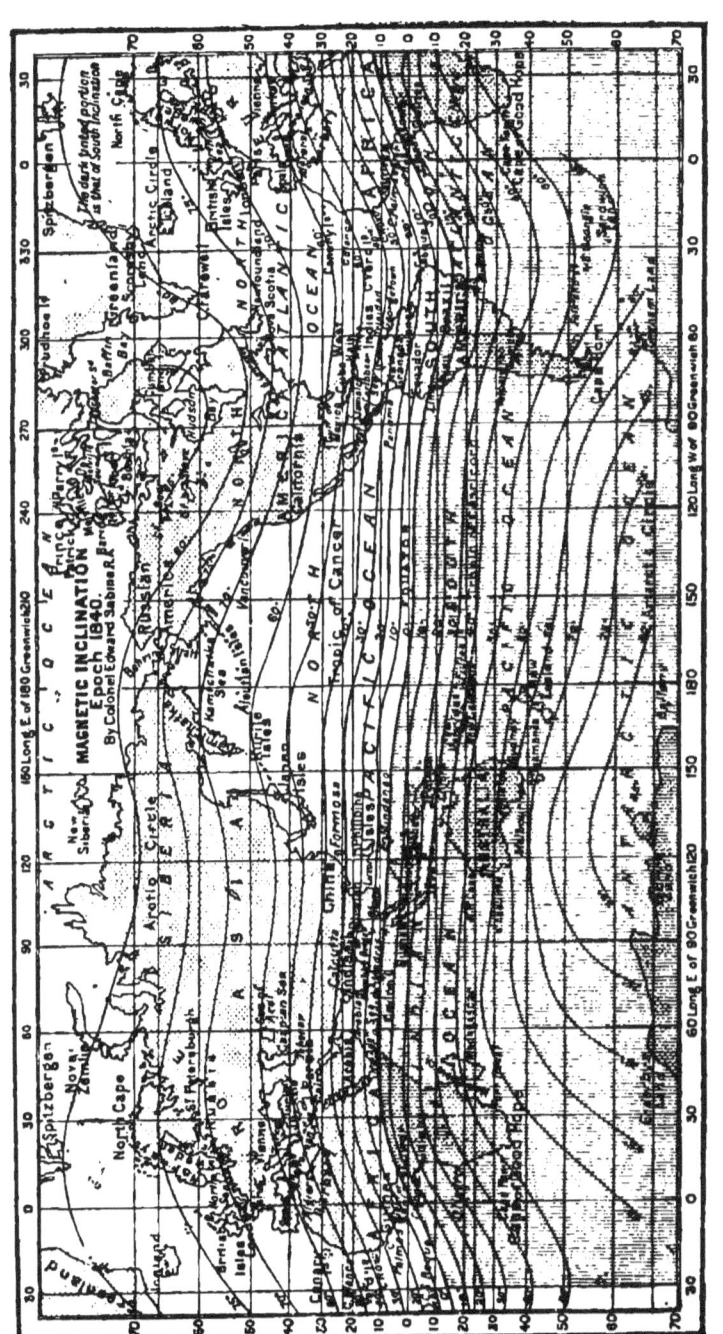

LINES OF EQUAL MAGNETIC INCLINATION.

force is vertical. These points are called the Magnetic Poles of the earth, though in a different sense to that in which we have defined the poles of a bar magnet. The term *Pole of Verticity* is sometimes applied to them. According to Captain Ross, this pole in the northern hemisphere is in lat. 70° 5′ 17″ N., and long. 96° 45′ 48″ W. In the southern hemisphere the pole has not been reached, but in 1841 Captain Ross found the dip to be 88° 35′ in lat. 76° 20′ S., and long. 165° 32′ E.

41. Isodynamic Chart.—On comparing the chart of isodynamic with that of isoclinal lines, we observe that the two sets do not coincide, the line of least general intensity not being the magnetic equator, and not being of equal intensity throughout. By the line of least intensity, we mean a line, such that the intensity increases as we pass off this line on one side or the other. There exists a particular point on this line at which the intensity is smaller than at any other point in the world. This point, according to Erman, is in lat. 20° S., and long. 35° 12′ W.

In the same way, by a point of maximum intensity, we mean a point such that the intensity diminishes as we pass from that point in any direction whatever. Of such points there are two in the northern hemisphere, and probably only one in the southern. The points are often also called magnetic poles, but should be distinguished as *Poles of Intensity*. The two poles in the northern hemisphere are not of equal intensity, the stronger lying in North America to the southwest of Hudson's Bay, about lat. 52° 19′ N., and long. 92° W., and the weaker lying in North Siberia. The positions of these poles are only known approximately, and that in the

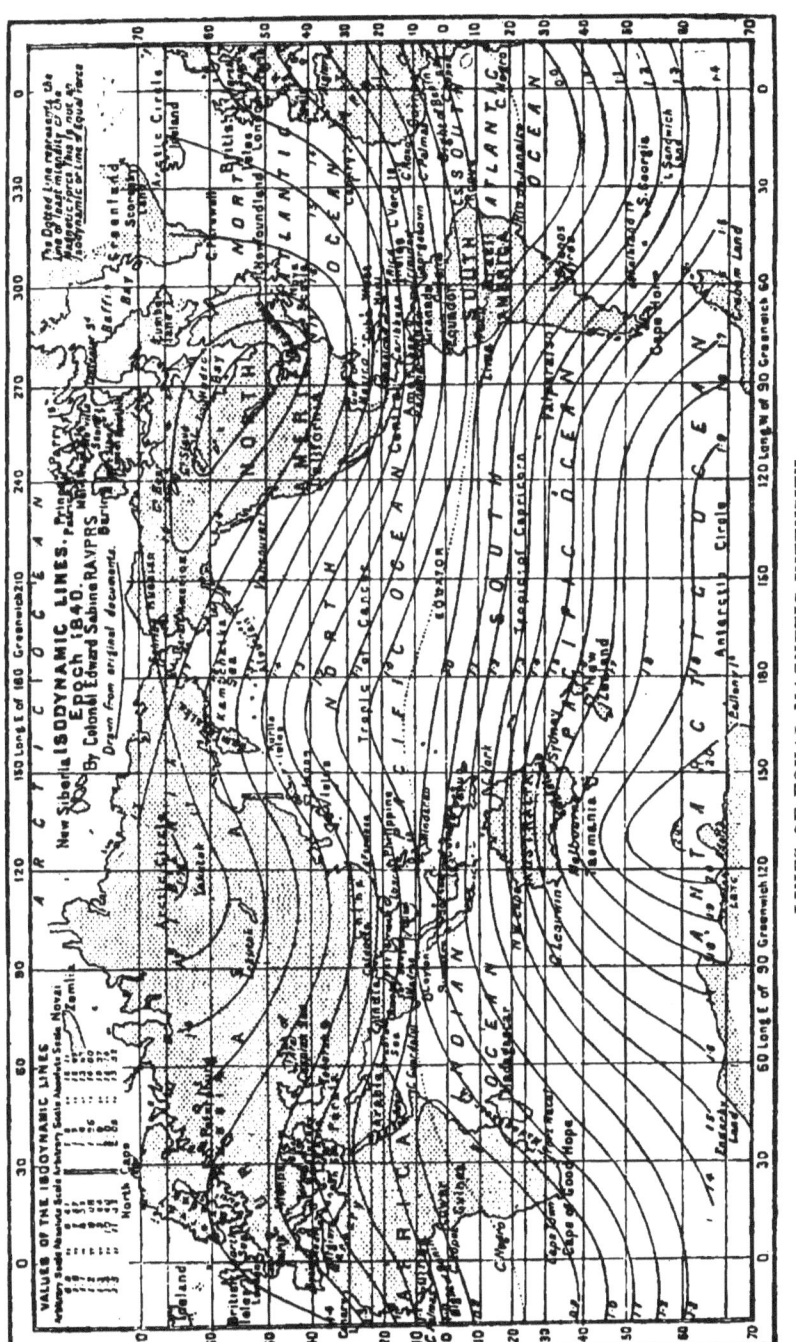

LINES OF EQUAL MAGNETIC INTENSITY.

southern hemisphere with still less exactness, the point of highest recorded intensity, according to the observations of Captain Ross, being in lat. 60° 19′ S., and long. 131° 20′ E.; but he had certainly not reached the actual point of greatest intensity, and was prevented by insuperable obstacles from proceeding further towards it.

These remarks are sufficient to show that the poles of verticity and intensity do not coincide in the northern hemisphere, and although their position is less certainly determined in the southern hemisphere, enough is known to say that they are not coincident.

42. Isogonic Chart.—Referring lastly to the declination chart, or chart of isogonic lines, we see that the line of 0° declination is not a great circle, but an irregular line passing through the poles of verticity and astronomical poles in both hemispheres. The lines of small declination follow its general direction, but the lines of higher declination form a series of loops in each hemisphere, connecting the pole of verticity with the corresponding astronomical pole.

There is to be noticed a remarkable oval patch extending over parts of North-East Siberia, China, and Japan, along the margin of which the declination sinks to 0°, and within it becomes westerly, though surrounded by a region of easterly declination.

There is also an area similar to this over the Pacific, in which the declination shows a curious decrease, but does not reach 0°.

43. Hypotheses of one or two Magnets.—The first attempt to explain physically the observed magnetic variations was the hypothesis of Bond (published in 1676), which

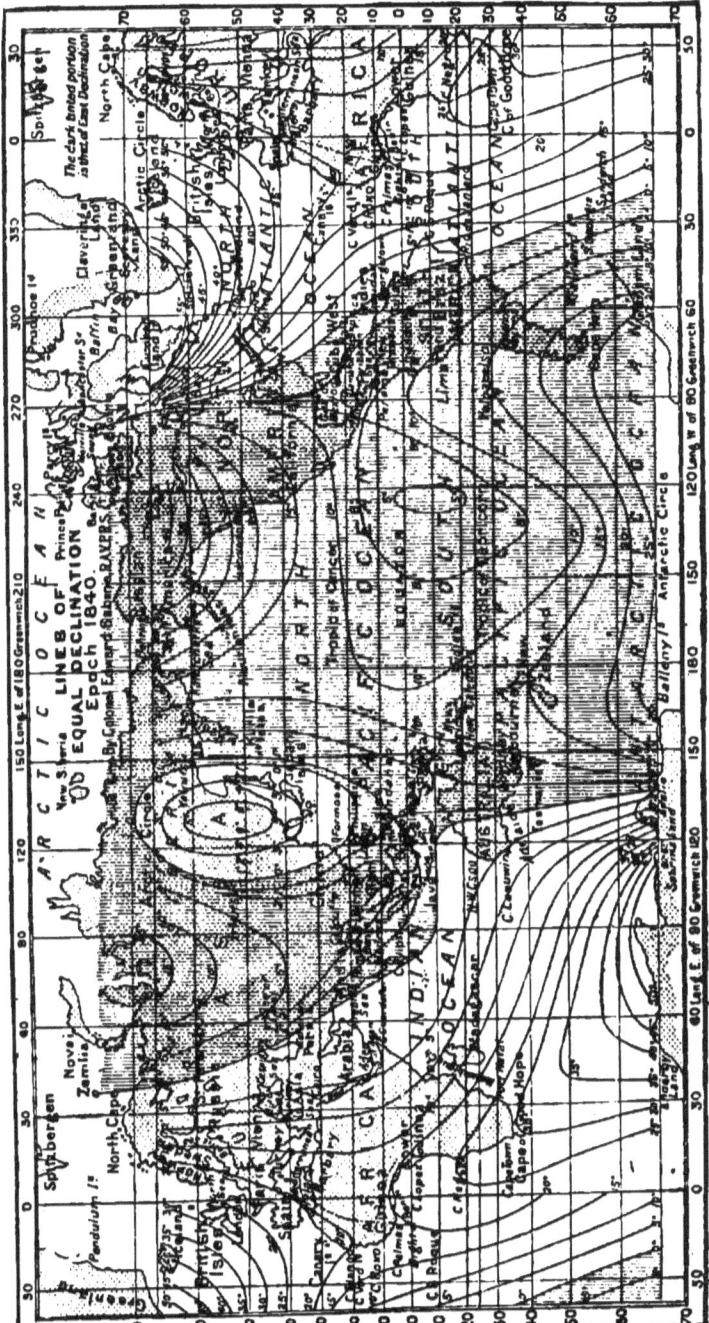

LINES OF EQUAL MAGNETIC DECLINATION.

assumed two magnet poles, one in the northern and the other in the southern hemisphere, but not coincident with the terrestrial poles. Of these poles the magnetic south was in the northern, and the magnetic north pole in the southern hemisphere. This hypothesis explained the general observation that in the northern hemisphere the north end of a needle dips down, and in the southern hemisphere the south end. It would require, however, the poles of verticity and intensity to coincide, and the lines both of equal dip and of equal intensity to be small circles round this common pole as their centre. We have already seen that neither of these is the case, and have no choice but to reject the hypothesis.

The existence of two poles of intensity in the northern hemisphere, inferred by Halley from his map of isogonic lines, led him to the hypothesis (published in 1683) of two magnets, of different strength, having their four poles at certain points in the two hemispheres. This hypothesis (developed mathematically by Hansteen in his *Magnetismus der Erde*, published in 1819) was found to correspond with observation much more nearly than that of a single magnet, but the discrepancies were too great to allow of its being accepted as a full explanation of the facts. We are then at present able only to say that the earth, as a whole, is magnetic, the northern hemisphere having a preponderance of south polar magnetism, and the southern hemisphere an equal excess of north polar magnetism. Of the distribution of this magnetism, over and through the earth, we know only what observation teaches us. Whether it is permanent or the result of cosmical induction or partly both, we know not; except that observation justifies us in saying that some variations in terrestrial magnetism, which depend on the position of the sun in his daily and yearly course, are likely to be due to solar induction or to some less direct solar influence (such perhaps as changes of temperature); while some remarkable perturbations seem to be associated with outbursts taking place in the solar atmosphere.

44. **The Mariner's Compass.**—The practical interest of terrestrial magnetism as applied to navigation is obvious. The only element with which the mariner is directly concerned

Fig. 39.

in steering his vessel is the declination, and in parts of the world where it is well known the course is directed by the compass alone in all weathers; astronomical observations being used only to correct, from time to time, the calculated position, derived from the rate and magnetic bearing. The compass usually employed consists of a flat circular card, on the under surface of which are secured four to eight light magnetic needles. The card swings in a compass-box on a pivot placed at its centre, the box having a pointer which corresponds to the direction of the ship's head. The box is supported on gimbals (Fig. 39)—an arrangement for preserving the box horizontal while the ship is pitching and tossing. The card is divided into thirty-two points by a star engraved on it (Fig. 40), and it is by these points the course is steered.

Fig. 40.

45. Effect of iron masses in Ships.—As soon as iron entered largely into the construction of ships, errors in the compass, depending on the terrestrial magnetic induction, appeared. This effect is illustrated by holding a bar of soft iron parallel to the dipping needle, when the lower end will, on testing, be found to be a north pole, and the upper end a south pole. If a piece of steel be held parallel to the dip and hammered, it can be converted into a permanent magnet. In this manner a fire-poker, which usually stands in a vertical position, and is frequently struck down on the solid hearth, is generally found to be a permanent magnet.

46. Semicircular Variation. — The rudder-post is a vertical mass of iron near the compass; it will, under terrestrial induction, always bring into existence a south pole nearly in the plane of the compass. It is obvious from Fig. 41 that the effect of this pole on the compass will be *nil* when it is in the magnetic meridian, either north or south; while to the west of the magnetic meridian it will cause westerly variation in the north end of the compass needle, and when east

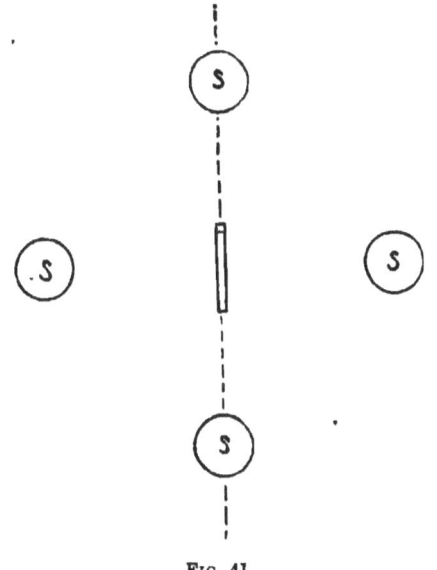

FIG. 41.

of the magnetic meridian an easterly variation. It is for this reason called the Semicircular Variation.

This variation can be neutralised by placing a smaller rod of iron on the opposite side of the compass-box, also in a vertical position. Its exact position must be found by experiment when the ship's head is east or west.

47. Quadrantal Variation.—A horizontal mass of iron in the ship—such as the guns and iron armour in an old man-of-war, or even a cargo of iron and steel—produce by their transient magnetism another variation in the compass. Each mass of iron becomes a magnet, always having its magnetic axis parallel to the meridian. The effect is seen on inspecting Fig. 42. In the four positions, *A, B, C, D*, of the mass—

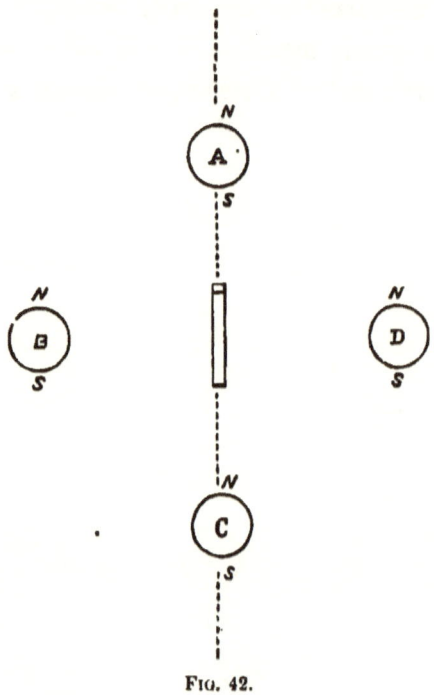

Fig. 42.

i.e. at the four cardinal points of the compass—the variation vanishes. When the magnetic mass is between *A* and *B*—*i.e.* in the north-west quadrant—the influence of the induced south pole on the north pole of the needle preponderates, and the variation of the north pole is west. Between *B* and *C* the north polar influence preponderates, and the variation is east. Between *C* and *D*, in the south-east quadrant, it is again west, and between *D* and *A*, or in the north-east quadrant, it is east. This variation, from changing its direction at each quadrant, is called quadrantal variation. It follows that two masses of soft iron fixed in the ship on opposite sides of the compass always increase each other's disturbance of the needle, but if placed so that the lines joining them to the compass subtend a right angle, they tend to neutralise each other's effect. To correct this variation a mass of soft iron must be fixed near the compass in a direction at right angles to that of the centre of the resultant disturbing mass.

48. Magnetism of Steel-plated Ships.—As soon as ships were constructed of iron plates riveted together, it was found that the hammering of the plates during construction converted them into permanent magnets, the total effect of which on the ship's compass was very large and very irregular; so much so that in one ship the compass varied 50° east in one position of the ship's head, and 50° west in another. It was found by theory, and confirmed by experiment, that the total permanent magnetism could always be resolved into two magnets, one along the ship's length, and the other transverse to the ship. Each of these was separately corrected by a permanent magnet fastened on the deck of the vessel.

After the first few voyages of an iron ship a considerable amount of the magnetism obtained during construction is lost, probably by beating about with the waves, and it is in consequence necessary, while the ship is young, to make a new correction for magnetism after each voyage. Very soon, however, the ship acquires a permanent magnetic condition, after which no further readjustment is needed.

The magnetism lost during the first few voyages is called *sub-permanent*, and that retained always *permanent* magnetism.

QUESTIONS ON BOOK I.

1. Draw a rough sketch of the lines of force for three equal and similar magnet poles placed at the angles of an equilateral triangle.

2. Draw the lines of force for two magnet poles of the same sign, but one stronger than the other.

3. On twisting the torsion circle in Coulomb's balance, through 40°, the needle is deflected from the meridian 5°. Find the torsion equivalent of the earth's directive action on the magnet. $\frac{T-A}{A}$
ANS.—7°.

4. The earth's directive action being measured by 5° of torsion, how far must the torsion circle be twisted round to bring the needle to 10°?
ANS.—60°.

5. The influence of the earth in Coulomb's balance being neutralised by external magnets, so that the needle is under torsion only; when the magnet pole is introduced the needle deflects 40°. How much torsion must be applied to bring the needle to 20° and to 10°?
ANS.—140° and 630° respectively.

6. The directive action of the earth being 5°, the introduction of the magnet causes a deflection of 40°. How much torsion must be put on to bring the reading to 20°?
ANS.—940°.

7. A short magnet needle suspended horizontally, and oscillating under the earth's action only makes 21 oscillations in a minute; when another magnet pole is distant 4 inches it makes 27 oscillations in the same time. Calculate the number of oscillations it will make when the second pole is distant 2 inches.
ANS.—40 per 1′ nearly.

8. A short suspended magnet, oscillating under the earth's force, makes 35 oscillations in a minute; when a south pole is placed in the meridian to the north of it, it makes 45 oscillations in the same time. How many oscillations per minute will it make if the pole be placed at the same distance to the south of it?
ANS.—21 per 1′ nearly.

Questions on Magnetism.

9. A needle makes 29 oscillations per 1' when a south magnet pole is 8 inches to the south of it, and 50 oscillations when the same pole is 4 inches to the north of it. Find how many oscillations the needle will make when under the earth's influence only.

ANS.—34 oscillations per 1' nearly.

10. Two magnet needles of equal size and weight, freely suspended, under the earth's action, make 40 and 36 oscillations respectively in the same time. Compare their magnetic strength.

ANS.—Ratio of 1 to ·81.

11. Two magnets 14 and 16 centimetres long, placed east and west of a suspended needle, with their nearer poles 7 and 8 centimetres respectively from the point of suspension, just balance each other. Compare the strengths of their poles.

ANS.—49 to 64.

12. Two equal magnet poles, placed 3 centimetres apart, exert on each other an attraction of 4 units. Find the strength of the poles in absolute measure.

ANS.—Each of strength 6.

13. Two magnet poles, whose strengths are in the ratio 3 to 2 when placed 10 centimetres apart, exert a force of 24 units. Find the strength of each pole in absolute measure.

ANS.—60 and 40.

14. Two magnets, the strengths of whose poles are 8 and 12, are placed in the same straight line, with opposite poles facing each other, at a distance of 4 centimetres. If the magnets are respectively 12 and 16 centimetres long, find the magnetic attraction between them.

ANS.—5·5 units nearly.

15. The same magnet needle, suspended horizontally under the earth's action, makes at two places 101 and 103 oscillations in the same time. Compare the horizontal component of the earth's magnetism at those places.

ANS.—1 to 1·04 nearly.

16. A short magnet, suspended horizontally, makes 29 oscillations in a minute; when a south pole is placed 4 centimetres from it on the north side, it makes 39 oscillations in the same time. Compare the strength of this pole with the horizontal component of the earth's magnetism. Explain fully what is meant by this comparison.

ANS.—12·9 to 1 nearly.

BOOK II.

FRICTIONAL ELECTRICITY.

CHAPTER I.

ELECTRIFICATION.

49. Definition of Electricity.—There are certain bodies which, when warm and dry, acquire by friction the property of attracting feathers, filaments of silk, or indeed any light bodies towards them. This property is called Electricity, and bodies which possess it are said to be electrified. The ancients were acquainted with it only in amber, the Greek name for which (ἤλεκτρον) is the origin of the term Electricity. Dr. Gilbert, physician to Queen Elizabeth, seems to have been the first who noticed the same property in other bodies, and we shall see reason to believe that any two bodies whatever of different structure, when rubbed together, develop electricity to a greater or smaller extent.

To exhibit this property all the apparatus employed must be kept warm and dry. With this precaution, absolutely necessary in all experiments on the present subject, it is easy to exhibit electricity in a very great variety of bodies. Glass rubbed with silk, sealing-wax rubbed with flannel, vulcanite or ebonite rubbed with any woollen material, or with silk, common writing-paper well warmed and rubbed with a bristle clothes-brush—all manifest electricity by picking up feathers, scraps of paper, silk fibre, or other light materials.

50. Means of detecting Electricity.—If we present an electrified body to a pith-ball pendulum—that is, a pith ball suspended by a silk thread—it is first drawn towards the excited body, and, immediately after contact, repelled, for a reason which we shall see presently. A skeleton-ball pendulum (Fig. 43) made of narrow strips of gilt paper, will answer equally well. A light lath (Fig. 44), about a metre long, poised on the convex surface of an egg or a watch-glass, will follow the movements of the excited body round a complete circle. These and other arrangements described later for detecting the presence of electricity are called Electroscopes.

FIG. 43.

If the body electrified be very light, it will cling to other bodies to which it is presented. The paper excited by a clothes-brush will be found to cling with some force to the table on which it was laid while being excited by brushing; on removal it clings to the hands of the operator, and may be made to cling to the walls of a room, or any other flat surface.

51. Action of Electrified Bodies on each other.—To investigate the action of electricity on other electricity, we will excite by friction a rod of sealing-wax, and either poise it on a convex surface, like the lath electroscope, or suspend it

Electrification.

in a paper stirrup (Fig. 45), like the magnet in Art. 3. If we bring towards its end another rod of sealing-wax, also excited,

FIG. 44.

we shall find repulsion between the two rods. If, on the other hand, we bring towards it an excited glass rod, we shall find

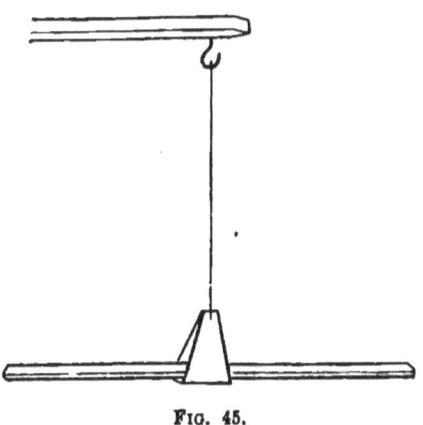

FIG. 45.

attraction. If instead we take an excited glass rod, and suspend it in a paper stirrup, or poise it on a point by means of a dimple blown in its surface (Fig. 46), we shall find it attracted by excited sealing-wax, but repelled by excited glass.

52. Vitreous and Resinous Electricity. — This teaches us that there are two different kinds of electricity:

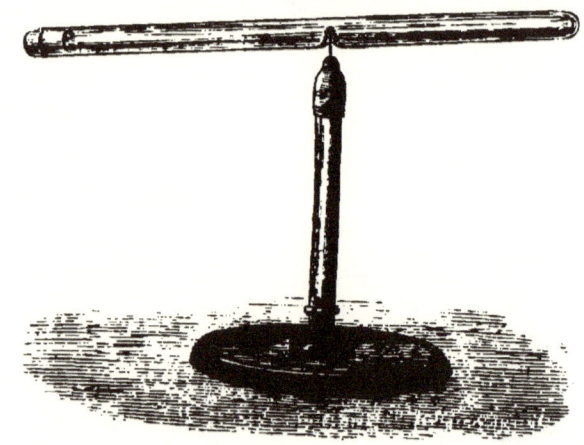

Fig. 46.

one developed in glass when excited by silk, called Vitreous or Positive electricity (written + E.); another developed in sealing-wax when excited by flannel, which is called Resinous or Negative electricity (written − E.). The experiments also show that like electricities repel, but unlike electricities attract, each other.

The suspended glass and sealing-wax rods when excited may be used to detect the kinds of other electrifications; for a body, if unelectrified, will attract both rods when presented to them in turn, but an electrified body will attract one and repel the other, as its electricity is of the opposite or of the same name. Thus paper electrified by rubbing with india-rubber will be found to have a charge of vitreous electricity, and the india-rubber will have a charge of resinous electricity.

If a silk ribbon (Fig. 47), a foot or a foot and a half long, after being rubbed several times over a glass rod, is folded in the middle, the two halves repel each other, being similarly excited by the glass, and, if suspended, remain for some time divergent. This may be used as an electroscope, for on bringing near from below a negatively-electrified body (an excited rod of sealing-wax, for instance), the ribbons diverge further, they being negatively electrified; and, conversely, on bringing near a positively electrified body they collapse.

FIG. 47.

In the same manner, if a sheet of paper, before it is excited, be cut up into narrow strips, only held together along one edge, after excitement the strips show a violent repulsion, curling up away from one another.

53. Conductors and Non-Conductors or Insulators.

—There is a class of bodies, of which the metals are the best

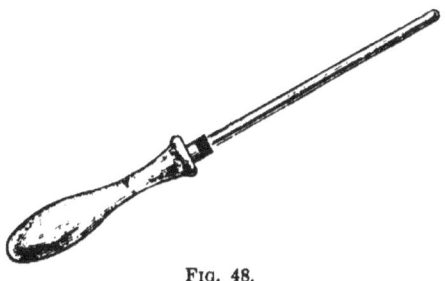

FIG. 48.

examples, which do not show any sign of electrification when excited by friction. This is the case with a brass rod held in the hand, and rubbed with a cat's fur or a silk handkerchief. If, however, the brass rod be supported on a handle of glass (Fig. 48) or ebonite, we shall find that, holding it by its handle, and rubbing it, it is immediately excited, and on testing is found to be charged with negative electricity. On touching the excited brass with the finger, or with another metal body in connection with the earth, all signs of electricity instantaneously disappear. We see therefore that the metal is capable of excitement like the other bodies we have considered; but the reason we do not observe it when held in the hand and excited is, that the electricity is drawn away by the hand as fast as it is generated. Bodies such as these are called *Conductors;* while other bodies, such as glass and sealing-wax, which do not carry away the electricity as fast as it is generated, are called *Non-conductors* or *Insulators*. These latter, which can be excited when held in the hand, used to be called *Electrics*, and those like the metals, which were not so excited, were called *Non-electrics*. These terms, however, are now misleading, and had better be abandoned.

Different bodies have very different powers of conducting electricity, all being intermediate between an ideal perfect conductor and perfect non-conductor. The best conductors are the metals, and the best solid non-conductor is said to be gum-lac. For our present purpose it will be sufficient to notice that such bodies as the following are, next to metals, the best conductors: Charcoal, graphite, water, mineral and vegetable substances (chiefly owing to the large amount of water they contain), and linen and cotton fibres. The best non-conductors or insulators after gum-lac are sealing-wax, glass, resin, sulphur, silk, paper, and caoutchouc. These are roughly in order of their powers of conduction and insulation respectively. It is doubtful how far air and gases are conductors in the proper sense of the word, but it is important to notice that dry air acts as an insulator of ordinary charges, while damp air allows the charge to pass away, though this effect is probably due to the film of moisture formed on the surface of the insulating supports of electrified bodies, and this liquid film is certainly an excellent conductor. In the case of liquids also we have mercury and the fused metals, which conduct well, and, just like the metals; aqueous solutions of acids and salts are fair conductors; pure water, alcohol, ether, are semi-conductors; while carbon bisulphide is a good non-conductor, though in these, excepting the metals, it is doubtful how far conduction is separated from another action (electrolysis), which we shall discuss later on.

Conduction in bodies is also affected by temperature. Some bodies which are insulators when cold become conductors when heated to fusion, or even considerably below fusing-point. This is the case with glass.

54. Effect of Damp or Dry Atmosphere.—We can now understand the necessity for drying and warming our apparatus, insisted upon above. Warming the air of a room in which experiments are performed dries the air, by removing it further from its dew-point, while warming the apparatus above the temperature of the air prevents the formation of the film of water on the insulating supports. Paper, being very hygroscopic, must be thoroughly dried by holding it before the fire for a minute or so, in order to drive out the moisture before it can be electrified.

55. Gold-leaf Electroscope.—The instrument most

commonly used for investigations in electricity is the Gold-leaf Electroscope. This consists of a brass rod (*A*) fastened to the centre of a brass circular cap (*B*), and having at its other end two strips of gold leaf (*CC*), which, when the instrument is unelectrified, hang down parallel to each other. This apparatus is insulated by supporting the cap on a glass tube (*D*), well varnished, which surrounds the brass rod. The tube is cemented into the top of a glass bell-jar (*E*). Two strips of tinfoil (*FF*) usually run from the base of the glass bell up to the level of the gold leaves. The base is of wood, sometimes covered with tinfoil, and usually supports a cup of sulphuric acid, or calcium chloride, to maintain dryness in the air.

FIG. 49.

On touching the cap of the electroscope with excited glass or sealing-wax, we communicate a charge which causes the gold leaves to diverge exactly like the excited silk ribbons in Art. 52. Otherwise a negative charge can be communicated by simply flapping the cap slightly with a silk handkerchief, affording another illustration of the electrification of an insulated conductor by friction. Further, when we have charged the electroscope, say with positive electricity, on bringing another positively electrified body near to its cap, we observe that the leaves diverge further: this is because the positive electricity tends to repel like electricity from the cap into the leaves, causing in this manner further divergence. In the same manner, on bringing a negatively electrified body near, the leaves are observed partly to collapse. In this manner we use the electroscope to distinguish even very feeble charges of electricity.[1]

56. Development of the two Electricities, simultaneous and in equal quantities.—It will now be easy to show that these opposite electricities are always developed together; that where the glass was charged with positive electricity, the silk used for the rubber carried off negative electricity, and that where the sealing-wax was charged negatively the flannel used as rubber carried off positive electricity.

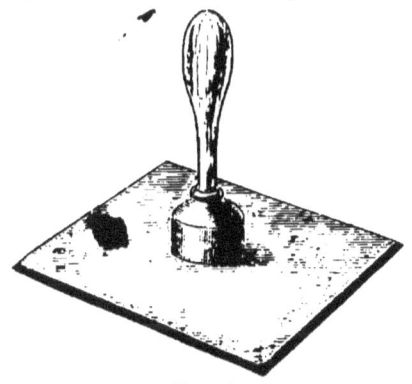

FIG 50.

This can be shown (Fig. 50) by taking a plate of window-glass, and a rubber made of leather covered on its flat surface with silk (better if amalgamated, as for the electrical machine), and furnished with a glass handle. On simply turning the rubber round on the plate a few times, the friction develops electricity; but on presenting the plate and rubber in contact to the previously charged electroscope, no indication of electricity appears. On presenting them separately, however, the glass is found to be positively and the rubber negatively

---

[1] For a similar reason to that noticed in Magnetism, we must observe the *first* movement of the leaves as the electrified body approaches the electroscope.

charged. Similarly, if a rod of sealing-wax (Fig. 51) be furnished with a flannel cap extending three inches down it (with a silk thread attached by which it can be drawn off), by twisting the rod round and round inside the cap electricity is generated; but on presenting them together to the electroscope, no trace of electrification is observed. When, after drawing off the cap by the silk thread, they are presented separately, the sealing-wax is found to be negatively and the flannel cap positively electrified.

FIG. 51.

This shows that the two electricities are always separated together, and since, while the two bodies are held in contact, there is no trace of electrification, the two quantities separated are always such as just to neutralise each other's attractive and repulsive effect on external electricity. This leads us also to say that the two electricities are separated in equal quantities. This statement we shall find to be of universal application; and we can no more develop a quantity of positive electricity without an equal (or complementary) quantity of negative electricity, than we can have a north magnetic pole without somewhere an equal south pole.

57. The Electrical Series.—The kind of electrification developed on a body depends not only on the body itself, but on the substance with which it is rubbed. Thus glass is positive when rubbed with silk, and negative when rubbed with the fur of the living cat. Minute differences in the surface texture of the substances rubbed leads to an electrical separation on rubbing. Thus white and black silk, when rubbed together, show a separation of electricity; probably due to a difference in surface caused by the dye; rough and smooth glass, when rubbed together, leave the smooth positively and the rough negatively electrified; and even two pieces of ribbon cut from the same piece, if drawn over each other, the length of one across the breadth of the other, will show a separation of electricities. The fur of the living cat, and, according to Clerk-Maxwell, that of the living dog, is found to be positive to a dressed cat's fur.

If we have any three substances (A, B, C), and find by experiment that A carries away positive electricity when rubbed with B, and B positive electricity when rubbed with C, we shall always find A positive to C when they are rubbed together. In performing the experiment care should be taken that all the bodies are neutral, to begin with. Suppose, for instance, that A, on being rubbed by B, left B with a high charge of negative electricity, the effect of rubbing B and C *might* then be only to divide B's charge between B and C, which would then both be found negative.

On this ground it is possible to arrange any given substances in an *electric series*, such that each member of the series is positive to all that come after it, but negative to all that go before it. From what we have just said, it will be clear that the order of the series will not be the same for all samples of nominally the same substance, and thus irregularities occur. Thus it is generally stated that cat's fur stands at the head of this series, but the present writer has found certain cleavage planes in calcite to be positive to the fur of at least one living cat, and has found specimens of glass positive to some dressed furs. The series given by different authors consequently differ a good deal; that which we supply here must therefore be understood as only true in a general way, with such limitations as we have noticed. It is that obtained with the substances generally used by the present writer.

+	
Catskin.	Metal.
Smooth Glass.	⎰ Caoutchouc.
The Hand.	⎱ Planed Dealboard.
Paper.	Ebonite.
Flannel.	Sealing-wax.
Silk.	Sulphur.
Roughened Glass.	Vulcanised India-
Cork.	rubber.

58. Electrification by Pressure and Cleavage.—There are other methods besides friction of causing electrical separation. We do not at present refer to electricity developed by contact in metals, or by chemical decomposition, or by heating the junction of two metals, all of which will be discussed in their due place. If two non-conductors be simply pressed together, and suddenly separated, they will be found to be electrified. This is easily shown by pressing a cork supported on a glass handle down on to a piece of india-rubber, or even on to a piece of orange-peel. Many minerals show an electrical separation on cleavage. If a block of mica be held by an insulating handle, and large flakes be separated rapidly from it, the block will be found to be electrified. The same thing appears on breaking up roll-sulphur. If the sulphur be supported on an insulating pad, a piece of india-rubber for instance, and be broken over an electroscope by smart taps of a hammer, the fragments which fall on the cap will generally make the leaves diverge. For the same reason, lump sugar, when broken in the dark, often shows a phosphorescence, due to the reuniting of the electricities separated by the fracture.

59. Pyro-Electricity.—There is also another mode in which electricity is developed, namely, when certain badly conducting minerals are heated or cooled. This is termed pyro-electricity. It is most strongly shown in tourmaline

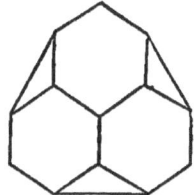 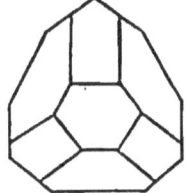

FIG. 52.

crystals which have the facets at the opposite ends of the crystal differently arranged (Fig. 52). The specimen should be suspended in a stirrup of fine wire over a metal plate warmed by a spirit lamp. Very soon one end will show positive, and the opposite negative, electricity, and this will continue as long as the temperature rises, till it reaches a temperature of about 350° C., when all trace of electricity ceases. On removing the plate, and passing the lamp flame over the crystal to discharge its electricity, and then allowing it to cool, that end which was positive when being heated becomes negative while being cooled, and *vice versa*. The end which is positive while being heated is called the analogue, and the opposite the antilogue, pole of the crystal. Suitable crystals are rare, but specimens in the form of long needles may be met with, which show pyro-electricity faintly, and especially while cooling, when observation can be more easily made. In Fig. 52 the left-hand drawing showing the terminal with fewest facets is the analogue, and the right-hand drawing is the antilogue pole.

No physical theory has yet been propounded to account for the electrical separations we have noticed. We may, perhaps, point out that they all seem dependent on a molecular strain in the molecules of different bodies when brought into very close contact by friction or pressure. The electrification by cleavage or heating in crystals may be referred to a similar cause, if we remember that in many crystals the arrangement of the molecules is such that their expansion by heating and all physical properties are different in different directions. In these, either cleavage or heating may establish a state of molecular strain which is accompanied by a separation of electricity. If the crystal is a conductor, the separated electricities of course immediately unite again, and the phenomenon cannot be observed.

We have, as in Magnetism, purposely avoided all reference to the various one and two fluid hypotheses, which were useful only in the infancy of those sciences.

CHAPTER II.

THE FIELD OF ELECTRIC FORCE.

60. The Electric Field.—We must now proceed to consider the laws of attraction and repulsion of electrified bodies, just as we did in Magnetism. We have seen that if we have a distribution of electricity, and an electrified body be brought near it, this latter will experience mechanical force. Just, then, as the air space round a magnet showed us a field of magnetic force, so the air space round an electrified body shows us a field of electrical force. To the air or other medium across which electrical forces are displayed, Faraday gave the name dielectric. It will simplify matters if we use for exploring the field of force a very small sphere, carrying always the same charge of electricity, and we may then assume that the action on this sphere is the same as if all the electricity were collected at some point within it, probably near its centre. We will suppose this an unit charge, and assuming the electrification positive, we will call it a plus unit (written + unit). At every point in the field of force there will be a certain definite direction in which the + unit put there will be urged, and this direction is called the line of force through that point. The whole field may therefore be mapped out into lines of force, which, as in Magnetism, cannot intersect each other. There will also be a certain force with which the + unit is urged along the line of force at each point in the field, and this force is called the

82   *Electricity.*   [Book II.

strength of the field at that point. We may also define the positive and negative direction of a line of force as the direction in which a + or − unit respectively would be urged.

61. Coulomb's Torsion Balance.—We have no means, similar to the magnetic curves, for exhibiting to the eye the form of the lines of force. We may assume, however, that

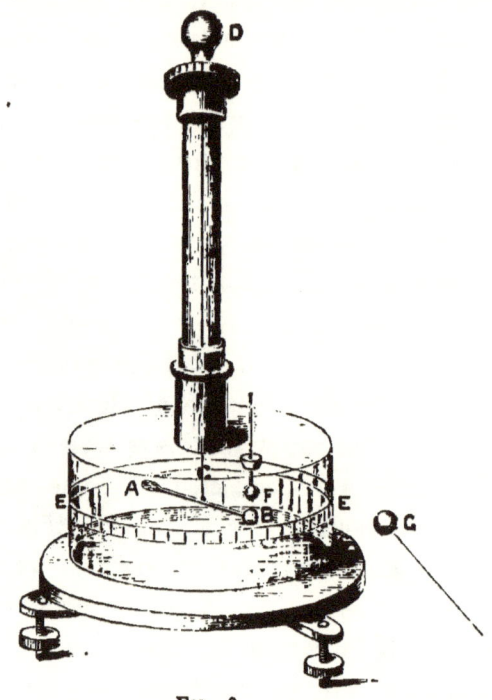

Fig. 3.

the lines of force for a small electrified sphere proceed out round it in all directions, and can then investigate the strength of the field at each point as depending (1) on the distance, (2) on the quantity, of electricity present. This was done by Coulomb, using a torsion balance very similar to that used by the same experimenter for magnetic forces.

The torsion balance (Fig. 53) consists of a glass needle (A) carrying at one end a gilt ball (B), and at the other a counterpoise, suspended by a fine wire (C), which is often a single capillary fibre of glass, attached to a torsion circle (D) above, the circle having a graduated rim by which the twist put on to the wire may be measured. The needle moves in a glass case (E), whose surface is graduated, the suspension of the needle being in the centre of graduations: by its means the movement of the needle may be read. In the upper part of the case there is a hole through which an insulated gilt ball (F) (the carrier ball), of the same size as the needle ball, may be introduced and placed in contact with the needle ball. Another insulated gilt ball (G) (the divided-charge ball), equal to the carrier and needle balls, and supported on an insulating stem, is required in the course of the experiment. The base is supported on levelling screws, by which the suspension of the needle is brought to the centre of the graduations on the case. Within the case is placed a vessel with drying material as in the gold-leaf electroscope.

When the whole system is unelectrified, the needle ball rests in the place which the carrier ball will occupy when in position; the wire being without torsion, and the needle and pointer each at its zero of graduation.

62. Law of Action at different Distances.—On electrifying the carrier ball, and introducing it, there is at first attraction, but after contact repulsion, of the needle ball. We will suppose it to be repelled, and to come to rest at 72°. The torsion on the wire is also 72°. To bring the needle back to 36°, it will be found necessary to turn the torsion circle backwards through about 250°. The repulsion at 36° will then be 250° + 36° = 286°, which we notice to be very nearly 4 × 72°. Thus we learn that the repulsion at 36° is four times that at 72°. To bring the needle to 24°, we must still turn the torsion circle backwards through one complete revolution, and 260° additional. The total torsion is then 360° + 260° + 24° = 644°, which is nearly 9 × 72°.

This will be sufficient to suggest the law of inverse squares, as that holding between two small electrified spheres placed at different distances from each other. In most instruments the torsion, when the needle and carrier balls are within 20° of each other, becomes less than this theory requires, the reason being that the electricities on the two balls mutually repel each other towards the more remote sides of the balls, and they in consequence act on each other at a distance somewhat greater than the distance of their centres.

We may infer that the strength of the electrical field, due to a quantity of electricity condensed in a point, is inversely as the square of the distance from the electrified particle, *i.e.* if distances be taken respectively as 1, 2, 3, . . . etc., the forces at those distances will be as $1, \frac{1}{4}, \frac{1}{9}, \ldots$ etc.

63. Law of Action with different Quantities.—We have seen nothing at present enabling us to measure quantities of electricity, but if we have two equal spheres, one charged with electricity, and the other insulated and neutral, we may assume that on bringing them into contact the charge will be divided equally between them. Thus, in the above experiment, when the carrier ball touched the needle ball the charge was equally divided between them, and we were therefore investigating the force between two equal charges. After turning back the torsion circle to its 0°, let us remove the carrier ball, and halve its charge by simple contact with the equal divided-charge ball. Reintroduce it into the instrument, carefully avoiding contact with the needle ball (this may be done by turning the torsion circle through about a quarter of a revolution), and regulate the torsion circle till the needle again stands at 72°. It will be found that the torsion circle stands at 36°, and the torsion on the wire is (72°−36°)=36°. Hence we see that the repulsive force is halved on halving the charge in the carrier ball. If we halve again the charge in the carrier ball, the torsion circle must be twisted through 54°, and the torsion is therefore (72°−54°)=18°, which is one fourth of its first value— when the charge of one of the balls is divided by four. Lastly, take out the carrier ball, and discharge by contact with the finger. On reintroducing it, the needle ball is attracted, and divides its charge with the carrier ball, so that each ball has half of its original charge. We shall then find that the torsion necessary to keep the balls at 72° is 18°, or $\frac{1}{2} \times \frac{1}{2}$ of that when each charge was unity.

From these experiments we may infer that the force at equal distances between two charges of electricity condensed in points is proportional to the product of the quantities, and that the strength of the field at a given distance from a charge condensed in a point is proportional to the charge.

*64. Absolute Measure of Electricity.—We may now explain how electrical quantities may, like magnetic, be measured in terms of the absolute system of units, explained in Appendix I. Thus we shall assume one absolute unit of electricity to be such a quantity that, when condensed in a point, it exerts unit force on another equal quantity placed at unit distance. We can then express the force between two quantities q and q' condensed in points at distance D cm. apart by $\frac{qq'}{D^2}$, and the strength of field at a distance D from a quantity q condensed in a point by $\frac{q}{D^2}$.

Coulomb, by vertical stops which prevented the needle swinging back to zero, showed identically the same laws to hold for the attraction between two quantities of electricity of opposite sign.

65. Use of the Proof-Plane.

Returning to our fundamental experiment of the attraction and subsequent repulsion by an electrified body of any light conducting body, we can

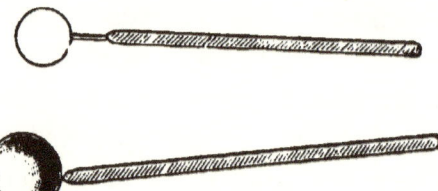

Fig. 54.

see that if we insulate by a glass handle a small gilt ball or paper disc, and apply it to the surface of an electrified body, it will, on removal, carry away some of its electricity, which may be tested by a charged electroscope at a distance. We may, in this manner, test the electrification of a body too feebly electrified to show directly attractions and repulsions. Such an instrument was called a *Proof-Plane* by Coulomb, and has since his time been widely used in testing electrification. It may be noticed that what we test by the proof-plane is really the strength of the electric field close to the point on the conductor at which it is applied, for this, and this only, determines the quantity of electricity which shall be repelled on to the proof-plane when brought into contact with the conductor, the flow continuing till the charge on the proof-plane and that on the conductor exercise equal and opposite repulsions. Assuming, then, that the proof-plane is so small that it can be charged from the conductor without

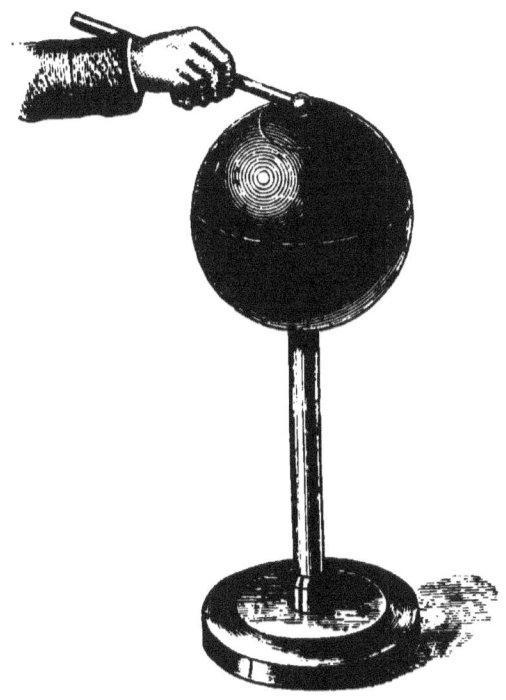

FIG. 55.

sensibly weakening its charge, or altering the distribution on it, the proof-plane carries away a charge proportional to the strength of the field of force close to the conductor at the point where it is applied.

66. No Electricity within a hollow Conductor.— We will employ the proof-plane to show that there is no electrical force inside a charged conductor, or, as it is usually expressed, that electricity resides only on the outside of a conductor.

Let us take an insulated hollow sphere (Fig. 55), or conductor of any shape, with a small circular aperture, through which the proof-plane may be easily introduced. Charge the conductor,[1] and charge with the same kind of electricity a gold-leaf electroscope at a distance. On testing with the proof-plane we find indications of a charge, on any external point, but on any part of the interior surface no charge whatever.

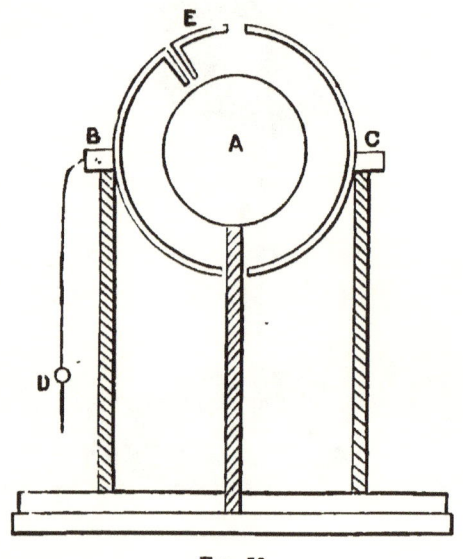

Fig. 56.

Otherwise take an insulated sphere (A), having two insulated hemispheres (BC), which envelop A, but are separated from it by an air-space (shown in section in Fig. 56). Let A be charged, and the hemispheres adjusted carefully without

---

[1] In this and the following experiments the charging of the conductors, but not of the electroscope, is done from an electrophorus.

The Field of Electric Force.

contact with A; then lift by its silk thread the metal wire D, and drop it through the aperture E in B, until it just rests on A, and then remove it again. On removing B and C, A will be found to be completely discharged, the charge having been by contact transferred to the external hemispheres.

Again, if we test the outside and inside of a hollow electrified cylinder, we shall find the inside charge insensible everywhere except very near to the edge. This will be true even if the cylinder be made of wire gauze with very large meshes. Faraday used an insulated cotton gauze bag, similar to a

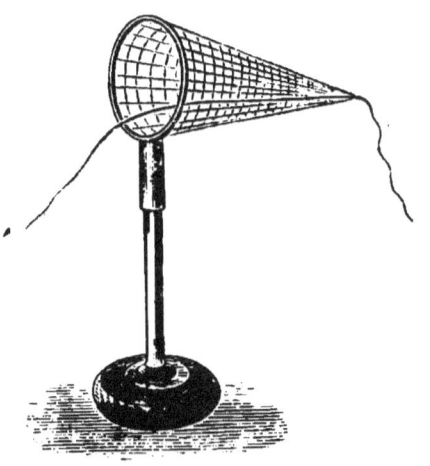

FIG. 57.

butterfly-net, fitted to a wire rim for support, and fastened on to a glass stem, the end of the bag being furnished with a silk thread passing through both sides, by which the bag could be turned inside out at pleasure. After charging he showed by the proof-plane that there was no sensible electrification on the inside. He then by the silk thread turned the bag inside out, showing again that there was no trace of electrification on the inside surface.

Faraday also constructed a cubical chamber, twelve feet wide, formed of a slight wooden framework, with copper wires passing along and across it in various directions, and then covered it with paper in close proximity to the conducting wires, and pasted bands of tinfoil over it in every direction. This chamber was insulated, and put in connection with a

Fig. 58.

powerful electrical machine, which was worked for some time. He then says :—"I went into the cube and lived in it, and using lighted candles, electrometers, and all other tests of electrical states, I could not find the least influence upon them, or indication of anything particular given by them, though all the time the outside of the cube was powerfully charged, and large sparks and brushes were darting off from every part of its outer surface."

We may imitate this experiment by placing a metal wire cage over a gold-leaf electroscope supported on a metal plate, which is insulated with a pad of india-rubber (Fig. 58). We may either leave the electroscope free or connect its cap by a wire with the outside surface of the cage; but on electrifying the cage, the leaves of the electroscope will not diverge, as we have seen they always do when the instrument is placed in a field of electric force.

67. Electrical Density. — These experiments show us that the field of force only exists in the dielectric surrounding electrified conductors, and does not extend inside them. They show not only that there is no electricity within the conductor, but also that the external electrification is so distributed that the resultant force at every internal point vanishes. The older theorists, assuming that electricity was of the nature of a material but weightless film investing the conductor, set themselves to discover the law of density of such a film that the condition thus stated might be true, and there came into use the term Electrical Density at a point on a conductor. We may use the term to denote the quantity of electrification per unit area on a charged conductor, and this implies no material idea of electricity, while our definition of quantity implies none. The term, moreover, is convenient, since we can clearly have the same quantity of electricity on a sphere of one inch or of one foot radius, and the density of the distribution must thus be inversely as the surface of the sphere, or as 144 to 1. It follows, too, theoretically, as a consequence of the general law of distribution stated above, that the force close to any point on an electrified conductor is proportional only to the density of the electrification at that point.[1] Hence for our purpose it matters little whether we speak of the force near a point on an electrified conductor, or the density of the electrification at the point.

Although we cannot lay down the law of density of distribution on a conductor, we can by the proof-plane show some

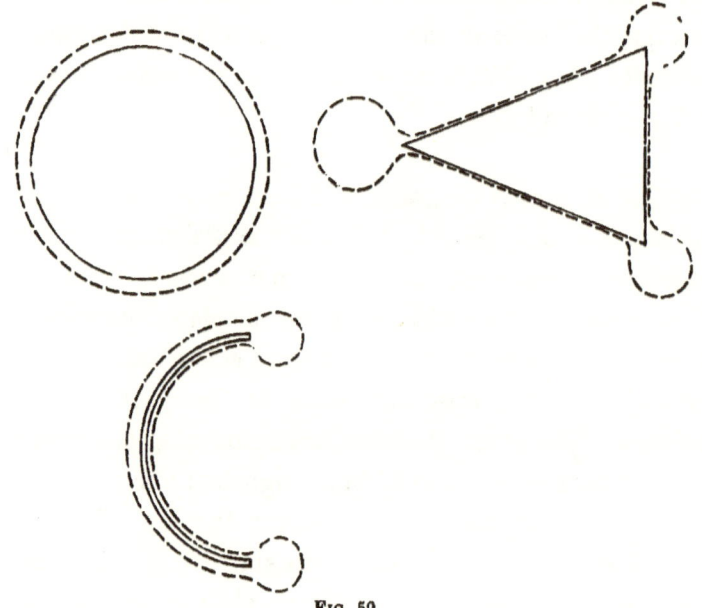

Fig. 59.

of its more general properties. To obtain numerical results we must employ the Torsion Balance, charging independently the needle ball; after touching with the carrier ball a certain part of the conductor, introduce it into the balance, as before carefully avoiding contact, and observe the torsion necessary to give a certain fixed deflection. This torsion

[1] Cumming's Introduction to the Theory of Electricity, Art. 62.

measures the quantity on the carrier ball, and is therefore a measure of the electrical density, which can be compared at as many points as we please.

It is, however, generally sufficient to show the more general laws by the proof-plane and gold-leaf electroscope. If we test a sphere, we shall find that its electrification has the same density at every point, as might have been expected from its shape. For other conductors it will be found that the density at points and angles is very high; that at the flatter portions small; while within hollows and cavities it almost wholly disappears.

If for the density we substitute depth of a liquid film supposed homogeneous, we may represent to the eye the depth of the imaginary electric stratum by the diagram (Fig. 59), which show it approximately for a sphere, a cone, and a hollow hemisphere.

68. Electrical Potential. — Let us next connect the proof-plane by a long wire with a gold-leaf electroscope at a distance (Fig. 60), and touch in succession various parts of any of the conductors we have been experimenting upon. We shall observe that for every point on or within each of these conductors there is a certain fixed divergence of the leaves which never alters, whether the proof-plane be applied to places of high or low density. This divergence depends on the electrification of the conductor as a whole, and we will for the present define it as the potential of the conductor, the experiment showing that all points on the conductor are at the same potential. This indication is of course the potential of the cap and leaves of the electroscope, and although this instrument is not adapted to give numerical measures, we can speak of a higher and lower potential according as the divergence of the leaves is greater or less. When the leaves diverge with negative electricity we have negative potential, which may have a greater or less value.

69. Capacity of a Conductor.—Take the hollow sphere having an aperture in its surface, and connect it with the distant electroscope. If we bring successive charges by means

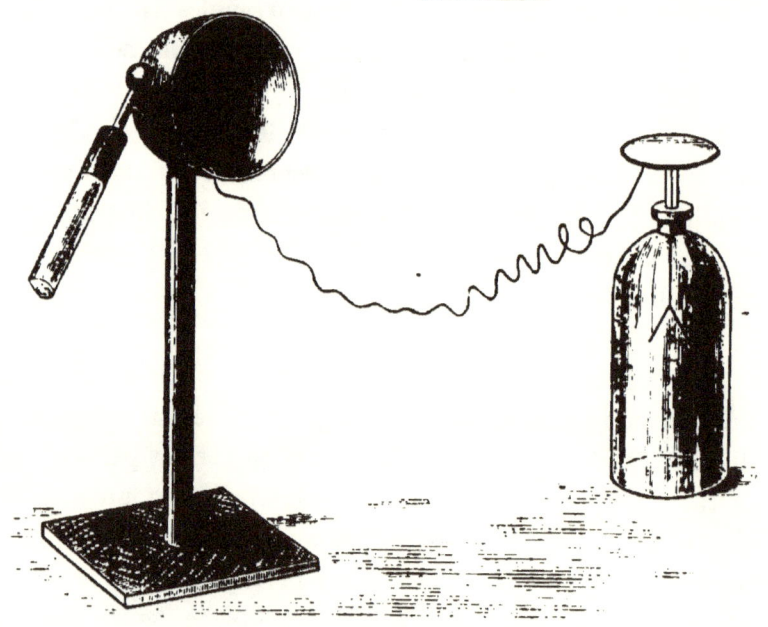

Fig. 60.

of a small insulated sphere or proof-plane, and introduce them through the aperture, on touching the inner surface the charge is given up to the sphere, and the proof-plane can be withdrawn uncharged. We now observe that the potential shown by the divergence in the gold leaves goes on rising with the charge, and we shall *assume* that the potential is proportional to the charge, so that for each conductor there is a fixed ratio between the charge and the potential, which fixed ratio is called the Capacity of the Conductor. If, then, we are able to obtain a numerical measure of the potential in terms of a suitable unit; for any given conductor, if Q represent the charge, V the potential, and C the capacity, we shall have $\frac{Q}{V} = C$, or $Q = CV$.

The capacity, so far as a conductor insulated in a large room is concerned, depends only on the shape and size of the conductor, but we shall learn presently that it depends also on the neighbourhood of other conductors. That the capacity depends on the form, and not only on the size of the conductor, may be shown by choosing two conductors of the same surface and very different forms; a sphere composed of two separable hemispheres (see Fig. 56), and one of the separate hemispheres answers well, since in the hemisphere both the outer and inner hemispheres become external. Charge one hemisphere and test its potential by connecting it with a distant electroscope. Then bring up the second hemisphere, and fit the two together without discharging, and you have the same quantity of electricity as before distributed over the same surface, the inner surface now not being electrified. It will be found, nevertheless, that the gold leaves have collapsed somewhat, proving that for equal charges the potential of the sphere is lower than the hemisphere, or that the capacity of the sphere is greater than that of a hemisphere of the same total area.

70. Potential Experiments with the Gold-Leaf Electroscope.—We can now examine more fully the action of the Gold-leaf Electroscope, especially with reference to the function of the tinfoil strips, which are attached to the glass case opposite to the gold leaves. We will at present assume that the whole base is covered with tinfoil in contact with strips, and that it extends outside the glass case by passing under it, as shown in section, in Fig. 61. We will now insulate the electroscope, and connect the cap with the base by strips of tinfoil outside the case (Fig. 62).

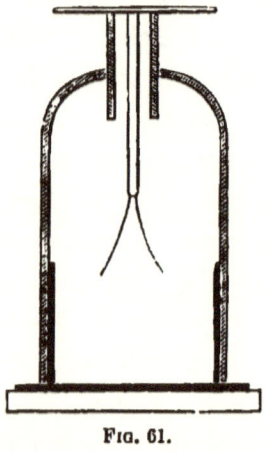
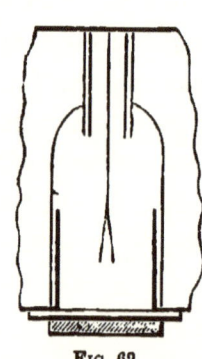

Fig. 61.   Fig. 62.

We shall now find, however highly we electrify the cap, there is no divergence of the gold leaves. The effect of joining, by the conducting tinfoil, the base and the cap is to bring them all to the same potential. We learn, therefore, that the *leaves will not diverge unless the base and cap are at different potentials.* To illustrate this further, remove the connecting strips, and charge, say with + electricity the base, leaving the cap uncharged; the leaves now diverge with − electricity. Next give a charge to the cap, and if it be of the right strength, the leaves collapse, since the base and cap are brought to the same potential. If the last charge be too strong the leaves diverge with + electricity. By giving alternate charges to the base and cap we shall find that the leaves may diverge with + or − electricity, though both cap and base are charged positively, just as the potential of the cap is higher or lower than that of the base.

71. Electrical Force requires varying Potential.— These experiments teach us that we can only have electrical force exhibited in a region in which the potential changes as we go from one part to another. In the last experiment the mechanical force which caused the leaves to diverge was exerted because a positive electrification tends to move from places of higher towards places of lower potential; and *vice versa*, negative electricity tends from places of lower towards places of higher potential. Every field of force therefore is a region of varying potential, but the space inside an electrified conductor, in which, as we have already seen (Art. 66), no divergence in the leaves of an unelectrified electroscope takes place, must be a region of uniform potential.

We may point out two useful analogies which these experiments suggest. First, that of temperature, in which a flow of heat takes place from hotter to colder bodies, *i.e.* from bodies at higher towards those at lower temperature. In this case heat is analogous to electricity, and temperature to potential, no exchange being apparent if the bodies are at equal temperatures. Secondly, that of level in gravitation—a liquid (water, for example) always tends to flow when a channel is opened from places of higher towards places of lower level, in which case level is analogous to potential, and water to electricity, there being no flow of water between two reservoirs at the same level.

CHAPTER III.

ELECTRICAL INDUCTION

72. Electrification induced on an Insulated Conductor.—If we introduce an insulated unelectrified body into a field of force, we find a separation of electricities by induction similar in general character to magnetic induction.

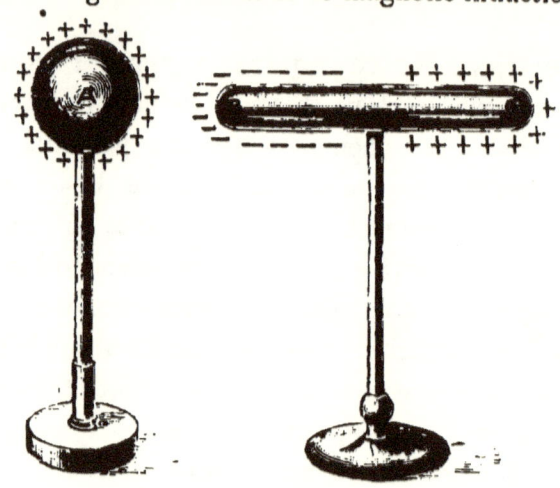

Fig. 63.

Thus if A (Fig. 63) be a body electrified, say positively, and BC an insulated unelectrified body, we shall find on testing BC with a proof-plane that there is a charge of negative electricity at B and of positive electricity at C. If we pass from B or C, testing with the proof-plane at each step, we shall easily see that the density diminishes continually, until at an intermediate point it vanishes. Such points of

Electrical Induction.

neutral electrification form a neutral line round BC. We thus see that the electrification of A acts on the conductor BC, separating its electricities, drawing electricity of opposite name towards B, and repelling electricity of like name towards C.

We infer that every electrical charge tends to separate electricity in all surrounding conductors, drawing to the parts nearest to it electricity of opposite name to its own, and repelling to the most remote part electricity of like name.

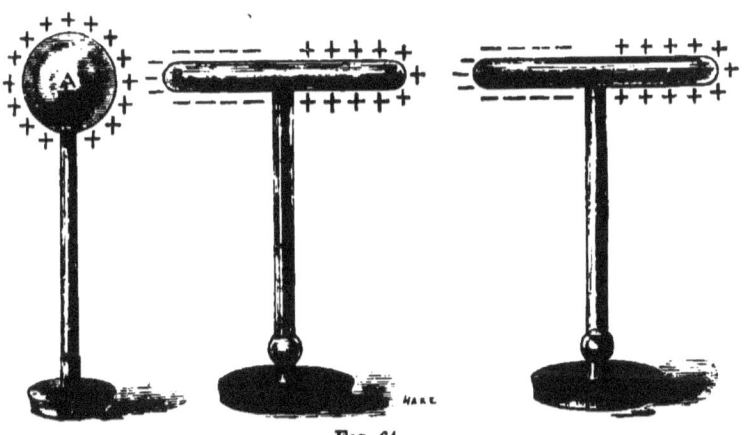

FIG. 64.

It is easy to see that these induced charges are able to cause fresh separations by induction in other bodies, as may be seen if we bring DE (Fig. 64) near to C, when we shall find negative electricity towards D and positive towards E.

If BC be divisible into two parts by a plane through its middle (Fig. 65), enabling us to separate B and C, while keeping them insulated, we shall find that B carries away a negative charge and C a positive charge.

We thus see that from a given electrical separation we can by induction make fresh separations in other conductors without limit, and this principle is used in many machines for generating electricity. It might at first sight appear that in obtaining an unlimited amount of electrical separation from a small initial separation we have a breach of the general law of conservation of energy. Such is not the case, however, since, in separating B and C in the foregoing illustration, just as much energy is expended as would have produced in any other way the separation in question.

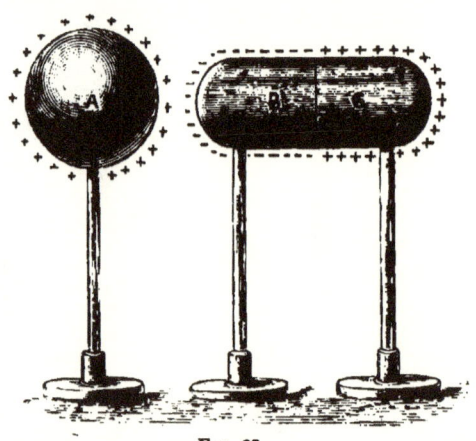

FIG. 65.

If, while BC is under induction, we test in the manner of Art. 68 its potential, we shall find it to be the same throughout, just as for a charged body. This potential is found to be lower than that of the charged body A, but nearer to A the nearer BC is brought to A. The function of the induced negative charge at B is to keep down the potential where it would be too high, and that of the + charge at C to keep up the potential where it would be too low.

We can now see that the attraction of light bodies in our earliest experiments was itself a consequence of induction. These bodies had a charge developed in them by induction opposite to that of the inducing body on the side next to it. The attraction between the opposite electricities caused the first attraction of the bodies. By contact the induced charge was neutralised, and the original charge distributed over both bodies, and then repulsion between the like electricities caused the observed repulsion between the bodies.

In the same way, in every case in which an electrical discharge takes place, that charge is preceded by induction, and may be regarded as a consequence of the increased inductive action as the bodies approach more and more near.

73. Induction on a Body connected with the Earth.
—If BC be touched for an instant with the finger, the leaves of an electroscope attached to it collapse. The reason is, that the human body, the floor, walls, and furniture of the room, are on the whole conductors, and through them the cap and base of the electroscope are brought into conducting contact, and, as we have seen, the leaves in that case collapse. The conductor BC, however, is not discharged, but retains an induced negative charge, which can be either tested by the proof-plane, or becomes sensible to the attached electroscope on the removal of A, the inducing body.

74. Electroscope charged by Induction.
—We can in this manner charge a body by induction with a charge opposite to that of the inducing body. This method is frequently employed for charging a gold-leaf electroscope (Fig. 66). Present to it an excited glass rod, charged + (Fig. 66a), and the leaves will diverge, owing to the inductive separation of electricities, + E. going to the leaves, and − E. to the cap, the potential of the leaves and cap, owing to the induction, being higher than the earth. Touch the cap with the

finger (Fig. 66*b*), thus bringing the cap and leaves to earth potential, or the potential of the tinfoil strips,—the leaves will collapse, the cap and leaves retaining a bound negative

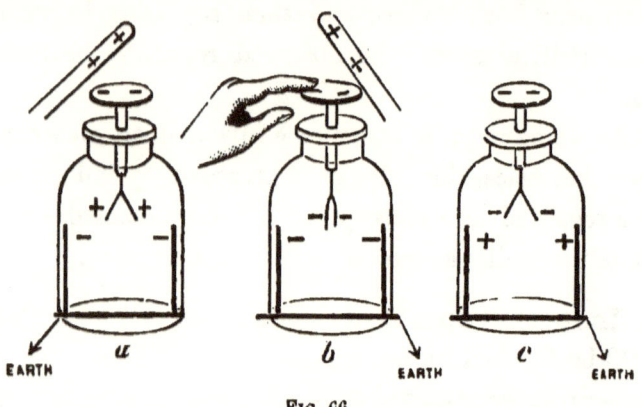

Fig. 66.

charge. Remove first the finger, and next the inducing body (Fig. 66*c*), and the electroscope leaves diverge with their negative charge now set free.

75. Faraday's Ice-pail Experiment.—To find the total amount of inductive action of which an electrified body is capable, Faraday adopted the following method, which is generally called the Ice-pail Experiment, from the use of an ice pail in the original experiment. Take a metal pail (A), closed at bottom, and open at the top, and support it on an insulating stand (Fig. 67). Connect its outside with an electroscope (B) at a distance. Electrify a brass ball (C), suspended by a silk thread, and lower it into the pail. The leaves will of course immediately diverge by induction, but after the ball has been lowered a third of the depth, no further divergence is perceptible as it is lowered further. And even after contact with the base of the pail, the leaves still retain the same divergence. On removing the ball by its silk thread, it is of course found to be completely discharged.

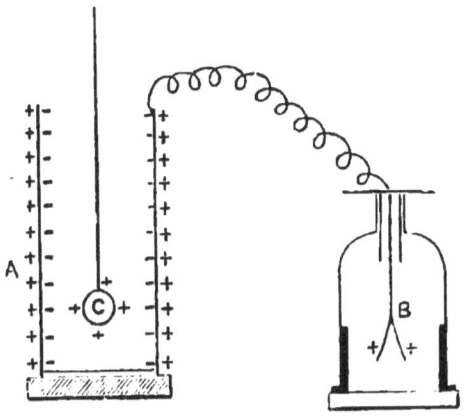

Fig. 67.

We see by this experiment that the brass ball, as soon as it was pretty well under cover of the pail, induced on the pail a certain definite quantity of electricity, negative on the inside, and of course an equal quantity of positive on the outside. By contact with the base of the pail, the ball was discharged, just neutralising the induced negative charge on the inside, leaving the positive charge on the outside quite unaltered. Thus we see the original induction on the surface of the pail was equal to the body's own charge, and this must be the expression of a universal law of induction.

Faraday repeated the experiment with a series of ice pails, one inside the other, but separated by insulating pads (Fig. 68). The result was precisely the same. When he lowered the electrified ball into the innermost pail (No. 1), the same effects were observed as before in the outermost (No. 4). On connecting 1 and 2 together by an insulated wire, there was still no change in the electroscope. On now removing No. 1

by silk threads there was still no change perceptible, every experiment only tending to confirm the preceding conclu-

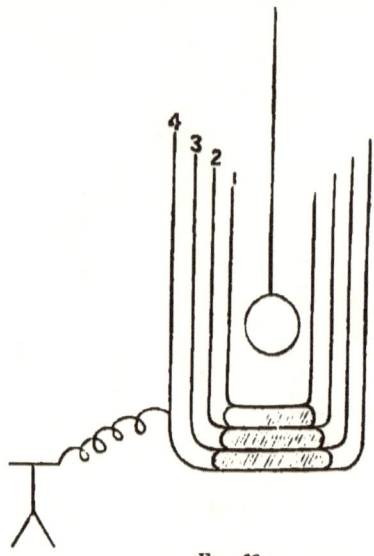

Fig. 68.

sion of the equality under all conditions of the charge, and the induced charge developed on surrounding conductors.

76. The Earth our Zero of Potential.—If we make electrical separations in an ordinary room, the foregoing experiments show us that the complementary distributions are bound across the air of the room to the distributions on the insulated conductors within. Outside the room there will be no electrical force due to the separation made inside. The earth, being a conductor, is at the same potential throughout, that potential being independent of any electrical separations made in cavities within it. This makes the earth a very convenient standard as our zero of potential. This zero of potential is as arbitrary as the zero of a thermometer scale. Whether the earth's potential is high or low we cannot tell;

but since all potentials we observe are ultimately compared with it, and its own potential can never be altered by any electrical separations we make within it, we choose it as our most convenient standard of reference, or our zero.

*77. **Potential in Absolute Measure.**—We have at present only referred to potential as the electroscope indication. We have proved by experiment these laws :—(1) The potential at every point of a charged conductor is the same; (2) The potential of a conductor rises with its charge; (3) Electrical force requires a region of varying potential; (4) Positive electricity tends to fly from places of higher towards places of lower potential. We may choose as our measure of potential any physical quantity which satisfies these four conditions. Now it is proved in works on the Theory of Electricity that these are all satisfied by measuring potential by the work done against electrical forces in carrying a + unit from the earth up to the point at which potential is measured. For it is shown (1) the work done in carrying a + unit up to any point on or within a charged conductor is the same; (2) the work done is proportional to the charge, thus confirming our assumption that there exists a constant ratio between the charge and the potential, which ratio we defined to be the capacity of the conductor; (3) the electrical force urging a + unit in any direction whatever is measured by the rate of change of the potential in that direction, thus showing that electrical forces exist only in a region of varying potential; (4) that the + unit is urged by the forces acting in the electric field from places of higher towards places of lower potential, since work is done when the + unit is carried in the opposite direction.

This shows that we may measure the potential of a conductor absolutely by the work done on a + unit in carrying it from the earth to the conductor. Should work be done in carrying the + unit from the conductor to the earth, the potential of the conductor is negative.

*78. Absolute Measure of Potential at a Point in the Field.—We can clearly take, for the absolute measure of the potential at a given point in the field, the work done on a + unit brought up from the earth to the given point, and it can be proved that this is quite independent of the path pursued in carrying up the + unit. The difference of potential between any two points in the field thus becomes measured by the work done in carrying the + unit from one point to the other, that being at higher potential to which the + unit is carried. This work done between the two points is also independent of the path pursued. Thus each point in the field has its own potential.

To connect this with our electrometer indication, we may conceive a very small insulated conductor placed at the point, and connected with an electroscope so charged that no electricity passes between the electroscope and the conductor to alter its charge. The electroscope indication would then give the potential at that point in the air. Otherwise assume a burning match placed at the point, and connected with the electroscope. Unless the match and electroscope are at the same potential as the point in the air, electricity tends to be thrown off, and the smoke and products of combustion fly off with their own charges of electricity until equilibrium is established. The electroscope indication is then the potential at the point.

*79. Equipotential Surfaces.

—There is no force on a + unit, and therefore no change of potential, if it is carried along a line which cuts lines of force at right angles. Therefore any surface drawn cutting all lines of force at right angles has the same potential throughout, and is called an equipotential surface. One such surface passes through every point in the field between the conductor and the walls of the room, both of which are also equipotential surfaces.

Again, there is no force inside a charged conductor. This shows that the whole space within the conductor is equipotential, and not merely the surface. We pointed this out experimentally (Art. 66) when we saw that a gold-leaf electroscope did not show divergence when placed in a wire cage highly charged. There was, at least, no difference of potential between the cap and base of the instrument, however placed, and therefore presumably no change of potential anywhere within the conductor.

*80. Application to a Sphere.

—It is a useful exercise to consider the case of an electrified sphere supposed to be suspended in a large room. The lines of force emanate from it at right angles, and we will assume that they are straight lines (the room being very large), and that the equipotential surfaces are spheres concentric with the conductor (Fig. 69). Since the electrification has uniform density, the force exerted by the charge on the sphere can be proved the same as if it were condensed in its centre. Thus, if the charge be Q, and the radius R, the force on a + unit at a distance D from the centre is $\frac{Q}{D^2}$, and that just outside the surface is $\frac{Q}{R^2}$. The density is $\frac{Q}{\text{area of surface}} = \frac{Q}{4\pi R^2}$, which shows that the density is proportional to the force just outside the sphere. It can be proved that the work done in bringing up a + unit to a point at a distance D is $\frac{Q}{D}$, which therefore measures the

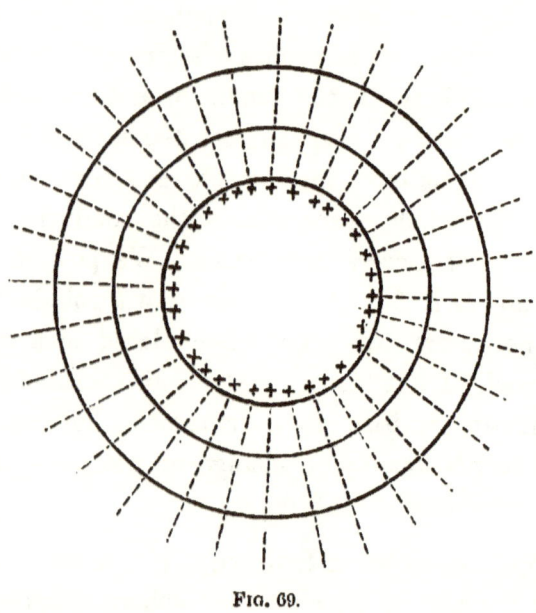

Fig. 69.

potential at distance D. Hence the potential close to the surface is $\frac{Q}{R} = V$ suppose. Hence $Q = VR$, and therefore R measures the capacity of the sphere, or the charge per unit potential (Art. 69).

81. Electrification of two Parallel Plates, one initially charged.—As an instructive example of the foregoing principles, we will consider the problem of the induction of one charged plate on another thin uncharged plate parallel, with it, whose distance from the first plate can be varied at pleasure. The arrangement is shown in Fig. 70

Fig. 70.

(1) Let the charged plate (*A*) (Fig. 71) be connected with

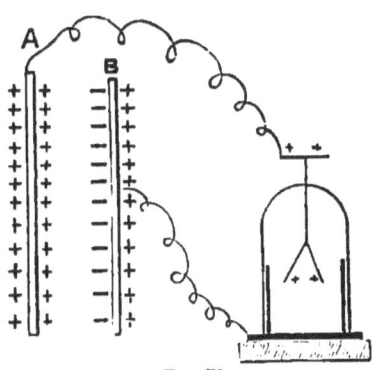

Fig. 71.

the cap, and the insulated but uncharged plate (*B*) with the base of the same electroscope. When *B* is brought up very near to *A*, but without actual contact, the leaves collapse, showing that the unelectrified plate is sensibly at the same potential as the electrified plate, but on moving it further away, the difference of potential goes on increasing, *A* of course being at higher potential than *B*. The potential at any point in *B* will be due to the three distributions, namely the + on *A*, and the + and − distributions on opposite sides of *B*. The two latter, from their symmetry, will neutralise each other's potential everywhere within *B*, and the potential of *B* will be that due only to *A*. When *B* is close to *A*, its potential will therefore be the same as that in air close to *A*, and as it retreats from *A* its potential will decrease just as the potential in air decreases.

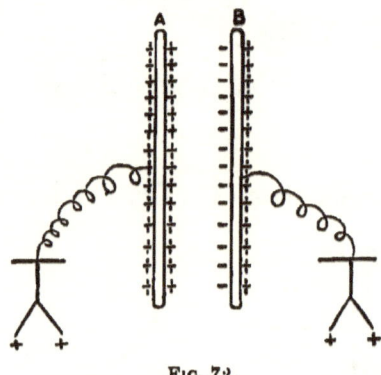

FIG. 72.

(2) Let us now test the potential of *A* and *B* relatively to the earth, connecting *A* with the cap of one electroscope, and *B* with that of another (Fig. 72). When they are close together, the two electroscopes indicate the same potential. As we separate them, we find that the potential of *B* constantly decreases, that of *A* remaining unaltered. The explanation is,

that the equal and opposite induced charges on B are so nearly at the same distance from every point on A, that their inductive effects on A are equal and opposite, and their potentials at every point of A are equal and opposite, and therefore do not affect the potential of A, which is still that due to its own charge.

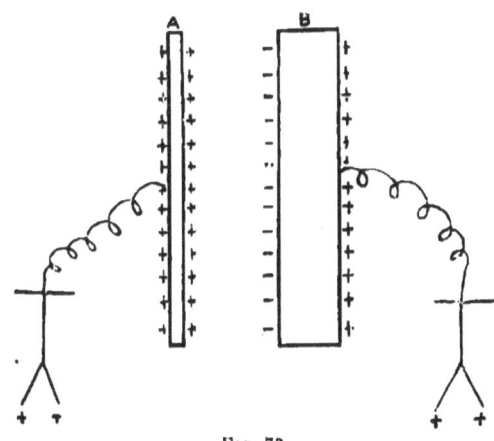

Fig. 73.

(3) Replace B by a thick plate (Fig. 73)—a hollow plate with two opposite flat metallic surfaces will do. We shall now find that the potential of A diminishes as B is moved up to A. Here the opposite charges called up by induction are not at the same distance from A, the negative charge being the nearer, and in consequence the potential of A is lowered.

(4) Replace the thin plate and touch it with the finger (Fig. 74). The potential of A at once falls, and the nearer B is to A the greater the fall in A's potential. This is due to the large negative charge induced by A, which, from its nearness to A, lowers A's potential. In other words, on bringing up the + unit to A, the work is almost *nil*, for B's attraction nearly equals A's repulsion.

(5) Place B at a certain distance from A, touch B, and connect it with an electroscope. The leaves of course collapse. On separating the plates further, however, the leaves of B's electroscope are seen to diverge with $-$ E., but on bringing them nearer together they diverge with $+$ E.

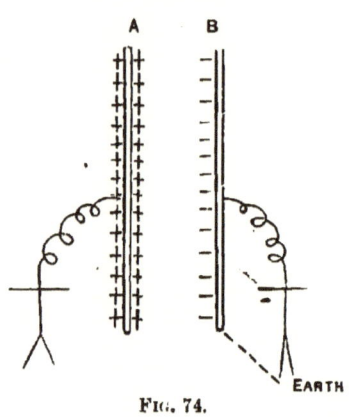

Fig. 74.

These are obviously the effects of increased and diminished induction, owing to the change in B's position. It shows also that a body having a $-$ charge may have a $+$ potential, owing to the presence of $+$ E. near to it.

82. The Leyden Jar.—These experiments show us that the capacity of a charged body depends not only on the geometry of the body considered, but also on the presence of other conductors. Since the potential of the charged body in the preceding experiment was lowered by bringing near to it a body connected with the earth, it follows that the capacity of the conductor was raised in the same proportion. This principle is used in the Leyden jar. This consists of a glass jar (Fig. 75), coated outside to about two-thirds of its height with tinfoil, and the inside is either coated with tinfoil or filled with sulphuric acid, or any conductor. A brass rod passes inside, with a brass knob on the outside. Here the inner coat is charged, while the outer is connected with the earth, and the capacity of the inner coat is thus enormously increased, as may be seen by first charging the jar from the same source with the outer coat insulated, and afterwards with the outer coat connected with the earth. The jar is discharged only by connecting the inner and outer coat, and the discharge produces an intense spark or shock. It is used where accumulations of large quantities of electricity are required for mechanical or other effects.

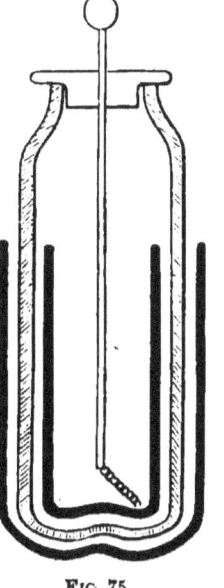

Fig. 75.

It may be remembered that in a Leyden jar the capacity is increased in direct proportion to the coated surface, and varies in inverse proportion to the thickness of the glass, supposing the glass to be always of the same kind.

83. Volta's Condensing Electroscope.

—On the same principle depends the condensing electroscope of Volta. The cap of the electroscope is ground perfectly plane, and another plane disc of brass with a glass handle is made to fit accurately on to it. The two are then separated by a thin layer of shellac varnish, which, when dry, forms an insulating layer of dielectric between the plates. It is only useful in cases where a large quantity of electricity is available, but of too low potential to be sensible to the ordinary electroscope. Connect the upper or condensing plate with the source of electricity, and the cap with the earth by touching it with the finger. There will be a large accumulation of electricity on the Leyden jar principle across the very thin layer of shellac. On removing the finger, the charge called up by induction is insulated, and

Fig. 76.

on lifting the cap becomes free, causing the leaves of the electroscope to diverge with electricity of opposite kind to that of the source. We shall illustrate the use of this apparatus hereafter.

*84. Discharge by Alternate Contacts.—Returning to the two plates in given position (Art. 81), A charged and B uncharged, we notice generally that the charge of A is divided, part on the side facing B, and part on the side away from B; while on B there is a $-$ charge opposite to A, and an equal $+$ charge on the other face. To the opposing charges, $+$ on A and $-$ on B, Faraday's ice-pail principle is applicable, showing that these charges are equal and opposite. These are frequently spoken of together as a bound charge. The charges on the outsides of A and B might be treated in the same way, they being bound to equal and opposite charges on surrounding conductors, only we assume surrounding conductors to be so distant that their effect on the distribution is inappreciable, and these charges are spoken of as the free charges of A and B respectively. Each of these systems will have its own capacity—that for the bound charge depending on the shape, size, and nearness of the plates, and that for the free charge only on the form of the external surfaces. If we call these C and C' respectively, every charge communicated to A will be divided between the free and bound charges in ratio of C' to C. If the whole charge on A be Q, the free charge will be $\dfrac{C'}{C+C'} \cdot Q = nQ$ suppose, and the bound charge $\dfrac{C}{C+C'} \cdot Q = mQ$ suppose; where of course $m+n=1$.

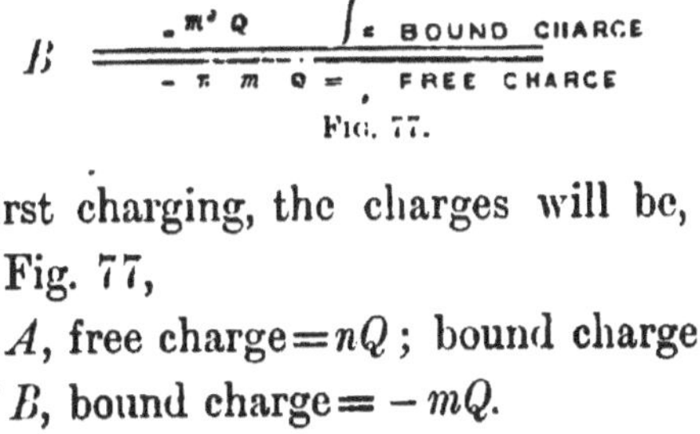

Fig. 77.

(1) At first charging, the charges will be, as in the first diagram of Fig. 77,

on A, free charge $=nQ$; bound charge $=mQ$;
and on B, bound charge $=-mQ$.

(2) Insulate B, and touch A, thus bringing its potential to zero. The bound charge on B is now divided in ratio $C':C$, and we have, as in the second diagram,

on B, free charge $=-mnQ$; bound charge $=-m^2Q$;
and on A, bound charge $=+m^2Q$.

116　　　　　　　*Electricity.*　　　　　[Book II.

(3) Insulate A, and touch B; the bound charge on A will now be divided in same ratio, and we have

on A, free charge $= nm^2Q$, and bound charge $= m^3Q$; and on B, bound charge $= -m^3Q$.

(4) By similar reasoning we see that after p contacts with the alternate plates the free charge will be

$\pm nm^{p-1}Q$, and the bound charge $\pm m^pQ$.

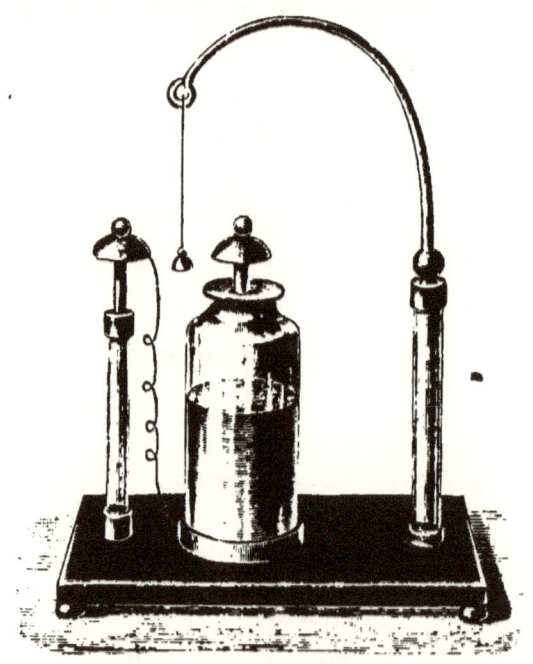

Fig. 78.

Since m is a fraction near to unity, m^p will be a considerable fraction when p is a large number, and hence in the discharge by alternate contacts the charge is dissipated very slowly indeed. This is illustrated in various ways, as by attaching a bell to the knob of the Leyden jar (Fig. 78), and placing another in connection with the earth in such a position that a small metal weight, suspended by a silk thread may strike first one bell and then the other, the motion being kept up by the successive attractions and repulsions between the metal and either bell. This arrangement will continue ringing for a considerable time if the jar be first charged by a machine.

85. Specific Inductive Capacity.—Returning once more to the parallel plates, let A (Fig. 79) be charged as before, and

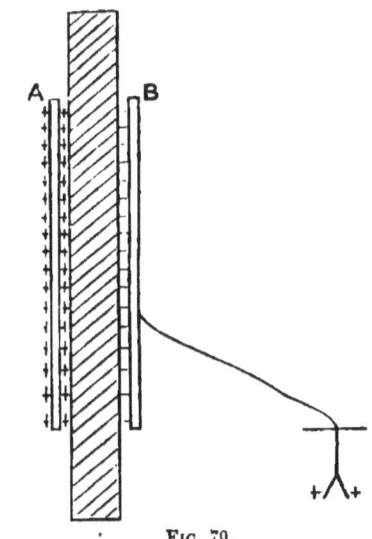

Fig. 79.

B be connected with an electroscope. Touch B with the finger, bringing its potential to zero. Take now a plate of solid paraffin larger than the plates, and whose thickness is a little less than the distance between the plates. On carefully introducing it between the plates without contact with either, the leaves of B's electroscope will be found to diverge slightly, showing, on testing, positive electrification, that is, just the same effect as if the plates were brought nearer together.

(Great care is necessary to prevent the electrification of the paraffin, by accidental friction with the hands or clothes, in which case the resulting divergence would be negative, since the paraffin becomes negative by friction.) This shows that induction depends on the nature of the dielectric. This phenomenon was discovered by Faraday, who experimented by constructing exactly equal Leyden jars, in one of which air was the dielectric, and in the other a substance like sulphur or shellac. On charging one, and then dividing the charge with the other jar, he found in the case of shellac that the jar having shellac retained two thirds of the divided charge, and that with air only one third. Since they were at the same potential, he inferred that the capacity of the jar with shellac as dielectric was just double that with air. This he expressed by saying that the inductive capacity of shellac was double that of air. He found dry air a convenient standard, since he found no sensible difference on either rarefying or compressing it, or on substituting for it any of the permanent gases. There were few solid substances in which the insulation was good enough to admit of Faraday's method of experiment. The only ones with which he expresses himself satisfied are sulphur and flint glass, in both of which he showed the specific inductive capacity to be greater than double that of air.

86. Condition of the Dielectric in a Leyden Jar.— That all electrical actions belong to the dielectric, and not to the conductor, is also shown by the Leyden jar with moveable coatings (Fig. 80). Charge this jar in the usual way, and place it on an insulator. Lift out the inner coat, and this will be found to carry away only a small fraction of the charge. Lift the jar out of the outer coat, which will also retain hardly a trace of the charge. The glass can now be handled inside and out, a slight discharge being perceptible when the outside and inside are touched at the same time; but on fitting up the jar again, and discharging in the usual way, there will be nearly as strong a spark as if the discharge had immediately followed the charge.

Fig. 80.

This shows that every electrification is not one of conductors in the field, but rather one of the field itself, the function of the conductor being only to determine the limits of the field.

Another illustration is given by the residual charge in a Leyden jar. Of whatever dielectric the condenser be made, except it be a gas, a short time after the first discharge has passed, another feeble discharge can be obtained, and this may be repeated several times in succession. This appears due to a want of homogeneity in the dielectric, and a partial conduction through it, causing a storing up of electricity within the substance of the dielectric, which begins to be conducted back again only after the primary discharge has passed.

87. Faraday's Theory of Induction.—Faraday has laid down a theory of induction agreeable to this conception, and this was the first step towards a true physical conception of electrical actions. He satisfied himself that induction was not due to action at a distance between the electrified body and the body under induction, and he substituted for it an action through the dielectric from molecule to molecule only. He assumes that every dielectric consists of molecules, each

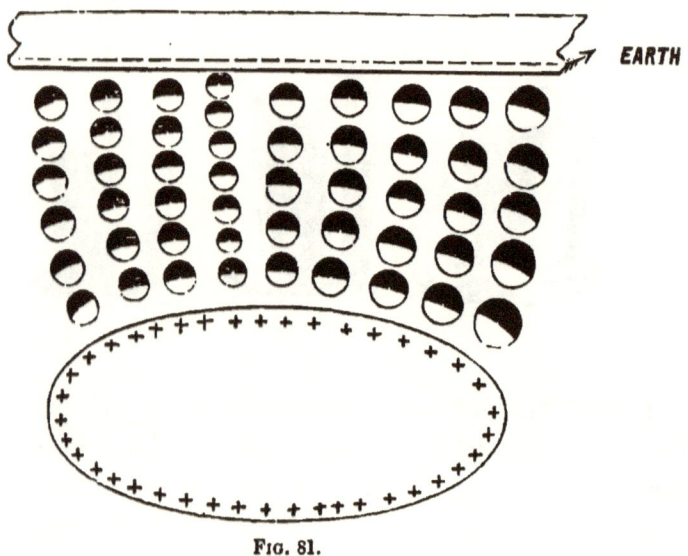

Fig. 81.

of which acts as a conductor, but which are separated from each other by a non-conducting medium, or, at least, non-conducting up to a certain limiting strain among the molecules. The electrification of the surface bounding the field (or of the conductor, if we choose still to speak of it) separates the electricities in the layer of molecules next to it. These act on the next layer, and so on through the field. The lines of force define the direction in which the separation takes place, the quantity separated being always equal to that in the proximate layer of molecules. Thus the electrification will consist of a flow of electricity equal to the original charge across each equipotential surface ; but instead of being a flow through a finite space, it is only a flow across the molecules which lie in that surface. This may be represented in a diagrammatic way, as in Fig. 81, supposing shaded parts to represent positive electricity.

Of a higher order is the theory of Faraday developed by Clerk-Maxwell, in which he regards the electrification as a state of molecular strain in the dielectric. In support of that theory is the observation of Sir William Thomson, that on charging and discharging a large condenser a peculiar noise is emitted, just as might be expected in a medium taking up or losing suddenly a strained condition. The same applies to the noise said sometimes to be heard at the instant of a flash of lightning.

CHAPTER IV.

ELECTRICAL MACHINES.

88. The Cylinder Machine.—There are two classes of electrical machines; that is, machines by which large quantities of electricity at high potential may be rapidly obtained, one depending on simple friction, and the other on an initial electrification by friction, from which an indefinite amount of electricity may be developed by induction.

FIG. 82.

The simplest form of friction machine is that known as the cylinder machine (Fig. 82). It consists of a cylinder of glass (B) fitted in a frame which allows it to rotate about a spindle running along its axis. The extremity of one horizontal diameter is pressed by a leather pad (*A*) coated with silk, on which is smeared an amalgam of mercury and tin, the pressure being increased by a spring controlled by a screw. The pad is usually insulated and furnished with a brass knob, from which negative electricity can be collected. Towards the opposite side of the cylinder points a comb, consisting of a row of very sharp brass points (*C*) attached to a large brass globe or cylinder (*D*), called the Prime Conductor, on which the positive electricity collects. This is always insulated by being supported on glass legs. A flap of silk attached at one edge to the rubber passes nearly over the upper half of the cylinder, and prevents the deposit of dust on the cylinder, by which the electricity would be dissipated.

On turning round the cylinder, the friction with the rubber separates electricity, the positive on the glass and the negative on the rubber. The glass with its positive charge is carried onwards till it is opposite the brass comb on the opposite side. Here it acts inductively on the points, and $-$ E. is drawn off, neutralising the $+$ E. on the cylinder, and causing a charge of free $+$ E. on the conductor. On turning the handle round this process constantly goes on, till the difference of potential between the prime ($+$) and negative ($-$) conductors is equal to that which can be obtained by the friction between glass and amalgamated silk. Sparks of positive or negative electricity can be obtained from the respective conductors. The difference of potential actually attained will always be less than the limit indicated, because of dust and moisture in the air, and also because of the want of perfect insulation in the glass supports. The advantage of a warm and dry state in the atmosphere is obvious.

In the ordinary working of the machine it is usual to connect the negative conductor with the earth by a metal chain. If the insulation of the rubber were perfect, we should, on drawing sparks from the prime conductor, at last reach a stage at which the potential of the negative conductor would be below the potential of the earth by the whole available potential difference, and then the prime conductor would be at zero potential, and no sparks could be obtained from it. The machine would apparently cease to work.

Again, the body which draws sparks from the machine is generally at the potential of the earth, and therefore the potential difference available for giving sparks is that between the earth and the prime conductor. But if the negative conductor be at a negative potential, this available difference is not the full potential difference of the machine, or the machine is practically not working to its full power. On connecting the negative conductor with the ground the potential of the positive conductor at once rises. The same effect may be gained by simply connecting the negative conductor with the apparatus by which sparks are to be drawn, keeping all insulated. In a fairly insulated machine the difference is well seen (1) by drawing a succession of sparks from the prime conductor while the rubber is insulated; (2) by drawing sparks, while standing on an insulating stool, and touching with one hand the negative conductor; (3) by drawing sparks, standing on the ground with the rubber to earth.

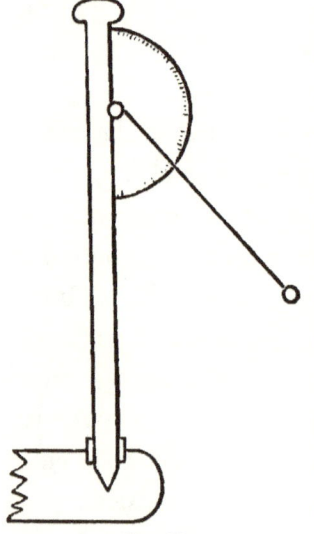

FIG. 83.

The prime conductor is frequently furnished with an electrometer, consisting of a vertical metal rod, from which is suspended, by a thin wire or linen thread, a pith ball (Fig. 83). The divergence is shown by a small graduated quadrant attached, which indicates the degree to which the machine is working. This is called Henley's Quadrant Electrometer— an unfortunate term, as the Quadrant Electrometer is an instrument of Sir William Thomson's, described hereafter.

89. The Plate Machine.—The Plate Machine (Fig. 84) is a circular vertical plate (A) of glass or ebonite, which is turned

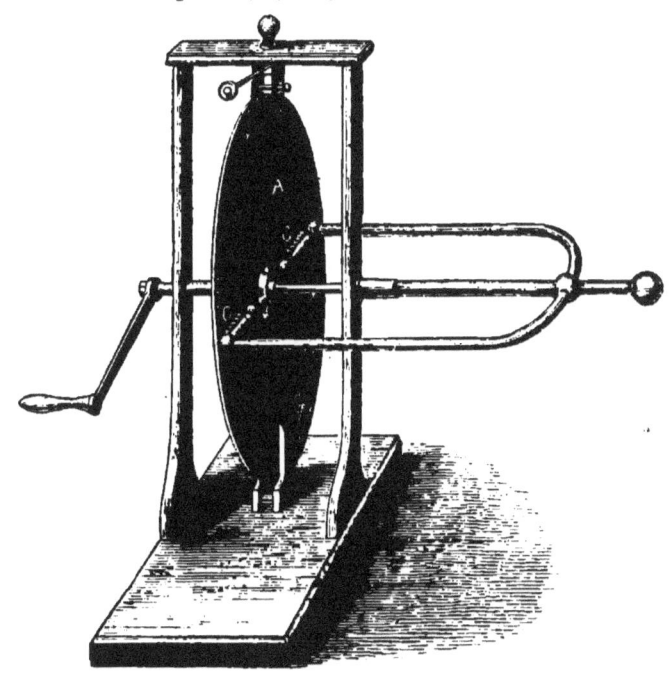

FIG. 84.

by a spindle through its centre. Two rubbers (BB) are attached at opposite extremities of the vertical diameter, each made double, and pressed by a screw clamp on opposite sides of the plate. Along a horizontal diameter are two combs (*CC*), each formed in shape of the letter U, so as to act on the two surfaces of the plate. These are connected by metal rods with the prime conductor, which is well insulated on a glass support. Flaps of silk (*EE*) extend over the quadrants from the rubbers nearly to the combs.

The action is identical with that of the cylinder machine. Its advantages are rather greater compactness, and the possibility of substituting ebonite for glass. The ebonite is as good in its electrical properties, but is less hygroscopic, and therefore the action is not quite so dependent on weather. Also the double action on opposite sides of the plate increases the rate at which electricity can be obtained.

90. The Electrophorus.—Of instruments depending on induction the simplest is the electrophorus (Fig. 85). It consists

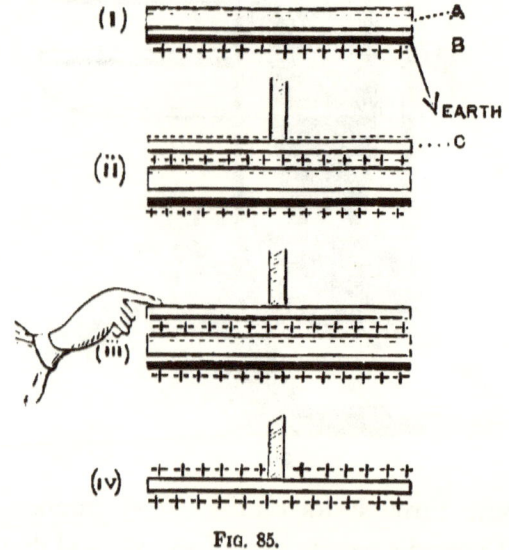

Fig. 85.

of a cake (*A*) resting on a metal form or sole (*B*), and of a cover (*C*). The cake used to consist of a resinous compound melted and poured into the form, but is now more commonly a plate of ebonite, with a sheet of tinfoil on its under surface forming the sole. The cover is a flat metal plate, having attached to it a glass handle, by which it can be raised and lowered. The charging of the electrophorus is done by rubbing or flapping the ebonite plate with a cat's fur (Fig. 85, i), by which a charge of − E. is developed on its upper surface. This acts inductively through the cake, and binds by induction a charge of + E. on the sole. By this means the potential of the charge on the cake is lowered, and the tendency of the electricity to escape into the air diminished. On putting the plate down on the cake there is only contact at very few points, and everywhere else a thin plate of air between the cake and cover. The induction will now be almost wholly between the cake and cover, owing to the much greater nearness of the cover. There will therefore be developed (Fig. 85, ii) a charge of + E. on the under surface of the cover very nearly equal to the whole − E. on the cake, while there is an equal free charge of − E. on the upper surface. On touching the plate with the finger (Fig. 85, iii), the complementary − E. is driven to earth. On lifting up the cover it has a strong charge of + E., which can be used for charging other conductors. The induction between the cake and sole is again restored, the cake returning to the state shown in Fig. 85 (i), and the charge is so well preserved that in a dry atmosphere the electrophorus may be used with only one charging for an hour or more together.

91. The Voss or Wimshurst Machine.—A great variety of machines have been invented, in which the induction of a small initial charge is employed for raising continually the initial charge in compound interest ratio, and also for giving the discharge whose power increases as the machine is worked to a degree only limited by the size of the machine and the perfection of insulation attainable. Of these we have only room to refer to two of the most modern.

FIG. 86.

We will take first the Voss or Wimshurst machine (Fig. 86), because its action is peculiarly simple when the difficulty of the initial charging has been overcome.

The machine consists of one glass plate, which is fixed, and of another glass plate parallel to the fixed plate, which is made to rotate rapidly in front of it. In Fig. 86 the larger plate is fixed, and the smaller rotates in front of it, admitting of our seeing the arrangement of the fixed plate through it. The fixed plate has two sheets of paper (*AA*), with tinfoil underneath it, pasted on to the glass, and called the armatures. From each of these proceeds a metal arm (*BB*) bent three times at right angles, and carrying on its end a metal brush, which sweeps over certain metal buttons as they pass by it.

The moveable plate has cemented to its front eight of these metal buttons (*a a . . .*), which come in contact with the successive brushes.

Fig. 87.

In front of the moveable plate, and facing it, are two brass combs (*CC*) which face the plate, and are cut away opposite to the buttons (Fig. 87), allowing them to pass without contact. These are connected by metal rods with the moveable conductors (*DD*), between which the spark passes.

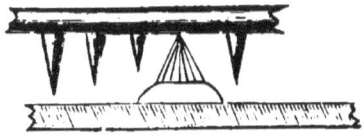

Fig. 88.

In addition there is a diagonal conductor (*E*) furnished at each end with a brass comb, of which the central tooth is replaced by a brush of metal wires which sweeps over the buttons as they pass under it (Fig. 88). The combs all extend the full width of the paper armature.

I

The knobs (*DD*) are in connection with the inner coats of two Leyden jars (*FF*) whose outer coats are to earth.

The peculiarity of this apparatus is that no special *priming* (that is, initial charging of the armatures) is required. It appears that from accidental surface inequalities a slight difference of potential is established by friction between the brushes and buttons, and the construction of the machine is such as to accumulate the initial charge, *however small*, on compound interest principle. In working the machine the plate is rotated in the direction of the arrows shown in Fig. 86. We assume initially a small potential difference between the armatures A, A, and will show how this difference is increased. Omitting the conductor CC, which takes no part in the initial stages of charging, each button passes during a revolution four brushes—two belonging to the armatures, and two to the diagonal conductor. Fig. 89 either shows one button in four consecutive positions, or four buttons simultaneously, remembering that pairs of buttons always occur at ends of a diameter.

Consider first the pair of buttons in position (i) and (iii) in Fig. 89, in which (i) represents a portion of the positive armature, and (iii) a portion of the negative armature. At (i) the positive armature induces a charge of $-$ E. on the button, while at (iii), which is connected with (i) by the diagonal conductor, the negative armature induces a charge of $+$ E. The button therefore leaves (i) with a negative charge bound across the air space, and leaves (iii) with a positive charge. The button, on passing from (i) to (ii), will give up its strong bound negative charge to the negative armature, retaining only a small free charge. Similarly, the button on passing from (iii) to (iv) will give up its bound positive charge, retaining only a very small free charge. We see therefore that each button which passes from (i) to (ii), or from (iii) to (iv), will enforce the charge of these respective armatures; and since at each point there is actual metallic contact, the electricity not having to break across an air space, the action will go on, however small the initial difference.

When the charges are high enough to act inductively across the air spaces between the plate and the combs (CC), the neutralisation which usually takes place in E will take place across the air space (DD), giving rise to the spark. As soon as this is the case, not only the metal buttons, but the whole glass surface between the combs and the armature, help to enforce the action.

After turning for a very short time, if the atmosphere be moderately dry and the machine warm, sparks four or five inches long may be easily obtained from a comparatively small machine (16-inch plates).

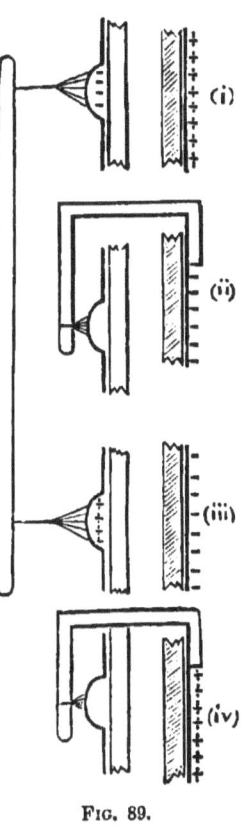

FIG. 89.

The use of the Leyden jars (FF) is to concentrate the spark. If they be removed, the discharge takes place by what is called the brush discharge, consisting of very fine branches, giving a slight pricking sensation if received on the hand, and making but very slight noise. If the Leyden jars be present, the first effect of the electricity developed in the conductors D, D, is to charge these jars, one with its inner coat positive, and the other negative, and these are discharged with their characteristic sharp report as each spark passes.

It may be noticed in illustration of the action explained, that when the machine is in action the diagonal conductor E may be removed without stopping the action of the machine until a discharge of the armatures takes place with one of the sparks, an accident to which all these machines are liable.

*92. The Holtz Machine.—This machine (Fig. 90), which was of earlier date than the Voss, depends on the same general principles.

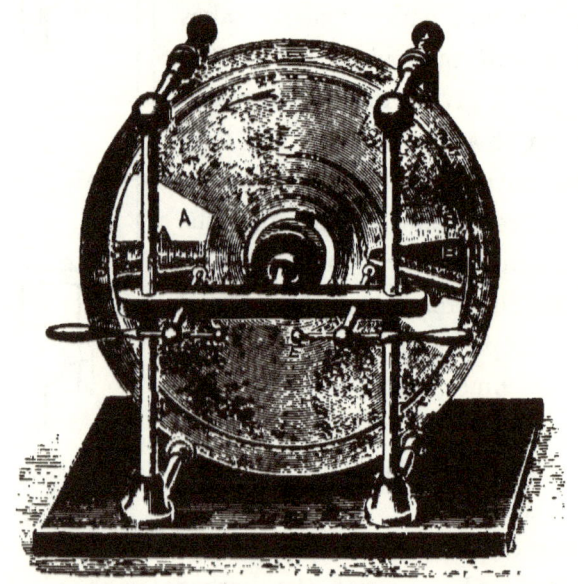

FIG. 90.

In it we have two plates, one fixed and the other revolving rapidly in front of and at a small distance from it, by means of a spindle through its centre.

The fixed plate (Fig. 91) has, at opposite ends of a diameter, two apertures or windows cut in the form of truncated sectors of a circle. Below one and above the other are two sheets of paper (*BB*), the armatures, glued to the glass, with two *tongues* or pointed strips, also of paper, projecting from them into their respective windows. In the centre is a circular hole through which passes the spindle of the moving plate.

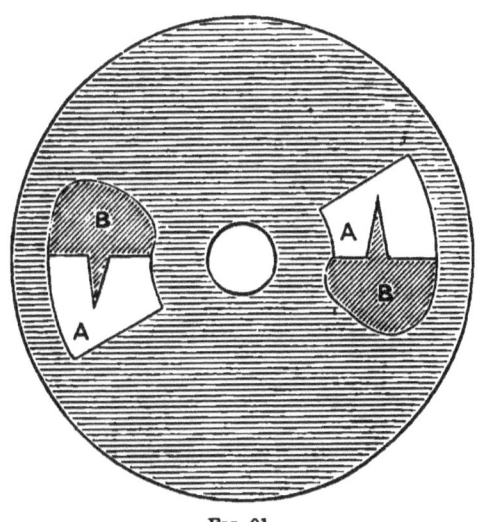

Fig. 91.

The moving plate is an entire circle with a hole in the centre for fixing the spindle, and, for mechanical reasons, having a diameter slightly less than that of the fixed plate.

The plate is fixed with the two armatures at opposite extremities of a horizontal diameter. Opposite to them, but on the remote side of the moving plate, are two brass combs (Fig. 90), as near as possible to the moving plate without actual contact with it. These combs are well insulated, and connected with two brass knobs (*EE*), whose distance apart may be adjusted by the insulating handles. These knobs are the positive and negative conductors. The relative position of the parts near one end of a horizontal diameter is seen in section in Fig. 92. In the section, *A* is the window, *B* the armature, *C* the tongue, and *D* one tooth of the brass comb.

Before working the machine, it must be primed. The brass knobs are brought into contact, and a piece of ebonite rubbed with flannel is held between the plates in contact with one armature, by which this armature receives a weak charge of negative electricity. Sometimes a small ebonite machine is fixed to the base in such a position that the electrified ebonite plate acts inductively on one tongue.

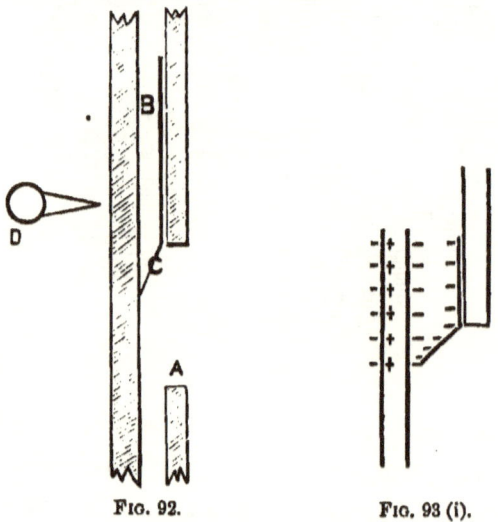

FIG. 92.   FIG. 93 (i).

The further action can best be understood if we consider the electrical actions which occur in six successive positions of a portion of the revolving plate in the course of a single revolution, just as we did in the Voss machine. The plate revolves in such a direction as to meet the tongues of the armature, as shown by the arrows in Fig. 90.

1st Position.—Opposite the window of the fixed plate containing the tongue of the negative armature, Fig. 93 (i).

The tongue, being pointed, reduces the inner surface of the glass plate to its own potential, giving it a negative charge. This charge acts inductively through the glass, binding on the opposite surface a positive charge, and leaving a negative charge free. This action through a dielectric, though an obvious consequence of Faraday's law of induction, was first pointed out by Reiss, and is often called Reiss's action.

2d Position.—Between the negative armature and the brass comb, as in Fig. 93 (ii).

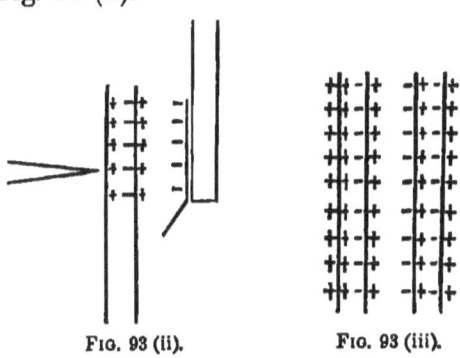

Fig. 93 (ii).   Fig. 93 (iii).

The brass points of the comb neutralise the free negative charge on the outer surface of the glass, and a redistribution of the induced charges takes place. The negative charge on the armature acts by induction both across the air and the glass, calling up a positive charge across the air space, leaving the negative charge bound to the positive charge on the outside surface of the glass.

3d Position.—After passing the armature, as in Fig. 93 (iii).

In this position the induction of the negative charge of the armature is removed, and in consequence a positive charge is set free on both sides of the moving plate. These charges of course act inductively on the glass of the fixed plate, as shown in the diagram.

4th Position.—Opposite the second window, which contains the tongue of the positive armature, as in Fig. 93 (iv).

This tongue will here take up the free positive charge from the inner surface of the glass plate, thus either charging or increasing the charge of the positive armature.

5th Position.—Between the positive armature and the brass comb, as in Fig. 93 (v).

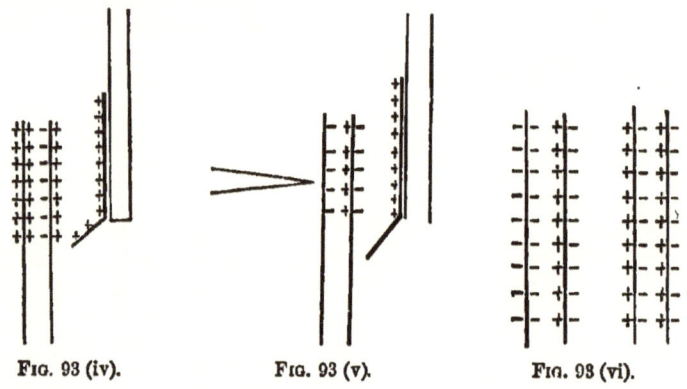

Fig. 93 (iv).   Fig. 93 (v).   Fig. 93 (vi).

The brass comb neutralises the positive charge on the outer face, and a new inductive distribution occurs: the armature acts inductively across both air space and glass, setting free an increased negative charge on the inner surface of the moving plate, leaving a positive charge bound to the negative charge on the outer surface.

6th Position.—After leaving the positive armature, as in Fig. 93 (vi).

The removal of the charge on the armature sets free a negative charge on both surfaces of the moving plate, leaving, however, a bound charge, positive on the inner, and negative on the outer, face. The reaction by induction on the fixed plate will occur again as in the third position. In this condition it comes round again to the negative armature, carrying a charge which will reinforce its electrification, after which the whole process goes on over again.

The action of the machine may be briefly described thus,—each portion of the moving plate as it passes from the induction of the negative armature has a positive charge on both faces, that on the inner face after half a revolution enforces the charge on the positive armature, and that on the outer face is taken up by the comb, and makes the spark. The same will be the case, *changing signs* with each portion of the plate as it leaves the positive armature.

For the neutralisation of the opposite electricities developed by the action of the machine on the combs and conductors, the knobs should be kept together till the charging has risen sufficiently for sparks to strike across, by which the neutralisation (only partial, of course) takes place during the whole time the machine is at work.

As in the Voss machine, two Leyden jars (not shown in the figure), having their outer coats connected by a brass band, are usually hung from the brass rods in connection with the conductors E, E. They are, of course charged, one positively and the other negatively, and their function is to store up the electricity developed, allowing, when they are charged, one strong spark to pass in place of a large number of sparks of much smaller quantity, which form a brush discharge. Occasionally the power of the machine is increased by having four plates instead of two, in which case the fixed plates are back to back, and the revolving plates outside; the brass comb being on the inside of a U-shaped rod to collect the electricity from both plates at once.

From a Holtz machine, with plates 2 feet in diameter, a brilliant discharge of sparks 6 to 8 inches long can be obtained.

93. Experiments with the Electrical Machine.—Almost an infinite variety of experiments, both instructive and amusing, can be exhibited by means of the electrical machine. We briefly indicate a few under general headings:—

1. *Subdivision of the Spark.*—This is done by means of small discs of tinfoil pasted on the surface of glass, leaving a very small interval between each two successive discs. In this way any pattern that can be traced by one continuous line can be formed, and when placed in the line of discharge of a machine, each interval is lighted up by a spark. The pattern traced by bright sparks can be seen in a darkened room.

2. *Attractions and Repulsions.*—A head is cut in wood, with long hair fastened on by a metal screw, which is in connection with a metal rod, by which the head is supported on the prime conductor: when the machine is worked, the hairs stand out, owing to mutual repulsion, and can be swayed about inductively in various directions by presenting the hand or any flat conductor near them.

The *Electrical Chimes* consist of bells, of which alternate ones are connected with the prime conductor and the earth. Between them hang by silk threads small masses of metal, which are attracted and repelled by the electrified bells in succession, keeping up a ringing while the machine is worked.

Electrical Hail consists of a number of pith balls placed in a glass cylinder, in the upper part of which is a moveable brass plate connected with the prime conductor, and the base is coated with tinfoil connected with the earth. On turning the machine, the pith balls fly about between the plate and base.

The same thing can be shown by figures cut in pith and placed between two brass plates, one of which hangs from the prime conductor, and the other is to earth. On working the machine, the figures continue dancing between the two plates.

3. *Conduction of the Human Body.*—By standing on an insulating stool, and holding the prime conductor of an electrical machine in the hand, a considerable charge may be imparted, of which the recipient is quite unconscious, unless it be by the standing out of the hair or of loose parts of the clothing by electrical repulsion. A spark can be taken from any part of the body of the person charged, just as from any other conductor, when a pricking sensation is felt just where the spark is drawn. Sparks drawn in this way are harmless, and almost painless.

With this experiment should be compared one in which the human body is in the line of discharge, and offers resistance to the passage of electricity. This may be done in a perfectly harmless manner by charging a Leyden jar with two or three turns of an electrical machine. A large class, on joining hands all round, the first holding the outer coat and the last touching the knob, will receive the discharge through the muscles of the arms and chest, and will receive a shock, most felt in the elbow joints, where the muscle is discontinuous. The arms and chest here act as a bad conductor, the right and left hands being brought to a slight difference of potential before the discharge takes place.

We have already noticed that conductors and non-conductors are only relative terms, and we have here two experiments in which the same body acts first as a conductor, and next as a dielectric.

5. *The Disruptive Discharge in Air.*—There are three ways in which an electrical discharge may be shown to take place.

The first is by the ordinary disruptive discharge. This occurs when the air becomes strongly strained by the potential difference, and, suddenly yielding, allows the discharge to pass, not freely as through a conductor, but by a violent disturbance of the molecules of air along the path, which become strongly heated, and make the visible spark. This spark is often spoken of very inaccurately as the electric fluid. The spark will be observed to take a zigzag and forked path. This seems due to the discharge passing along the line of least resistance, which, owing to conducting motes in the air, is not the straight line. The snap which accompanies the discharge has never been fully explained, but is no doubt due to the disturbance in the air caused by the passage of the discharge.

6. *The Glow Discharge.*—This takes place on sharp points, either in connection with the machine or on pointed conductors connected with the earth presented towards the machine. It may be seen in the dark as a faint purplish glow on the brass combs connected with the various forms of machine. If a pointed rod be placed on the prime conductor, the glow will immediately appear, and it will be found impossible to draw a spark from the machine, the electricity being discharged silently from the point. If the hand be placed near the point a strong current of air will be found setting from the point.

A method of discharge, similar to that from points, is afforded by a flame, which we have already noticed (see Art. 78), and by any form of water-dripping apparatus, in which the water dropping away from an insulated vessel carries off a charge until it brings the nozzle from which the water drips to the same potential as the air in contact with it. The electrical watering-pot depends on this principle. A metal vessel, having a capillary outlet by a syphon, is suspended from the prime conductor. Before electrification the water drips only one drop at a time, but on turning the machine the water flows out in a continuous stream, owing to the repulsion between the electrified vessel and the similarly electrified water which is leaking away from it.

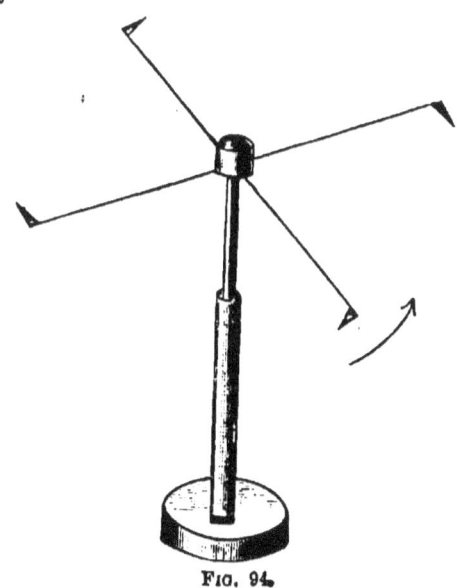

Fig. 94.

It appears from the current of air which proceeds from the points that the particles of the air themselves become charged at the point, and are then repelled, carrying their charge with them, and discharging as they come against the walls of the room or other conductors. This current of air is accompanied by a recoil if the pointed conductor is free to move. It is employed as a source of motion in the electrical whirl (Fig. 94) and electrical orrery, in both of which points are so placed that the recoil sets the apparatus of which they are parts spinning, the direction of rotation being against the points.

7. *The Brush Discharge.*—This is best seen between the conductors of a Voss or Holtz machine after the Leyden jars in the interior have been removed. It seems intermediate in character between the spark and glow discharges. It sometimes rises out from wooden knobs or conductors about the machine like the stem of a tree, and spreads out in the air like its branches.

The connection of these forms of discharge with the phenomena of lightning cannot be overlooked. The spark discharge is identical in character with the flash of forked lightning, the forking and zigzag path being often seen in the spark from the machine.

The glow discharge is known as St. Elmo's Fire, which is frequently seen on the tops of the lightning-rods connected with the masts of ships, and also upon other pointed objects—even on the tops of umbrellas or walking-sticks—when the atmosphere is much disturbed electrically.

The brush discharge may occur in some varieties of summer lightning, though what is most commonly called so is only the lighting up of the edges of cloud-masses by electric discharges taking place behind them, or at points below the horizon of the place of observation; the discharge being too distant for thunder to be audible. Thunder, for the volume of its sound, is audible for an exceedingly short distance—very much less than the report of a cannon.

The only other form of discharge, that known as the fire-ball, has not yet been explained or imitated experimentally. It appears of the nature of a Leyden jar very powerfully charged, which may move about through rooms, playing about the furniture, quite harmless till the instant of discharge, which takes place with a terrible explosion and a deafening noise.

94. Experiments with a Leyden Jar Battery.— Many striking effects of electricity can only be shown by the help of Leyden jars of large size, or batteries of several jars charged powerfully by the machine. Batteries of several jars

FIG. 95.

are made by having all the knobs in metallic contact, and the outer coats all to earth. Great care must be taken that the discharge from such arrangements is not allowed to pass through the body. For discharging them, either discharging tongs (Fig. 95) must be employed, or, better, some form of self-discharger like Lane's (Fig. 96), which only allows the charge to pass when it has reached a certain degree. This latter consists of two knobs (AB) placed one above the other;

the lower (*B*) is insulated, and connected with the knobs of the Leyden jars. The upper (*A*), which is also insulated, moves about a pivot within the hollow ball (*C*). It is counterpoised by a weight (*D*) on the opposite side of the pivot, so as to be held up, away from the lower knob, in contact with a fixed knob *E*, until the knob *B* reaches such a charge that its pull on *A* draws *A* and *B* into contact, and

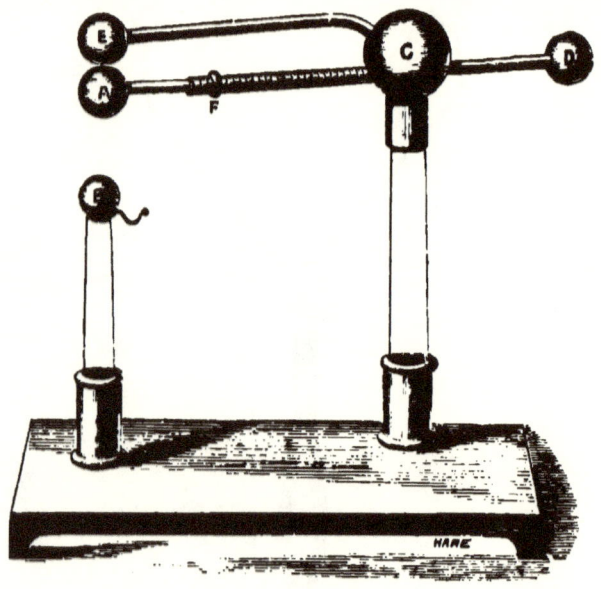

Fig. 96.

the discharge takes place between them. On the lever between *A* and *C* is a small sliding weight (*F*), which can be shifted along so as to alter the degree of charge necessary to bring down the upper knob. The experiments here given can easily be done by a Leyden battery of four quart jars charged by a Holtz or good plate machine, and several of them with a single jar.

The ignition of coal-gas is seen by simply bringing the

knob of a single charged jar into contact with a gas burner from which gas is issuing, the outer coat being connected by a chain with the gas pipes. It may also be shown by corking up in a metal tube a mixture of coal-gas and air. The tube is furnished with an arrangement by which the spark passes through the mixed gas within the tube. On passing the spark an explosion takes place by which the cork is driven out.

The explosion of gunpowder is not effected by passing the spark in the ordinary way. It appears to be too rapid, and in consequence the gunpowder is scattered about without being ignited. On introducing a piece of wet string, which is only a semi-conductor, in some part of the line of discharge, the spark is retarded, and the powder then explodes. The accompanying diagram (Fig. 97) shows an arrangement by which this and several following experiments can be performed, using Lane's discharger, already described, and Henley's discharging table for supporting the apparatus through which the discharge takes place. The Henley's table consists of a table (A) supported on an adjustable stem, having a strip of ivory or some bad conductor across its top. On opposite sides are two insulated arms (BC), passing through a ball and socket which has universal motion. These arms can be adjusted with their lower ends at any position on the table. The Leyden battery (D) has its knob connected simply with the lower knob of the Lane's discharger (E), and wires connect the upper knob (F), through the Henley's discharger, with the outer coat of the jars. For exploding gunpowder, the gunpowder is laid on the discharging table, the points of the arms being placed in it, and the wet string replaces part of one of the wires.

146   *Electricity.*   [Book II.

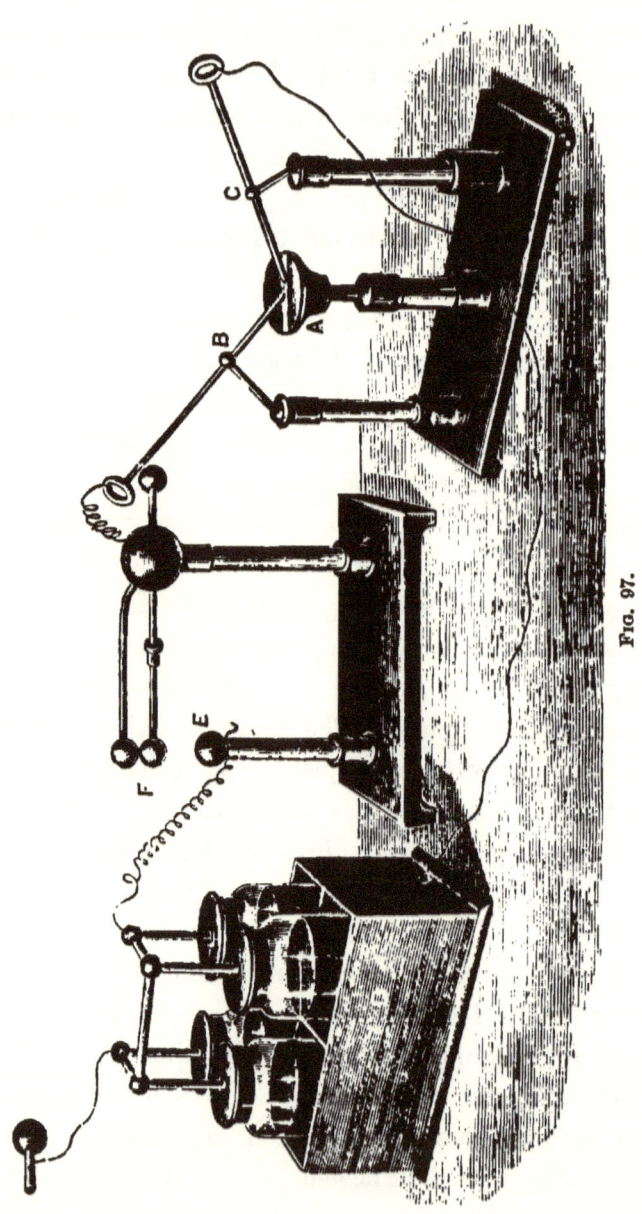

Fig. 97.

The powder may be put in a small ivory mortar, with an ivory bullet fitting into its mouth. If the discharge be made across two wires which enter the mortar rom opposite sides, the bullet will be expelled with some force.

Ether may be ignited by simply putting it in a metal cup connected with the earth. If the knob of the Leyden jar whose outer coat is also to earth be approached towards the ether the discharge passes and ignites the liquid.

If the charge from several jars be passed through gold leaf or very fine wire, the metal offers resistance, and the charge in passing may completely deflagrate the metal. This can easily be shown with gold leaf. The gold leaf should be gummed on a piece of cardboard, tinfoil being also gummed on to the card in contact with the gold leaf, and projecting from the ends. The card must then be put in a screw-press, which replaces the top of the table on Henley's discharger, and the arms must be brought into contact with the projecting tinfoil. After the explosion has passed, the gold will, in part or whole, be deflagrated, leaving a purplish stain on the card where the discharge has passed. To show the mechanical effects, such as splitting wood and puncturing glass, more powerful Leyden batteries are required. An interesting experiment, which can be shown with one or two jars, is that of passing the discharge through a card held in the screw-press, with the arms just on opposite sides. By the discharge a hole is pierced through the card, and a burr is left round its edges on the negative side, as if a material body, such as a needle, had been pushed through from the positive to the negative side.

An instructive experiment is that known as the Thunder House, illustrating the effect of a discontinuous conducting line for a powerful discharge (Fig. 98). A conducting wire passes down the end of a wooden model of a house gable, except about half an inch where the discharge has to pass across a piece of wood (A) fitted loosely into the wall. On discharging a Leyden jar through it, the loose piece of wood, which occurs in the line of discharge, is frequently projected several yards. If the wood be turned round, making the conducting wire continuous, as at B, the discharge passes quietly through it without dislodging the wood. In a similar way, a pyramid built of loose bricks may be thrown over by a discharge, if the conducting line is broken near the base.

Fig. 98.

This illustrates the effect of lightning when the conductor does not terminate in "good earth"—that is, earth constantly damp, and continuous with the conducting body of the earth. The lightning rod under these conditions becomes itself a source of danger to the building it is intended to protect, since the lightning no longer passes to earth by the rod, but flies from it across walls and other bad conductors, rending them in pieces, in its passage to the gas or water supply pipes of the house, which are certain to be in "good earth." Similar accidents may happen through not connecting by metal bands the lightning rod with all external masses of metal, such as gutters, spouts, and lead on the roof.

95. Chemical Decompositions by the Machine dis-

charge.—The power of the machine discharge to perform chemical decompositions was originally shown by Faraday, and can be repeated easily by the discharge of a Voss or Holtz machine. In the case of iodide of potash it is only necessary to place, on a piece of platinum foil, a few thicknesses of bibulous paper soaked in the solution. Then bring a platinum wire from the positive terminal of the machine on to the folds of moist paper, and connect the foil with the opposite terminal. On turning the machine, a brown spot, due to iodine, soon appears round the platinum point, proving the decomposition of the salt.

For the decomposition of copper sulphate we have only to bring two platinum wires, in connection with the terminals of the machine, into a large drop of the solution on a plate of glass. After turning the machine, the platinum wire in connection with the negative conductor will be found coated with copper.

CHAPTER V.

ABSOLUTE MEASURE OF ELECTRICITY.

96. The Unit Jar, and Experiments with it.—We have in previous articles referred to changes and differences of potential, and have explained how they theoretically might be measured, but have not described any instruments by means of which these measurements could be reduced to practice. The instruments we have used have been essentially electroscopes—means of detecting the presence of a difference of potential; and not electrometers—means of actually measuring the difference. All instruments for measuring differences of potential we owe to Sir William Thomson, but, before referring to them, there is an earlier instrument invented by Snow Harris, called the Unit Jar, by means of which the quantity of electricity communicated to a given conductor can be measured, and some of the laws of electrification can be verified.

This (Fig. 99) consists of a small Leyden jar, placed on an insulating stem, whose inner coat is connected with the electrical machine, and outer coat with the body to be charged. It is furnished with two balls, whose distance apart can be adjusted, one connected with the inner, and the other with the outer coat. When the jar reaches a certain definite charge, a discharge takes place between the balls. The positive electricity from the outer coat, instead of going to earth, goes to charge a conductor connected with it, and therefore at each discharge of the unit jar a certain definite amount of electricity has left the outer coat and gone to the conductor, this amount being unaffected by the discharge of the bound charges of the jar. We may take this amount as our provisional unit, and so charge conductors with a certain number of units measured by the number of sparks which pass between the coats of the unit jar. As long as the conductor is the same, the rise in charge is of course proportional to the rise in potential.

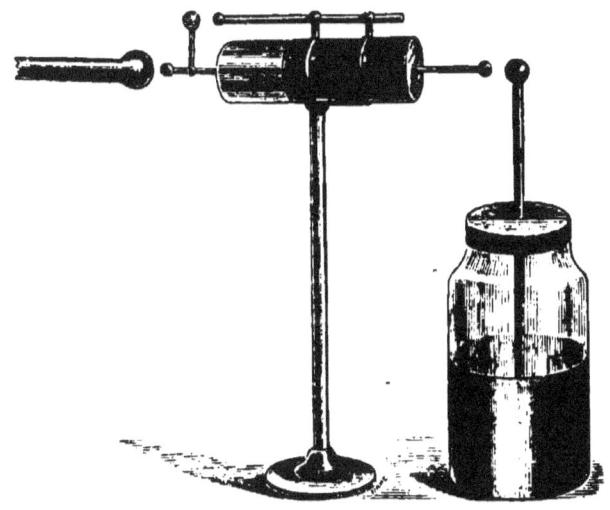

Fig. 99.

The inventor of the unit jar investigated several laws of electrical action by its means, of which we will take two as illustrations, the one referring to the striking distance, and the other to the capacity of a Leyden battery or jar.

The striking distance really depends on the form and size of the conductors between which the spark passes, but for two nearly equal spheres it is approximately proportional to the difference of potential. This may be shown by help of the unit jar. We must arrange on the knob of the jar to be experimented with a self-discharging arrangement, such as Fig. 100, where the distance between the knobs *A* and *B* connected with the inner and outer coats can be varied and measured by the sliding rod, which is graduated. If now, by the arrangement of Fig. 99, we charge the Leyden jar, we can count how many units leave the unit jar by the number of sparks which pass in it, before the Leyden jar has received a charge which will strike across any given measured air space. If we double

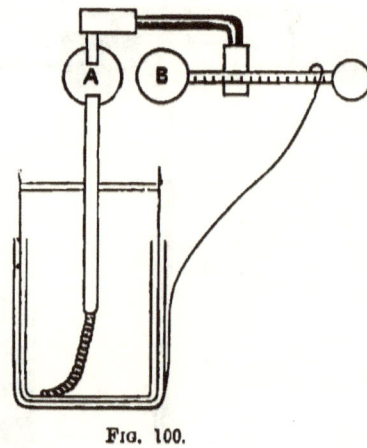

FIG. 100.

the air space, we shall find that we have to double the number of units admitted before discharge takes place, and so on. In making the experiment, the Leyden jar must be *completely* discharged after each experiment, as the passage of a spark across a considerable air space by no means produces complete discharge.

We may also easily show that the capacity of a battery is proportional to the quantity of coated surface, assuming that we have three or four jars of nearly equal coated surface and thickness of glass. Set the discharging electroscope at a

Chap. V.] *Absolute Measure of Electricity.* 153

certain distance on the knob of a single jar, and observe the number of units required to produce discharge, that is, to produce a certain definite potential difference between the inner and outer coat. This number will be a measure of the capacity. Connect another equal jar with the first mentioned jar, in a battery of two jars. It will be found to require twice as many units to produce a discharge. With a third jar it will require three times as many, and so on.

*97. **Theory of Thomson's Electrometers.**—It is proved in works on the theory of electricity, that if we have two plates parallel to each other, one insulated and electrified and the other to earth, the lines of force proceed from the plate at higher to that at lower potential in parallel lines at right angles to either plate, if we exclude a portion round the edge of each plate, which is subject to the induction of surrounding bodies. If, then, we take two spaces, each of area S, opposite to each other and near the middle of two parallel plates, it appears that the capacity of the system formed by the two surfaces is $\frac{S}{4\pi t}$, where t is the distance between the plates, and π is the ratio of the circumference to the diameter of a circle, and very nearly equal to $\frac{22}{7}$. All the measures are of course referred to the absolute system.

It also appears that the attractive force between the portions indicated of the two plates is given by $\frac{V^2 S}{8\pi t^2}$, measured in degrees or absolute units of force.

In applying this theory, Thomson has two parallel plates, which are brought to the potentials whose difference is to be measured. In one of these he makes an aperture, into which a moveable disc almost exactly fits, and he then measures the force exerted on this disc alone; taking care that when the reading is taken, the disc is at the same potential and in the same plane with the annulus or "guard ring" surrounding it. This position is often called the "fiducial position."

*98. **The Absolute Electrometer.** — Sir William Thomson divides his electrometers into two classes, Idiostatic, in which the electrification to be measured is the only one employed, and Heterostatic, in which the electrification is measured by means of an independent electrification, made in the electrometer. In one of his earliest forms of absolute electrometer (Fig. 101), the moveable disc (A) was suspended

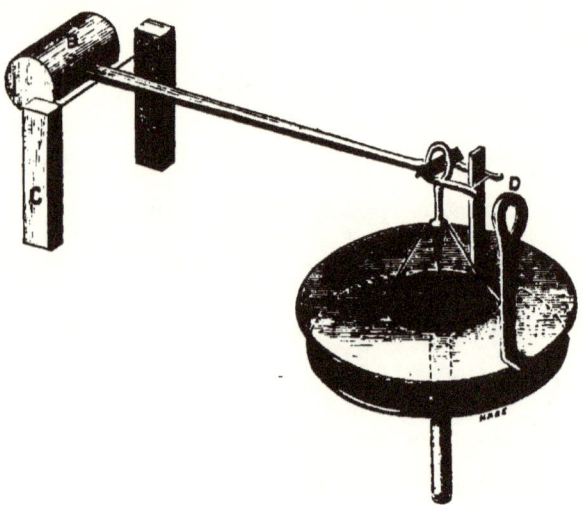

FIG. 101.

by three metal wires from one end of a long metallic lever, and counterpoised by a weight (B) at the other end. The fulcrum consists of a wire stretched between two metal supports (CC), to which a certain amount of torsion is given, so as to keep

Chap. V.]   *Absolute Measure of Electricity.*   155

the metal disc, when unelectrified, above its fiducial position. Its register is made by the fine hair which joins the ends of the arms (D) projecting from the lever, and moving with its motion over the surface of an upright enamelled rod, on which are two black dots separated by about a hair's-breadth. The hair and dots are viewed simultaneously through a strong convex lens, and the fiducial position is registered when the hair bisects the distance between the centres of the two black dots.

All the parts of the instrument we have described, as well as the guard ring, are in communication with the earth.

The lower disc, whose potential is required to be measured, is insulated on a glass stem, and has its distance from the first plate adjusted by a micrometer screw.

Before using the instrument the guard ring is placed in metallic connection with the lower disc, so that there is no electrical attraction. The disc or trap-door is above its fiducial position, owing to the torsion of the wire. By means of weights placed on the moveable disc, and a light wire rider on the arm, the disc can be brought to its fiducial mark. The force acting on the disc when in fiducial position will then always equal the weights which had been used in this experiment. In making a measure of potential the lower disc is connected with the body whose potential is required, and by turning the micrometer screw the distance between the discs is adjusted till the register is brought to its fiducial mark. Then, knowing the attraction F by the weights previously used,[1] the distance t by the micrometer screw, and the area S of the moveable disc, the difference of

---

[1] F, the weight in grams, must be multiplied by the absolute measure of gravity to reduce it to absolute units of force. This may be assumed 981.

potential becomes known in absolute measure by the formula
$$\frac{V^2 S}{8\pi t^2} = F, \therefore V = t\sqrt{\frac{8\pi F}{S}}.$$

In the drawing we have omitted the external case, the mechanical arrangement of the micrometer screw below, and the vessel containing pumice-stone moistened with sulphuric acid for securing dryness.

*99. The Portable Electrometer.—Where small potential differences have to be measured, the absolute

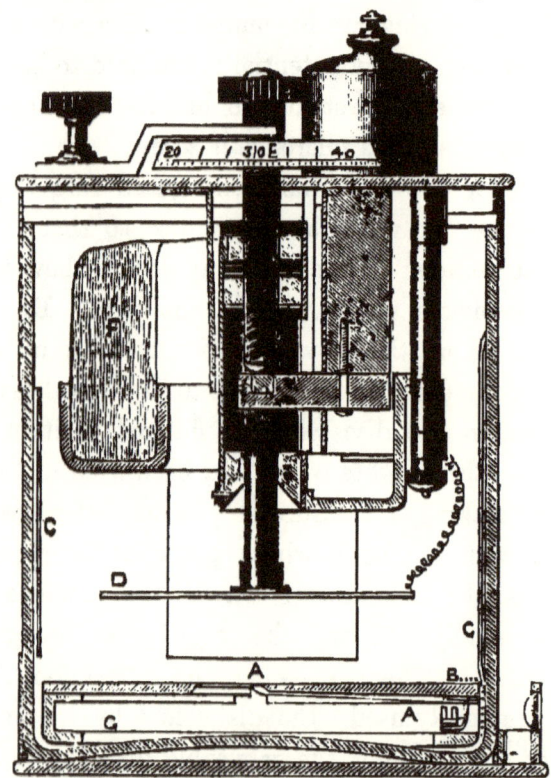

Fig. 102.

electrometer is not sensitive enough. In these cases heterostatic instruments have to be employed. Fig. 102

represents the Portable Electrometer, constructed specially for observations on atmospheric electricity. The attracted disc (A) consists of a very thin sheet of aluminium held below its fiducial position by the torsion of a wire which supports it. The movements of the disc are registered by a long arm (AA), also of aluminium, whose end is divided into two arms crossed by a hair, which moves over an enamel plate, as in the absolute electrometer. The case containing the instrument is a Leyden jar, and all the parts we have named are in connection with its inner coat (C). This is charged independently by an electrophorus. The plate (D) is supported on a glass stem, and its movements registered by a micrometer screw (E). It is connected by a spiral wire with a terminal which passes through the case, but is insulated from it (Fig. 103). This terminal is connected with the body of which the potential is to be measured. F represents pumice-stone moistened with sulphuric acid to secure dryness in the instrument.

Fig. 103 gives a sketch of the brass umbrella, which, by sliding on the terminal in connection with D, either, when raised, insulates it from the earth, or, when lowered, puts it in connection with the earth. The importance of this will be seen in taking an observation.

Supposing the Leyden jar charged, we first determine the earth reading. This is done by depressing the brass umbrella, thus bringing the plate D to earth. On turning the micrometer screw we can bring the disc to its fiducial mark, and read off its exact position by means of the micrometer screw. Now raise the umbrella, and put D in connection with the body whose potential is to be found. Turn round the micrometer screw until the disc is in fiducial position, and again read the micrometer screw.

The difference between the two readings is a measure of the potential difference between the body and the earth, independent of the charge given to the Leyden jar.

To prove this, let U be the unknown potential of the charge in the Leyden jar. Connect the moveable plate with

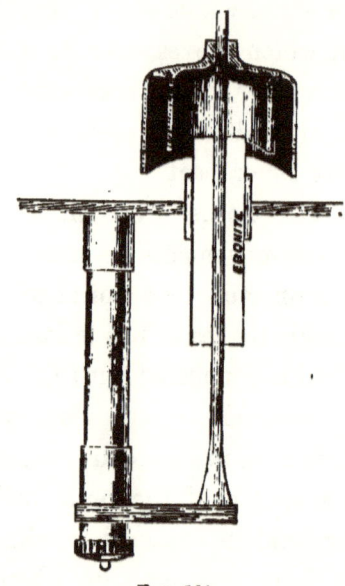

Fig. 103.

the earth, and suppose that the observed distance between the plates is t_0. Then we have (Art. 97)

$$U = t_0 \sqrt{\frac{8\pi F}{S}} \quad \ldots \ldots \ldots (1).$$

Next let V be the potential required to be found, and let t be the second reading of the micrometer. Then

$$U - V = t\sqrt{\frac{8\pi F}{S}} \quad \ldots \ldots \ldots (2).$$

$$\therefore \quad V = (t_0 - t)\sqrt{\frac{8\pi F}{S}},$$

showing that the measure obtained is altogether independent of the charge in the jar. The constant multiplier $\sqrt{\dfrac{8\pi F}{S}}$ can be found once for all by comparison with an absolute electrometer, and the readings reduced to absolute measure ever afterwards.

This instrument is most frequently used for finding the difference of potential at a point in the air and at the earth's surface. For this purpose a wire is attached to the terminal which carries on its further end a burning slow match, the effect of which is to reduce the conductor (D) to the potential at the point in the air at which the products of combustion are escaping.

100. **The Quadrant Electrometer.**—To the same class belongs Sir William Thomson's earliest electrometer, the Quadrant Electrometer, which is adapted to detect and measure very minute potential differences. The principle of the instrument is, that when one conductor is under the cover of another, so that the induction on external bodies may be neglected, the force between them, whatever their forms, is proportional to the square of their potential difference. Thus if U be the potential of the internal body, which we will suppose at the higher potential, and V the potential of the external body, the force between them is $C(U-V)^2$, where C depends only on the geometry of the two bodies. Next let the body of potential U be placed symmetrically between two bodies alike in all respects whose potentials are V and V'. It will be urged in opposite directions by the forces $C(U-V)^2$ and $C(U-V')^2$, and therefore will be urged towards the body of lower potential by the force

$$C(U-V)^2 - C(U-V')^2$$
$$= 2C(V'-V)\left(U - \frac{V+V'}{2}\right).$$

If U be very large compared with both V and V,' then the force

$$= 2CU(V'-V).$$

This theory is carried into practice by making the external conductors in form of four quadrants cut from a shallow circular closed box of brass (Fig. 104), the opposite pairs

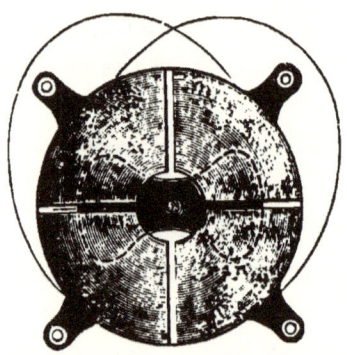

Fig. 1 .

being joined by wires. These are separately insulated, and within them hangs horizontally a light needle made of aluminium, maintained at a high potential by being connected with the inner coating of a Leyden jar. When the four quadrants are at the same potential, the needle is kept either by a magnet attached to it or by a bifilar suspension symmetrically over one of the planes of division. If the pairs of quadrants AA are at different potentials from BB, the needle will be urged at both ends in the same direction of rotation, with a force proportional to the product of the potential of the needle and the difference of

Chap. V.] *Absolute Measure of Electricity.* 161

potentials of A and B. It will, acting against the torsion or magnetic force, be slightly deflected towards the quadrants at lower potential, and in this case the amount of deflection is also proportional to the disturbing force. In the form of the instrument (Fig. 105) now commonly used, the quadrants (AA,

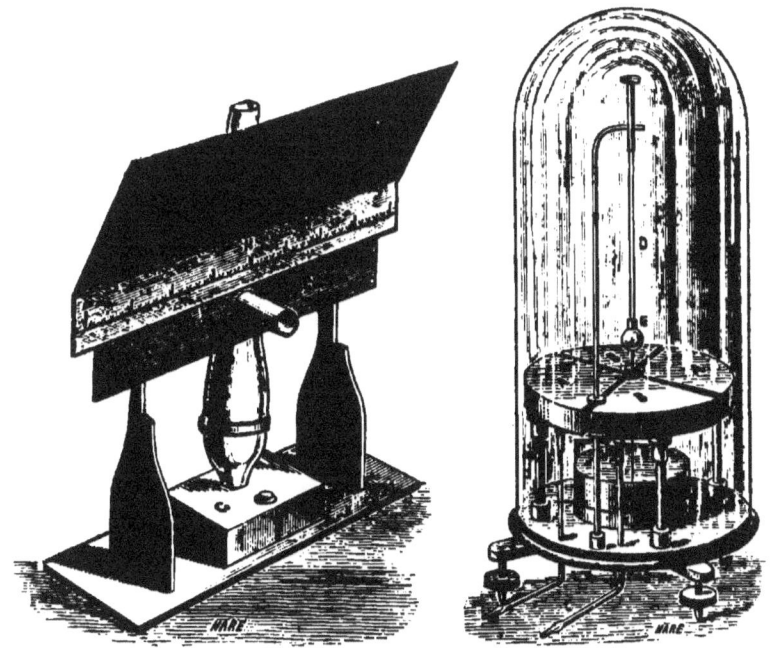

FIG. 105.

BB) are supported on the base by four glass stems; the opposite pairs are connected by wires, and each pair is connected with a terminal passing through the base, but insulated from it. Under the quadrants is a glass vessel, coated on the outside with tinfoil, and containing sulphuric acid, which forms the inner coating of the Leyden jar, and also keeps the instrument dry. The aluminium needle has a platinum wire passing vertically through its centre, whose

L

lower end dips in the sulphuric acid, and whose upper end is formed in a T, to the top of which the bifilar suspension (*D*) is attached. To register the movements of the needle a light concave mirror (*E*) is cemented to the wire immediately under the head of the T. The whole is enclosed under a bell-glass, and supported on levelling screws. By means of a lens (*F*) the light from a narrow slit in front of the flame of an oil lamp (*G*) is thrown on the mirror, reflected from it, and focussed on a graduated screen (*H*) placed above the slit. As the distance between the slit and the mirror is about 18 inches, the smallest movement of the mirror causes a considerable movement in the image of the slit on the graduated screen.

*101. **The Gauge.**—In Sir William Thomson's original form the bell-glass itself formed the Leyden jar, and the parts

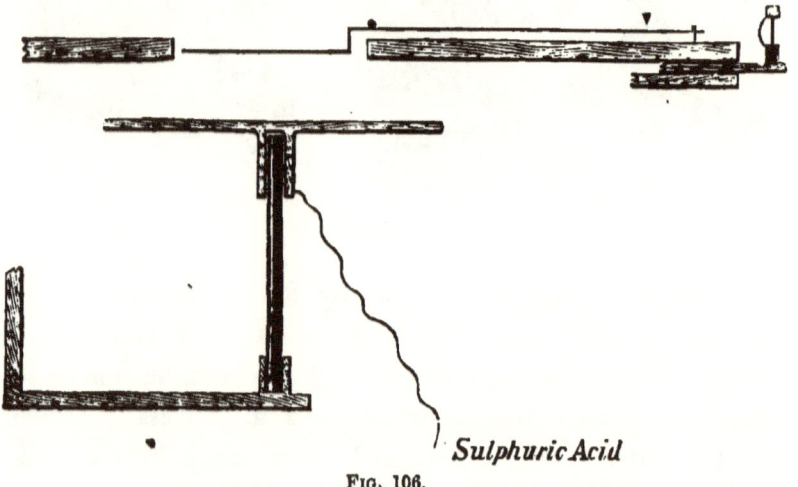

FIG. 106.

of the apparatus were suspended from a metal plate which closed it at the top. This form is still adopted where there is an arrangement for maintaining the charge of the jar constant, without which the observations made at considerable intervals of time are not comparable, owing to the unavoidable leakage of the Leyden jar. This consists of a gauge for showing when the acid of the jar is at its normal potential, and a replenisher to bring it back to its normal charge when it has fallen below it.

The gauge consists simply of an attracted disc electrometer, of which the attracted disc is in the cover plate, and the attracting disc is placed below and parallel with it, insulated, but in connection by a wire with the sulphuric acid in the jar. The diagram (Fig. 106) gives a section.

*102. **The Replenisher.**—The replenisher (Figs. 107 and 108) is a small inductive electrical machine. It consists of

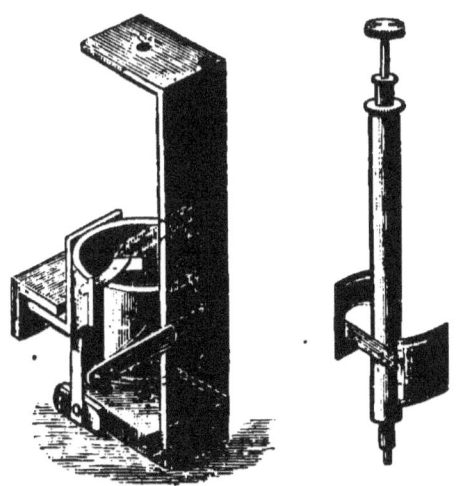

Fig. 107.

two inductors (AB) in the form of half-cylinders separated by a small air space, and two insulated metal carriers (CD)

attached to an ebonite spindle, by which they can be rapidly rotated between the inductors.

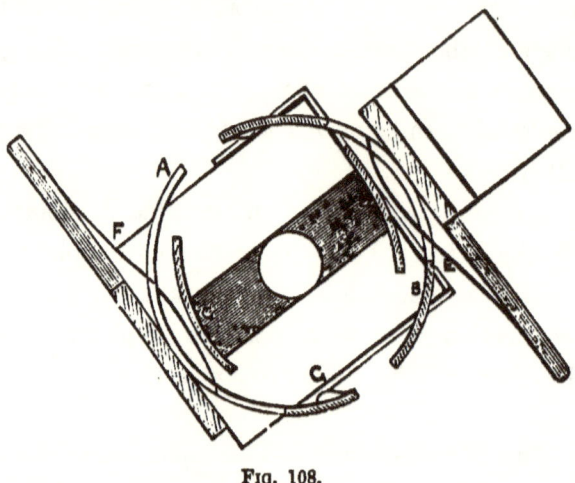

Fig. 108.

One inductor is insulated, but connected by a wire with the acid in the jar, and the other is to earth. By means of two springs (E and F) which pass without contact through slits cut in the faces of the inductors, the two carriers come for a moment into contact with each other when under full induction of the two inductors. These springs are connected by a metal band under the instrument, but insulated from the earth.

Assuming A connected with the inner coat of the Leyden jar, charged positively, the carrier C under the inductor A receives a *minus* charge, and D similarly a *plus* charge. The carrier (D) which has the + charge comes by rotation under cover of the + inductor (A), from which a spring (G) projects internally, just touching the carrier before it comes in contact with the spring (F). This carrier gives up its charge to the inductor, and thus strengthens the charge of the jar. The opposite carrier at the same time gives up its charge by a spring to the opposite inductor, by which it passes to earth. A few turns of the milled head at the top of the ebonite spindle will then bring up the charge if it be too low; and it can easily be seen that turning the head in the opposite direction will bring down the charge should it be too high.

*103. Uses of Quadrant Electrometer.—By the Quadrant Electrometer differences of potential can be shown and measured which are quite insensible to the gold-leaf electroscope. The pyro-electricity of tourmaline can be shown by it in very short broken crystals. It is only necessary to bind a platinum wire round each end of the crystal, connecting the opposite ends with the electrometer terminals. By placing the crystal without contact over a metal plate, under which a lamp is lighted, the needle will soon deflect, showing the presence of the pyro-electricity. Its chief use, however, is in investigating differences of potential on which current electricity depends, and which form the subject of our next Book.

QUESTIONS ON BOOK II.

1. A sheet of paper well dried and rubbed with a brush will adhere to the wall of a room, but it will remain longer adherent the drier the air of the room. Explain this.

2. Two gold-leaf electroscopes, charged with opposite electricities, are approached towards each other till the caps nearly touch. Explain the effect observed on the leaves.

3. A gold-leaf electroscope is taken from a colder room and at once placed on the table of a warmer room; a charged body is brought in contact with the cap. Describe the effect on the electroscope.

4. A crystal of tourmaline is suspended by a silk fibre between two bodies, one positively and the other negatively electrified; the whole system is enclosed in an oven, which is gradually heated from outside. Describe the behaviour of the tourmaline crystal during heating, and also during cooling.

5. Explain why, after heating a tourmaline crystal, it is usual to draw the flame of a lamp across it before observing the phenomena on cooling. Explain the effect on the observed phenomena, consequent on neglect of this precaution.

6. A piece of glass rubbed with cat's fur is pivoted freely, and approached by another piece of glass rubbed with silk. Describe the action between them.

7. A silk glove is drawn off the hand. What will be the electrical condition of the glove?

8. A gold-leaf electroscope is charged by flapping it with a silk handkerchief, and a piece of roll-sulphur, rubbed with cork, is approached towards its cap. Describe the observed effect.

9. In Coulomb's Balance, when the carrier ball is introduced, the needle ball, after contact, shows a deflection of 30°. Explain how the torsion circle must be treated to bring the balls 15° apart, and also to bring them 60° apart.

ANS.—105° in the negative direction, *i.e.* opposite to the deflection; 52° 30′ in the positive direction.

10. If the balls in the balance had been at first 30° apart, and 260° of torsion had been put on in a negative direction (*i.e.* opposite to the deflection of the needle), find the position of the needle.

ANS.—At 10°.

11. If the balls in the balance show at first charging a deflection of $a°$, and torsion $\beta°$ in the negative direction is applied, write down an equation for finding the position of the needle.

ANS.—If $x°$ be the position required, $x^3 + \beta x^2 = a^3$.

12. A fixed charge is given to the needle ball, and the carrier ball introduced without contact, carrying charges from successive conductors, show that the charges can be compared by turning the torsion circle till the balls are at a constant distance apart, and observing the torsion on the wire. These charges will then be simply proportional to the torsion in each case.

13. If the balance be discharged completely before each observation, and the carrier ball introduced several times successively with different charges, show that the charge in each case will be proportional to the square root of the cube of the observed deflections.

14. The charge on the carrier ball of the balance, which at first shows a deflection of 36°, is halved, and the ball introduced again without contact with the needle ball. Find the reading of the torsion circle when the balls again diverge 36°.

15. The needle ball of a balance is electrified, and charges are carried from three selected points on a conductor by the carrier ball, which is introduced each time into the balance without contact. The readings of the torsion circle corresponding to the three charges are respectively $-35°$, $+3°$, and $+20°$, the deflection of the needle being in all cases 45°. Compare the electrical density at the three points.

16. A sheet of tinfoil, of which two opposite edges are held by insulating handles is charged, and has a gold-leaf electroscope connected with its surface. What change in the indication of the electroscope would be noticed, supposing the sheet rolled up like a wall map?

17. A gold-leaf electroscope has its base to earth, and an electrified wire cage is lowered over its cap, just avoiding contact with the base. Describe the changes in the electroscope as it is lowered.

18. A gold-leaf electroscope has a sharp point attached to its cap, and a glass rod, charged by friction with silk, is held over the point for a short time, and then removed. Describe all the indications of the electroscope.

19. A person on an insulating stool draws a silk glove off his hand, and, holding the glove in the opposite hand, presents the ungloved hand to the cap of an uncharged electroscope. What indications will be obtained? If he now drop the glove on the floor what change will there be?

20. A glass funnel with a narrow tube is filled with copper filings, which gradually flow out on to the cap of a gold-leaf electroscope; a rod of sealing-wax rubbed with flannel is held over the funnel as the copper filings are discharged. Show that the electroscope acquires a permanent charge.

21. A platinum dish is placed on the cap, and over it a glass funnel with a capillary tube, filled with acidulated water. Show that

on holding an excited sealing-wax rod over the funnel the liquid will flow through the capillary tube into the platinum dish, and will communicate a permanent charge to the electroscope. What is its sign?

22. A sphere whose radius is 5 cm. has a charge of 10 absolute units communicated to it. Find its potential and the density of its electrification in absolute measure.

23. A sphere whose radius is 10 cm. is brought to potential 5 in absolute measure. Find its charge.

24. Spheres whose radii are 5 and 6 cm. are connected by a long wire (whose capacity is *nil*). Find how a charge communicated to the system is divided between them.

25. Spheres whose radii are 1, 2, and 3 cm., are charged to potentials 1, 2, 3 in absolute measure, and are then suddenly connected by a long wire. Find the potential of them all after contact.
    Ans.—$\frac{7}{3}$.

26. The radii of two spheres are as $2:3$, and the density of their electrification as $9:8$. Compare their potentials.
    Ans.—$3:4$.

27. An electrophorus cake excited by friction is dropped face downwards on a metal plate connected with the earth. What is the electrical condition of the sole?

28. One of two insulated hollow vessels has a weak charge of electricity. A carrier ball, supported on a silk fibre, is brought near the outside of the charged vessel, touched by the finger, and then dropped into the second vessel. It is lifted out, approached to the outside of this vessel, when near it touched by the finger, and then dropped into the first vessel. The whole process is repeated over and over again. Show that the potential difference of the two vessels rises in compound interest ratio.

29. If one thousand spherical mist particles, all at the same electrical potential, fall together into a single rain-drop, the potential of the rain-drop is one hundred times that of each mist particle.

30. Compare potential in a battery of 6 jars charged by 12 turns of a machine, with that of a battery of 12 jars of equal area charged with 36 turns of the same machine working at the same power.
    Ans.—As 2 to 3.

31. Compare the quantity in a fully-charged battery of 8 jars with that in another battery of 12 jars, the quantity of coated surface in each jar of the latter being double that in each of the former, and the thickness of the glass one half.

Ans.—As 1 to 6.

32. In a certain trap-door electrometer the trap-door was brought to its fiducial position by a weight of ·0133 grams, the whole being unelectrified. The disc is a square whose side is ·8 cm., and in a certain experiment the trap-door was brought to its fiducial mark when the moveable disc was distant ·5 cm. Find the potential difference in absolute measure.

Ans.—11·3 nearly.

33. The replenisher in a quadrant electrometer is a modified Voss machine. Trace out the corresponding parts of the apparatus in the two instruments.

34. Point out the exact source of danger in holding a piece of metal in the hand during a thunderstorm.

35. Show, on the general principles of induction, that a person may be killed at the instant of a lightning discharge without the discharge passing through his body (the return shock).

36. When the electrification of the earth is resinous, what would be the electrical condition of rain falling to the earth, and of smoke rising from the earth?

37. Show that a knight of the middle ages in a coat of mail could not be injured by lightning.

38. Why should you not in a thunderstorm take refuge under a tree?

39. Would you in a thunderstorm feel yourself secure in a house built of sheet-iron?

40. Show why a house in which a gas or water supply exists is more liable to damage from lightning than one without them.

BOOK III.

VOLTAIC ELECTRICITY.

CHAPTER I.

THE BATTERY.

104. Electrical Conditions of a Zinc-Copper Couple.
—Voltaic Electricity may be defined as the electrical conditions developed in metals and liquids when in contact. As an illustration (Fig. 109) we take a strip of zinc (amalgamated by dipping it in dilute sulphuric acid, and rubbing it over with mercury) and a strip of copper of the same size. Dip them, without contact between them, in a vessel of water, slightly acidulated with a few drops of sulphuric acid. If we now connect the plates with the terminals of a quadrant electrometer, or with the plates of a condensing electroscope, it will be found that the copper is positive to the zinc. It can be shown that in this, as in other cases, there is not a development of one kind of electricity only, for on insu-

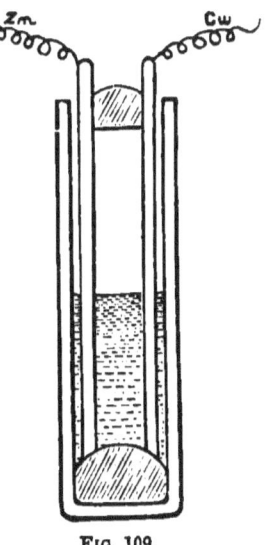

Fig. 109.

lating the vessel it will be found that the copper is positive to the earth, and the zinc negative to the earth.

If we now connect the copper and zinc by a thick wire, all trace of electrification disappears, but on separating them again the difference of potential instantaneously reappears. On substituting a very thin wire for the thick wire, we find that the difference of potential is diminished but does not disappear, but can be made less and less by shortening or thickening the conducting wire. This shows that there is in this case not a single discharge of electricity, as in a Leyden jar, but a continuous discharge depending in some way on the connecting arc.

105. Chemical Conditions of the Cell.—If we next examine the fluid in the vessel, we shall notice that while the zinc and copper are in contact, bubbles of gas stream up from the copper plate. This gas can be collected and proved to be hydrogen. On separating the plates the stream of hydrogen bubbles ceases. After the contact has lasted for some time, on taking out a few drops of the liquid and evaporating it, we shall find that it leaves a white residue of sulphate of zinc, and on removing the zinc plate, washing, and drying it, we shall find that it has lost in weight.

If, for comparison, we leave the zinc and copper in the liquid without contact for the same length of time, we shall find no hydrogen evolved, no deposit of zinc sulphate on evaporating the liquid, and no loss of weight in the zinc.

We have thus shown that when zinc and copper are dipped in acidulated water they assume different potentials, without any sensible chemical action taking place; but as soon as they are in contact with each other, the potential difference is diminished, and as long as contact continues, chemical action takes place in the liquid; zinc, being dissolved, forming zinc sulphate in the liquid, and hydrogen being evolved at the copper plate.

If the weighed amalgamated zinc and copper plates be placed under an inverted glass jar in a pneumatic trough, and there brought into contact, the hydrogen can be collected and its weight computed. If the loss in the weight of zinc be also determined, these two weights will have a constant ratio —hydrogen to zinc—of 2 to 65, which is the ratio of their chemical equivalents. We see, therefore, that the action in the cell is purely the chemical action of the fluid on the metallic zinc, although the action on the zinc takes place at the zinc plate, and the hydrogen is given off at the copper plate.

106. Thermal Condition of the Cell.—While the zinc and copper are in contact, we shall find that the temperature both of the liquid and the solid conductors has risen, and by performing the experiment in a calorimeter it can be shown that the total heat evolved is exactly equal to that which would be evolved on dissolving the same weight of ordinary granulated zinc in dilute acid. This further confirms the conclusion that the action in the cell is a purely chemical one.

107. Source of Energy of the Current.—From the experiments on the simple zinc-copper cell, we see that, although we may have difference of potential, we cannot have a flow of electricity maintained in the conductor, without a sensible amount of chemical action in the cell. This might have been in a measure anticipated, by considering that the current in the conductor is a form of energy (developing heat, and capable of doing work in a variety of ways), and can therefore only be maintained by an expenditure of energy. This source of energy is found in the energy of chemical combination in the battery. For the maintenance of the current it therefore appears necessary that we should have at least one fluid capable of decomposition, and of forming compounds with some other body with which it is in contact. Thus we might in the cell have substituted, for sulphuric acid, hydrochloric or nitric acid, or even pure water, and the action would, initially at least, have been much the same. We might also have varied the metals, provided we still had one of them capable of being dissolved by the liquid. Thus if we had used copper and platinum, we should have had the copper attacked by the acid, taking the place of the zinc in the typical cell; but if we had used gold and platinum, neither of which is acted upon by sulphuric acid, we should have had no current. We should also find, in all changes of the metals, that that which is acted on by the acid is always at the lower potential.

For convenience of reference, the plates in the liquid are called electrodes, that which is consumed by the acid being called the zincode, and the opposite plate the platinode, from their analogy to the zinc and platinum in a typical zinc-platinum cell.

108. Local Action.—In all the older forms of cell some modification of the zinc-copper cell of Volta was used, in which zinc was the metal dissolved, and dilute sulphuric acid the liquid.

When only commercial zinc is used in making the cells, a rapid evolution of gas takes place from the zinc plate, accompanied by the corrosion of this plate when the zinc and copper are not in contact, thus causing a waste of zinc, a weakening of the current, and obliging the use of a very weak acid solution in the cells. This is called local action, and can be avoided by rubbing the zinc plate—first dipped in dilute acid, to remove oxide—with liquid mercury. In this way an amalgam of zinc and mercury is formed on the surface of the zinc. The cause of this local action, as it is called, in the zinc plate, seems to be the existence of other metals as impurities in the zinc. These with the zinc and the acid set up small voltaic couples, by which the zinc is consumed and hydrogen evolved. The presence of the mercury seems to keep a uniform amalgam of zinc and mercury always in contact with the acid, and prevents these local circuits. When the battery is in action the zinc alone is consumed, the mercury amalgam being constantly replenished from the solid zinc behind. This allows a much stronger acid to be used for charging the battery.

109. Action of Evolved Hydrogen.—In every battery in which there is employed one fluid and two metals, a further defect consists in the deposit of the hydrogen gas on the platinode, forming a layer of hydrogen instead of metal. This, in the first place, acts as a non-conductor to the electricity, so weakening the current; in the second place, its contact with the copper plate lessens its potential, so that, after the battery has been working for a short time, the potential difference between the terminals is much lessened. It also decomposes the zinc sulphate in the liquid, causing a deposit of zinc on the copper plate.

110. Smee's Cell.—These effects are somewhat obviated

by Smee's battery, in which the platinode consists of thin sheets of silver or platinum, in either case covered over with finely divided platinum. This roughened surface discharges the hydrogen in a very remarkable degree, so that this form of cell is far more constant than any other one fluid arrangement. In this cell there are generally two amalgamated zinc plates on opposite sides of the platinised plate, all bound together by a metal clip (A, Fig. 110). The platinised silver plate is very thin, and supported on a wooden frame (B) placed between the opposite zinc plates.

Fig. 110.

III. **The Bichromate Cell.**—The only other one-fluid cell now commonly used is the bichromate cell, which is useful for ringing a bell, or other purposes where the current is intermittent.

In this, as in other cells described later, the platinode is of gas coke, a substance obtained from the inside of gas retorts, very hard, not attacked by any acids, and a good conductor. The other plate is of zinc, and the exciting liquid is a solution of bichromate of potash, acidulated with sulphuric acid. The zinc is often attached to a sliding rod (A, Fig. 111), by which it can be lowered into the acid when wanted to be used. There is often a single zinc opposed to two carbon plates in the cell.

The chemical action in this cell is somewhat complicated. The potassium bichromate ($K_2Cr_2O_7$) parts with some of its oxygen to the zinc, forming zinc oxide 3(ZnO), three atoms of zinc entering into the action, and the salt, in doing so, is decomposed into potassium oxide (K_2O) and chromium sesquioxide (Cr_2O_3). Each of these oxides, in the presence of free sulphuric acid, forms a sulphate, the ultimate products being zinc sulphate and a compound sulphate of potassium and chromium ($KCr2SO_4$) called chrome alum, which gives a green colour to the liquid after the cell has been in action for some time.

112. Daniell's Cell.—In two fluid and two metal batteries the hydrogen evolved acts chemically on some other substance, and causes a solid or liquid to be formed at the platinode which has no injurious effect.

A great variety of such cells are in existence for various purposes, of which we shall describe those most commonly used.

FIG. 111.

Daniell's Cell is constructed in a great variety of forms, but consists essentially of a zinc rod immersed in dilute acid, separated by porous earthenware, or some material gradually permeable by liquids, from sulphate of copper in which a copper rod is immersed. In this case the hydrogen set free by the action of the acid on the zinc attacks the copper sulphate, forming sulphuric acid, and causing a deposit of metallic copper on the copper plate.

This cell continues working apparently at the expense only

of the zinc and the copper sulphate, the latter of which can be replaced by packing crystals of copper sulphate round the copper plate, and in this case the working of the cell continues till the zinc is consumed. The formation of zinc sulphate in the zinc cell appears not to be injurious till a deposit of crystals occurs, as the cell is found to work equally well when the zinc cell is filled with a concentrated solution of zinc sulphate instead of acid. In this latter case the zinc sulphate has no direct action on the metallic zinc, except when the terminals are joined. The chemical action originating the current in this case is the tendency, in the presence of free zinc, to replace copper sulphate by the more stable compound zinc sulphate,—an action which can only take place in the pores of the material separating the zinc sulphate from the copper sulphate.

The form given to this cell may be an outer glazed porcelain cell containing the zinc plate and acid, with an inner vessel of porous porcelain filled with copper sulphate with the copper rod immersed, shown in section in Fig. 112. Another form is to have the outer vessel entirely copper, containing the copper sulphate, and an inner porous vessel with the zinc rod immersed in acid (Fig. 113).

On the same principle are constructed specific-gravity batteries, of which one form is shown in section in Fig. 114. It depends on the difference in specific gravity of zinc sulphate and copper sulphate. At the bottom of the vessel lies a copper plate embedded in crystals of copper sulphate, and a saturated solution of the salt is poured over it to about half fill the vessel. A copper wire is fastened to the plate, and, passing through the liquid (insulated by a coating of gutta-percha), is connected with a terminal outside. On the top of the copper

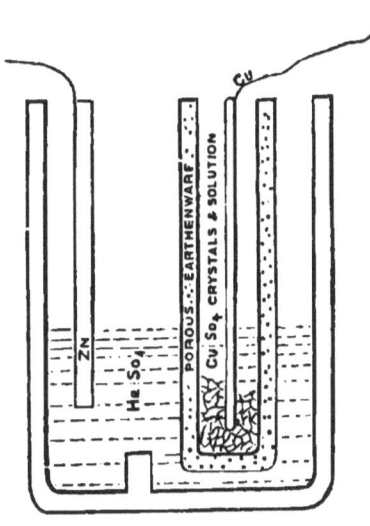

Fig. 112.

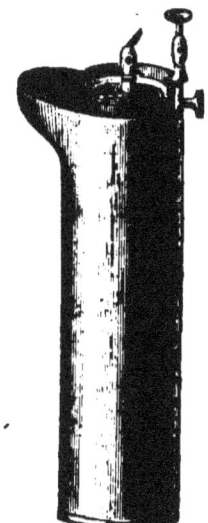

Fig. 113.

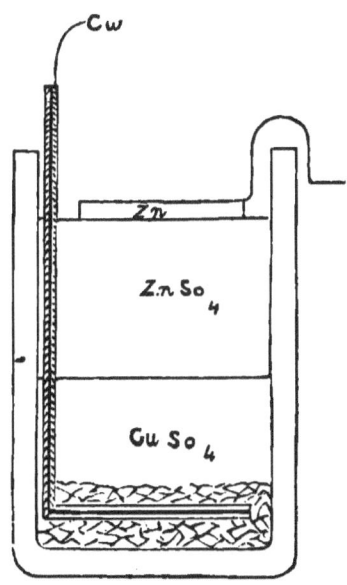

Fig. 114.

sulphate is carefully poured a solution of zinc sulphate or dilute acid, which, being specifically lighter, rests upon it without mixing. In contact with this is suspended a zinc plate. Menotti's battery differs from this only in placing a layer of sawdust or sand over the copper sulphate crystals, which takes the place of the porous cell.

113. Grove's and Bunsen's Cells.—In Grove's Cell (Fig. 115) the outer porcelain or glass vessel contains the

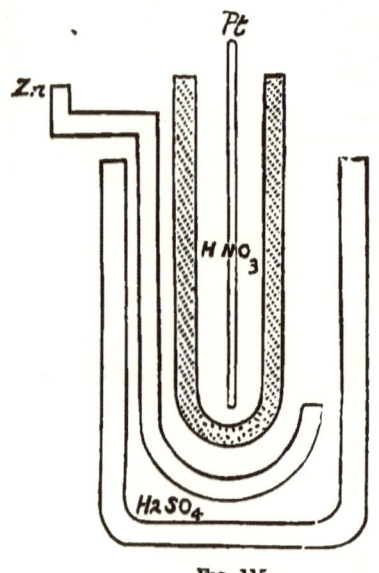

Fig. 115.

zinc plate immersed in dilute acid, and the porous vessel contains a sheet of platinum immersed in strong nitric acid. In this the hydrogen set free by the corrosion of the zinc attacks the nitric acid, reducing it to water and one or more compounds of nitrogen and oxygen, which are soluble in the water and nitric acid to a large extent; but the continued working of the battery causes them to be evolved in the form of red fumes.

The evolution of gas may be avoided by substituting chromic acid for nitric acid in the cell. The hydrogen then acts on the chromic acid, forming chromic oxide and water, the oxide being insoluble.

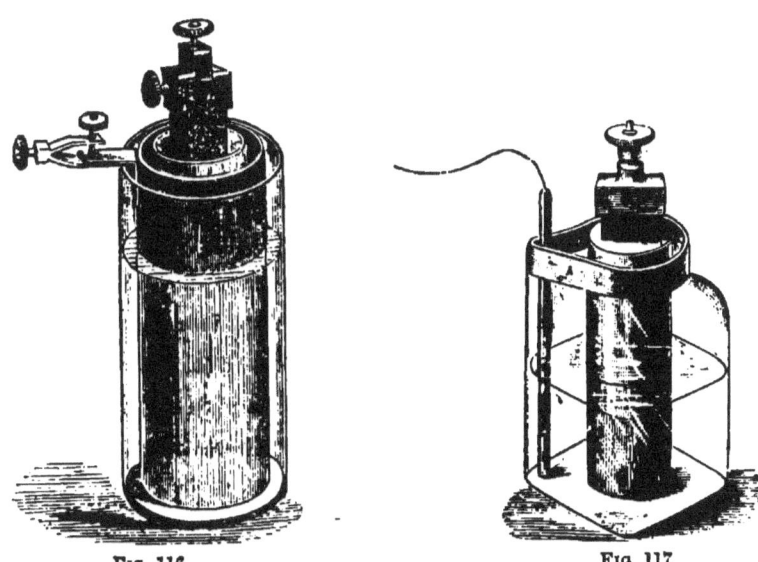

Fig. 116.   Fig. 117.

Bunsen's Cell differs from Grove's only in the substitution of gas graphite for platinum in the porous vessel. This diminishes the cost of the cell, but makes it less compact, and, on account of the porous texture of the carbon, less cleanly to work with (Fig. 116).

114. Leclanché's Cell.—In this cell (Fig. 117) the porous pot contains a rod of gas carbon, tightly packed round with fragments of the same gas carbon and manganese binoxide, this packing being covered over by a layer of pitch. The gas carbon which projects has a lead socket cast on to it, to which a binding screw is attached. The outer cell contains a zinc rod immersed in a solution of sal-ammoniac. The sal-ammoniac or ammonium chloride (H_3NHCl) attacks the zinc, forming zinc chloride ($ZnCl_2$), which combines with the ammonia (H_3N) to form a compound ($2H_3NZnCl_2$), and liberating hydrogen. The hydrogen reduces the manganese binoxide (MnO_2) in the porous vessel to a lower oxide (Mn_2O_3) and water. This cell continues working till the whole of the manganese binoxide has been reduced, if occasionally filled up with the sal-ammoniac solution.

115. Marie Davy's Cell.—In this the porous vessel contains a paste of mercury sulphate, in which the carbon rod is immersed; the outer vessel contains a zinc rod immersed in brine. In this cell zinc chloride is formed, and the sodium set free attacks the sulphate of mercury, forming sodium sulphate, and liberating mercury, which is found in a metallic form at the bottom of the cell. This can easily be reconverted into sulphate, and used over again without any loss.

116. Becquerel's Cell.—This, called by its inventor the

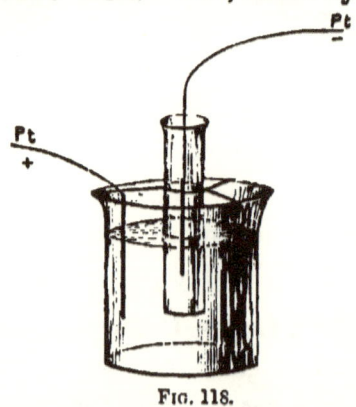

FIG. 118.

"oxygen battery," is of rather theoretical than practical importance, being constructed without the use of two metals. It consists (Fig. 118) of an outer vessel containing nitric acid, and a porous vessel containing caustic potash, platinum plates dipping into each vessel from the terminals. On joining the terminals a current flows from the platinum in the acid to that in the alkali, sulphate of potash being formed in the pores of the diaphragm.

117. Electromotive Force.—In dealing with voltaic cells, a very important element in their working is the difference of potential of their terminals when separate. This is commonly called the Electromotive Force (written E.M.F.) —though of course not a Mechanical Force.

The unit used for E.M.F. is not the ordinary unit of potential which we used in Electrostatics, but a unit obtained in a theoretical manner, and called a Volt. For the present there will be no appreciable error if we take it as the E.M.F. of a Daniell's cell formed of an amalgamated zinc rod in saturated zinc sulphate, and a copper rod in semi-saturated copper sulphate. The actual value of this E.M.F. is found to be 1·07 Volt.

In terms of this unit we can express the E.M.F. of different cells by simply connecting their terminals with those of a quadrant electrometer and observing the deflections, which are directly proportional to the E.M.F.s of the different cells experimented with. By this means the following values may be approximately verified (slight differences being unavoidable owing to variation in the metal and fluids) :—

Volta (zinc, acid, copper), . . .	about	1
Smee (zinc, acid, platinised silver), . .	,,	1
Bichromate (zinc, potas. bichromate, carbon when freshly prepared), . . .	,,	2
Daniell (zinc, acid, copper sulphate, copper), .	,,	1 to 1·14

Grove (zinc, acid, nitric acid, platinum),	about 1·94 to 1·97
Bunsen (zinc, acid, nitric acid, carbon),	,, 1·75 to 1·96
Leclanché (zinc, sal-ammoniac, manganese dioxide, carbon),	,, 1·41
Marie Davy (zinc, acid, mercurous sulphate, carbon),	,, 1·2

118. Battery arranged in Simple Circuit.—According to the purpose for which a battery is to be used, the cells are grouped either in simple or compound circuit, or in a manner compounded of the two.

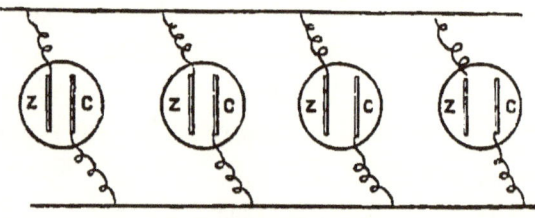

Fig. 119.

In a simple circuit arrangement, called also multiple arc, all the cells have their zincs connected to a common terminal, and all the coppers connected to another (Fig. 119). Since the zincs are all connected together, as also the coppers, they are respectively at the same potentials, and the battery is equivalent to a single cell with the size of the plates increased in proportion to the number of cells. The E.M.F. of the battery will be found to be the same as for a single cell, since it is independent of the size of the plates.

119. Battery arranged in Compound Circuit.—In this arrangement (Fig. 120) the copper of the first cell is connected to the zinc of the next, the copper of that to the zinc of the third, and so on. The cells arranged in this manner are often said to be in series.

In this case the E.M.F. rises in proportion to the number of cells, for there is a certain potential difference between the zinc and copper of the first, and the same between the zinc and copper of the second; but the copper of the first and zinc of the second are in contact, and therefore at the same potential; hence the whole potential difference will be double that of one cell. The same reasoning applies however many cells there may be in the battery.

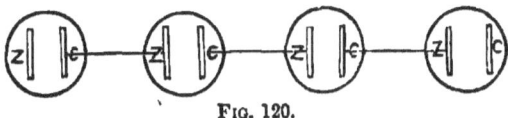

FIG. 120.

This arrangement was used by Volta, and termed by him "a crown of cups." He also constructed on this principle what is known as Volta's pile. This consists of a series of zinc and copper discs soldered together by their backs, and piled up with thicknesses of flannel between them, always retaining the same order, flannel, zinc, copper, flannel, and so on, the first and last plates being copper and zinc respectively. On fitting the pile into a wooden framework, by which the elements are pressed together, and dipping the whole into brine or dilute acid, the flannels become saturated, and act as liquid in the successive cells. Electrical indications were easily obtained from the terminals of a pile consisting of fifty or sixty couples.

Since Volta's time various modifications of this arrangement have been made. In the trough battery the compound zinc copper plates are let into grooves cut in the sides of a wooden trough, covered internally with pitch, to secure insulation, the space between the plates making a series of cells into which the liquid is poured. In this arrangement there is no means of removing the zinc plates for amalgamation, great local action being the consequence, necessitating the use of very weak acid.

Batteries of five or six cells, either of Smee's or the bichromate type (sufficient for most experimental purposes), are now constructed with the plates all attached to a wooden framework. This, by a rack-and-pinion motion, can be lifted wholly out of the acid, which is contained in ebonite or stoneware cells. Such a battery is figured in Fig. 121.

Fig. 121.

For post-office and other work, it is found more convenient to use series of Daniell's cells, which, when the plates are well amalgamated at first, remain in action without further attention for several weeks. The same is true of series of Leclanché cells, provided continuous currents are not required. They are excellent for bell-ringing and other purposes, and require less attention even than Daniell's.

120. Frictional Electricity obtained from a Battery.

—M. Gassiot, and since him other experimenters, have constructed many thousand cells, carefully insulated and arranged in compound circuit. By this means the E.M.F. is vastly increased, so much that sparks can be obtained, electroscopes and Leyden jars charged, and all the phenomena characteristic of frictional electricity demonstrated.

To compare the effects of frictional with those of voltaic electricity, it may be instructive to give the results obtained by Messrs. De La Rue and Müller, working with silver chloride cells, whose potential difference is about the same as that of the zinc copper cell we are using. They found that

1,000 cells in series gives a striking distance of	·0205	cm.
5,000 ,, ,, ,,	·1176	,,
10,000 ,, ,, ,,	·2863	,,
15,000 ,, ,, ,,	·4882	,,

These confirm what was said above, that the striking distance is not strictly proportional to the potential difference when that difference is very small.

121. Comparison of Frictional with Voltaic Electricity.

—Faraday has, on the other hand, compared the quantities derived from frictional and voltaic electricity both by their magnetic and chemical effects. He found that "two wires, one of platina[1] and one of zinc, each one-eighteenth of an inch in diameter, placed five-sixteenths of an inch apart, and immersed to the depth of five-eighths of an inch in acid consisting of one drop of oil of vitriol and four ounces of distilled water at a temperature of about 60° (Fah.), and connected at the other extremities by a copper wire eighteen

[1] Called by modern chemists *Platinum*.

feet long and one-eighteenth of an inch thick . . . yield as much electricity in . . . $\tfrac{8}{150}$ths of a second as . . . thirty turns of the large electrical machine in excellent order." "The electrical machine," he says, "is fifty inches in diameter; it has two sets of rubbers; its prime conductor consists of two brass cylinders connected by a third, the whole length being twelve feet, and the surface in contact with air about 1422 square inches. When in good excitation one revolution of the plate will give ten or twelve sparks, each an inch in length. Sparks or flashes from ten to fourteen inches in length may easily be drawn from the conductors."[1]

From these two results we learn that in frictional electricity the potential differences are very high, but the quantity of electricity concerned is very minute, while in voltaic electricity the differences of potential are very small, but the quantity enormously great. Returning to our hydrostatic analogy, we may say that the machine discharge is as the tiniest rill falling down a very steep hill; the voltaic current is like a vast river flowing through a nearly perfectly level valley.

122. Dry Piles.—On the principle of the compound series are constructed certain modifications of Volta's pile, called Dry Piles. In these the liquid is replaced by paper, which, unless specially dried, contains a large quantity of water. The only one now used is Zamboni's. This consists of paper coated on one side with tinfoil and rubbed over on the opposite side with manganese dioxide slightly moistened. The sheets are then cut out with a punch and piled together in the order, tinfoil, paper, binoxide of manganese. With

---

[1] Faraday, *Experimental Researches*, Series III., Jan. 1833.

several thousand sheets a high electromotive force is obtained, though the current is insignificant. The most remarkable thing about them is their permanence of action. By affixing suitable terminals the pile can be discharged by alternate contacts, giving motion to a light pendulum or see-saw, which under suitable conditions has been known to keep up its motion for several years. This pile is also used in Bohnenberger's electroscope, in which a single gold leaf is suspended between two parallel plates near together, which are connected with the terminals of a dry pile. The gold leaf then shows electrification by diverging to one side or the other.

This, however, as well as every other form of electroscope, is superseded by Thomson's Quadrant Electrometer, which can be made to measure the hundredth part of the E.M.F. of a single Daniell's cell.

CHAPTER II.

ELECTROLYSIS.

123. Phenomena of the Current.—We now proceed to consider some of the actions belonging to the electricity in motion as they are presented in the wire joining the terminals of a battery. These are the peculiar phenomena which form the subject of voltaic electricity. The properties of the current may be classed as Chemical, Magnetic, and Thermal. In the present chapter we consider the Chemical phenomena.

124. Direction of the Current.—As the phenomena of the current all depend on certain directions, it is convenient to have conventional rules by which these directions can be remembered. We have seen that in a zinc-copper cell the copper is at a higher potential than the zinc, and consequently when they are joined by a conductor, a neutralisation of electricity takes place along the conductor. This can best be represented by a movement of + E. from the copper to the zinc, and an equal movement of − E. from the zinc to the copper. The motion of the + E. may be called the positive current, and we fix our attention on this, and speak of it as the direction of the current. This is only a convention or *memoria technica* to represent to our mind the neutralisation of unequal potential, and does not imply any theory as to the nature of the current.

If we always had a flow of + E. to the zinc plate, and − E. to the copper, without any compensating flow in the opposite direction, the potential of the zinc would constantly rise, and that of the copper constantly sink. Hence we infer that there is a flow of electricity through the liquid of the cell equal in amount and opposite in direction to that in the conductor. That is to say, the current will flow in the liquid from zinc to copper, and in the external conductor from copper to zinc, making a complete circuit (Fig. 122). This assumption of the current in the liquid will be confirmed through all our experiments, since we shall find that the liquid obeys exactly the same laws as the solid conductor while the current is passing.

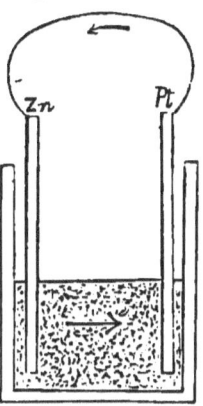

FIG. 122.

In every battery, then, we shall assume that the current in the liquid is from the *zincode* to the *platinode*, and in the external conductor from the *platinode* to the *zincode*.

125. Electrolysis of Potassium Iodide.—Let us now place the terminals of a zinc-copper or other cell on opposite sides of a piece of blotting or other kind of bibulous paper moistened with potassium iodide. Near the end of the wire in connection with the copper will appear a brown discoloration owing to the liberation of iodine. If the bibulous paper be first soaked in a solution of starch, the discoloration becomes blue owing to the action of the liberated iodine on the starch. To actions of which this is the type Faraday gave the general name of *Electrolysis*, and to him we owe the very full investigation of the general laws on which the action depends.

126. Electrolysis of Water.—Although the decomposition of potassium iodide can be shown by a very weak cell, many substances can only be decomposed by very powerful batteries. The decomposition of water is easily shown with a battery of four or five Grove cells.

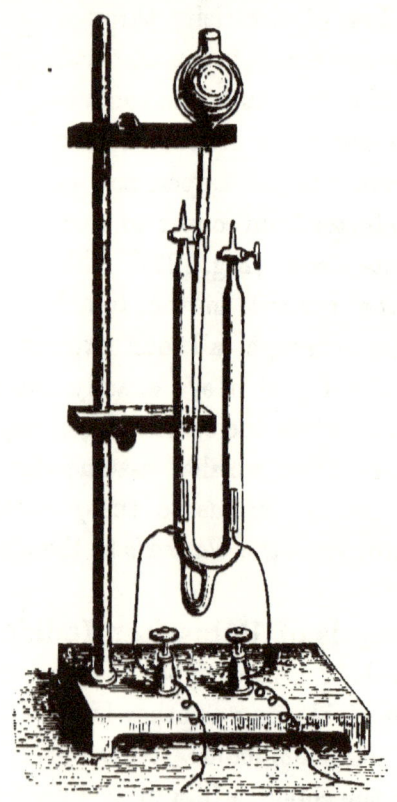

Fig. 123.

For exhibiting the decomposition, some kind of voltameter must be used. This, in the form shown (Fig. 123), consists of two glass tubes, calibrated to measure the volumes of the gases given off. In each tube is a platinum plate half an inch wide and four or five inches long, with a platinum wire welded to it, which is fused through the glass tube, and enables communication to be made with the battery. These tubes communicate either by being parts of the same U-shaped tube (Fig. 123), or by being inverted over water in an independent vessel. The apparatus must be at first filled with water, slightly acidulated with sulphuric acid, for which the third upright tube is provided. On passing the current, the gases are rapidly evolved, hydrogen bubbling up from the platinum plate connected with the zincode of the battery, and oxygen from the plate connected with the platinode. If we measure the volumes of the hydrogen and oxygen evolved, after reducing them to the same pressure, we shall find that the hydrogen occupies exactly double the volume of the oxygen, and if we compute their weight, we shall find the weight of the oxygen to be exactly eight times that of the hydrogen. In practice it will be impossible to collect the whole of the gases, since the oxygen is to some extent soluble in the water.

127. **Electrolysis of Hydrogen Chloride.**—Hydrogen chloride or hydrochloric acid may be decomposed by a similar arrangement, but the terminals must be made of carbon, since platinum is attacked by the "nascent" chlorine (*i.e.* chlorine at the instant of its separation from hydrogen). Moreover, the chlorine is soluble in water, but its solubility is much diminished by putting common salt in the water. With these precautions it will be found that very nearly equal volumes of hydrogen and chlorine are given off, the hydrogen as before collecting on the terminal connected with the zincode, and chlorine on that connected with the platinode of the battery.

In both these cases we see that the substance is decomposed into its elements in exactly the proportions in which chemistry teaches they enter into the substances, and which are indicated by the form of their chemical formulæ, H_2O for water, and HCl for hydrogen chloride.

128. Secondary action in the Decomposition of Sulphates, etc.—In many cases the electrical decomposition is accompanied by a secondary action which *may* be purely chemical. Thus if by means of two platinum plates we pass the current through copper sulphate ($CuSO_4$), we shall find pure copper deposited on the plate next to the zincode, and oxygen only given off from the plate next to the platinode. In this case the copper sulphate appears to be electrically decomposed into copper, and the radical SO_4, which is unstable, and cannot exist alone. It consequently attacks the water of the solution, taking up hydrogen from it, and forming H_2SO_4, liberating only the oxygen. The presence of the free sulphuric acid around the plate can easily be shown by performing the decomposition in a V-tube. In the case of the sulphates of the metals, potassium and sodium, which cannot exist as metals in the presence of either water or air, we have a double decomposition. Take, for instance, sulphate of sodium (Na_2SO_4) solution, and decompose it, when only oxygen and hydrogen will make their appearance at the plates. In this case it appears that sodium is set free by electrolysis at the plate next the platinode, but immediately attacks the water, forming soda (NaHO) and liberating hydrogen. At the same time SO_4 is set free at the opposite plate; it, too, cannot remain free, but attacks the water, forming with it sulphuric acid (H_2SO_4), and liberating oxygen.

We thus have exact equivalents of hydrogen and oxygen set free, as though water had alone been the electrolyte. The presence of the acid and alkali are shown by performing the decomposition in a V-tube (Fig. 124), and colouring the sodium sulphate solution with a little syrup of violets, which, when neutral (*i.e.* neither acid nor alkaline), exhibits a violet tint. On passing the current the liquid on one side becomes blue, proving the presence of an alkali, and on the other side becomes red, proving the presence of free acid.

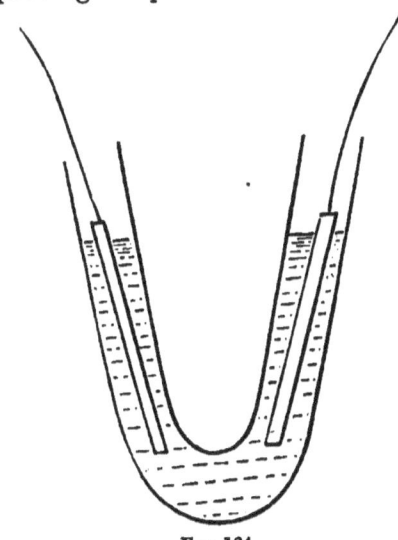

FIG. 124.

129. Potassium set free by Electrolysis.—Under proper conditions, potassium has been obtained in a pure state as a product of electrolysis. Its existence was thus demonstrated by Davy. He applied to the surface of a fragment of caustic potash, slightly moistened by exposure for a few minutes to the air, the terminals of a battery of about 200 zinc-copper cells, when globules of the metal appeared at the terminal of the wire connected with the zincode of the battery. These were preserved by performing the decomposition under naphtha.

The experiment may be repeated with a battery of five or six Grove cells, by making a hollow in the surface of a block of caustic potash, and putting in it a globule of mercury. If the block be rested on a platinum plate, and the current passed from the platinum plate to a wire dipping in the mercury, the potassium is liberated and forms an amalgam with the mercury, from which it can be separated by distilling away the mercury in the absence of air.

130. Faraday's Terminology for Electrolysis.—In
all the foregoing experiments it can hardly have escaped notice that hydrogen and the metals have appeared uniformly at the terminal connected with the zincode of the battery, while oxygen, chlorine, iodine, and acids have appeared at the opposite terminal, and this will be found the case in almost every decomposition into which these substances enter. To avoid confusion, Faraday, with the help of the late Dr. Whewell of Cambridge, invented certain terms for expressing the observed facts of electrolysis apart from any theory as to their cause. The process of separating by voltaic action chemical compounds into their constituents he termed *electrolysis*,[1] and any substance which could be thus decomposed he called an *electrolyte*. We have already employed the term *electrode*,[2] by which he means "that substance, or rather surface, whether of air, water, metal, or any other body, which bounds the extent of the decomposing matter in the direction of the electric current." It will be noticed that our use of the term for the plates of the battery is strictly in

---

[1] ἤλεκτρον and λύω, *to set free*.   [2] ἤλεκτρον and ὁδός, *a way*.

accordance with this use. "The surface at which the current," according to our present notion, enters "the electrolyte is called *the anode*[1]: "it is the *negative* extremity of the decomposing body, is where oxygen, chlorine, acids, etc., are evolved, and is against or opposite the positive electrode (platinode)." "The *cathode*[2] is that surface at which the current leaves the decomposing body, and is its positive extremity; the combustible bodies, metals, alkalies, and bases, are evolved there, and it is in contact with the negative electrode" (zincode).

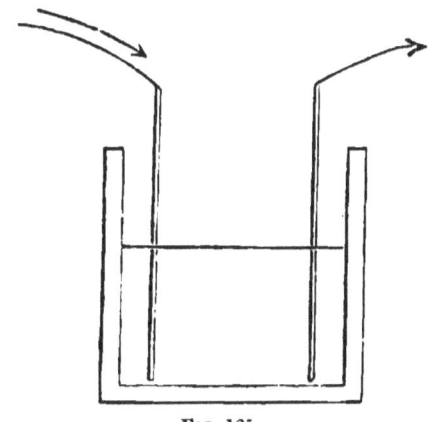

FIG. 125.

For the purpose of distinguishing the substances which are set free at the electrodes, Faraday continues, "I propose to distinguish such bodies by calling those *anions*[3] which go to the anode of the decomposing body, and those passing to the cathode, *cations*,[4] and when I have occasion to speak of these together I shall call them *ions*."[5]

Thus in the decomposition of water hydrogen and oxygen

---

[1] ἄνω, *upwards*, and ὁδός. [2] κατά, *downwards*, and ὁδός.
[3] ἀνιών, *that which goes up*. [4] κατιών, *that which goes down*.
[5] Faraday, *Experimental Researches*, Series VII., vol. i. p. 195.

are the ions, oxygen being an anion, which is set free at the anode, and hydrogen the cation, which is set free at the cathode.

131. Quantity of Ions separated by the same current.—As to the quantity of the ions separated at each electrode, we may notice first that if any number of voltameters be placed in different points in the same circuit, the amount of decomposition is the same in all. This will be true even though some of the voltameters have large plates and others small; some with plates near together, and others with plates far apart. The amount of electrolytic decomposition

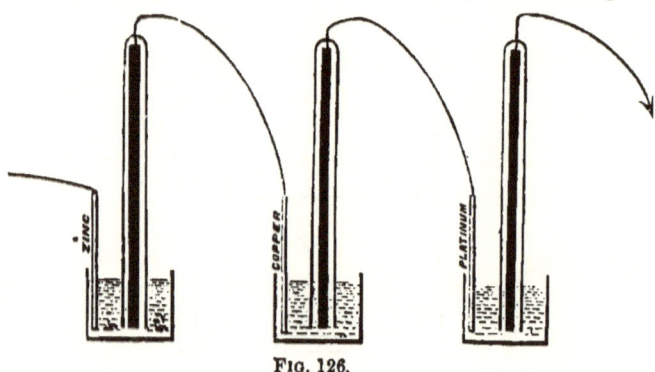

FIG. 126.

is also the same in all, even when secondary and local actions are taking place in some or all the voltameters. Faraday showed this by including in the same circuit three decomposition vessels filled with the same dilute sulphuric acid. The anodes in the three were of zinc, copper, and platinum respectively. But the cathodes were all of platinum, and were fixed in glass vessels, closed above, and filled with the liquid, so that the amount of hydrogen given off could be measured. At the zinc anode there was violent local action, while both the zinc-platinum and copper-platinum cells formed voltaic couples, zinc sulphate forming at the zinc, and copper sulphate at the copper anode. In the cell with both anode and cathode of platinum there was of course no chemical action beyond the direct decomposition of the liquid. After passing the current through this compound arrangement till a measureable amount of gas was collected at the three cathodes, it was found that the amount of hydrogen in all three was absolutely the same.

From these and numerous experiments, comprising nearly all the electrolytes with which he was acquainted, and experiments both with frictional and voltaic electricity, Faraday was enabled to lay down the principle that the quantity of any given element separated in a given time by electrolytic decomposition is simply proportional to the strength of the current. Having established this, he used a voltameter in the circuit as the measure of current strength in many experiments with strong currents.

Further than this, if the current were passed through a series of cells, some of which contained acidulated water, and others contained hydrochloric acid, the quantity of hydrogen collected at the cathodes of all the cells was found to be the same.

Or again, if we take a series of cells containing different electrolytes, *e.g.* (1) acidulated water, (2) copper sulphate, (3) fused chloride of tin, (4) hydrochloric acid, when proper precautions are taken for collecting the whole of the products of decomposition, it will be found that the hydrogen collected at the cathodes of (1) and (4), the chlorine at the anodes of (3) and (4), the copper at the cathode of (2), and the tin at the cathode of (3), will have certain definite ratios to each other which will be absolutely invariable wherever any of these substances form the ions in any electrolytic decomposition.

132. Electro-Chemical Equivalents.—Having seen, then, that (1) the quantity of any given electrolyte decomposed in different cells in the same circuit is always the same, (2) that the amount of any ion set free from different compounds is the same for the same current, (3) that the different ions are set free in quantities which bear a certain definite relation to each other in respect of quantity when liberated by the same current, we conclude that passing unit current for unit time causes the separation of a certain definite amount of each elementary substance which forms an ion which may be expressed in grains or grams, and is independent of everything but the kind of ion and the arbitrary unit of current we choose to adopt. This amount of each ion is called its *electro-chemical equivalent*.

We have assumed in the above statement, as Faraday did, that only one compound of each pair of ions is an electrolyte, being generally that in which, according to the chemical notation of his time, one atom of each ion entered. Later researches have shown that in many cases two compounds of the same ions (*e.g.* cupric and cuprous chloride) are both electrolytes, thus giving rise to two or more electro-chemical equivalents.

When these electro-chemical equivalents are calculated, they are found to have the same ratio as the ordinary chemical equivalents; but while these latter are only the ratios in which certain substances enter into chemical combinations, the former are perfectly definite masses of the substances. Thus it is found that for every 65 grams of zinc consumed in each cell of the battery, there will be set free in a voltameter 2 grams of hydrogen, and 16 grams of oxygen, and in a series of decomposition cells included in the circuit, and containing solutions of metallic salts such as Faraday contemplated, there will be set free 254 grams of iodine, 71 of chlorine, 63·3 of copper, 207 of lead, 200 of mercury, 78 of potassium, 216 of silver, 118 of tin, etc. The equivalents obtained from other salts will be simple multiples or submultiples of these numbers, generally either double or one half.

133. **The Battery obeys the Laws of Electrolysis.**
—The same laws which hold in the decomposition cell also hold in each cell of the battery. Thus for each electrochemical equivalent of zinc consumed in each cell of the battery, without local action, there will be an equivalent of each ion separated in every cell through which the battery current passes. This can easily be demonstrated by allowing a Daniell cell to decompose copper sulphate, making both electrodes in the decomposition cell of copper. Taking the precaution that all the copper plates, both of the battery and the decomposition cell, are cleaned and weighed before the action begins, it will be found, after the current has passed for any length of time, that the increase of weight of the battery plate and of the plate forming the cathode are exactly the same.

134. **E.M.F. necessary for Electrolysis.**—It is now easy to understand, on the ordinary principles of energy, why we require a high E.M.F. to decompose certain compounds in which chemical affinity is strong. If the decomposition, say in a water voltameter, is effected at all, we must have an equivalent of water separated for each equivalent of zinc

consumed in the battery cell. If the cell be a simple zinc-copper couple, the total thermal energy due to the consumption of an equivalent of zinc in the battery is simply the number of thermal units evolved during the conversion of that weight of zinc into zinc sulphate. This is a superior limit to the amount of energy available in the circuit, since in every circuit some energy is expended in heat developed in its solid and liquid parts.

Again, the combustion of an equivalent of hydrogen in an equivalent of oxygen evolves a certain definite amount of heat which may be measured in thermal units, and this number of thermal units must be expended in decomposing the equivalent of water into its elements. If then the energy (measured thermally) required for the decomposition of an equivalent of any substance be greater than the thermal energy developed per equivalent of zinc in the battery, that decomposition cannot take place.

*135. **E.M.F. measured thermally**. — Again, the E.M.F. of the battery cell may be measured by the thermal energy developed by the decomposition of an equivalent of zinc in each cell. For the E.M.F. is by definition measured by the work done in bringing a unit of electricity from the negative to the positive pole, and is therefore measured by the energy developed in the passage of the same quantity of electricity from the positive to the negative pole. If the unit of electricity be that which passes in our arbitrary unit current in unit time, the thermal energy developed by the passage of unit current for unit time through the battery will be a measure of the E.M.F. of the battery.

Hence, if we are able to express in thermal units the

amount of all the chemical actions which takes place in any battery cell, we have a thermal measure of its E.M.F. This Sir William Thomson has done for a Daniel cell (*Phil. Mag.*, May 1851). In this cell there is (Art. 112) a zinc plate in zinc sulphate, and a copper plate in copper sulphate. The chemical actions may be represented thus—

(1) Zinc decomposes the water, and forms zinc oxide.
(2) Zinc oxide combines with sulphuric acid, and forms zinc sulphate.
(3) Copper oxide is separated from the copper sulphate.
(4) Copper is separated from the copper oxide, the oxygen recombining with the hydrogen liberated in (1).

In (1) water is decomposed, and in (4) the elements of water recombine. These may be neglected, since they are equal and opposite in their thermal relations, the same amount of heat being evolved when the elements recombine, as was absorbed in their separation. Again, the action in (1) and (2) is of the nature of a running down of energy, and therefore accompanied by an evolution of heat; while (3) and (4) are of the nature of a building up of (potential) energy, and therefore are accompanied by an absorption of heat.

The following data are supplied by experiment :—

(1) The heat evolved in the combustion of one gram of zinc in oxygen produces $1 \cdot 246$ grms. of oxide $= 1301$ thermal units.
(2) The heat evolved by $1 \cdot 246$ grms. of zinc oxide in combining with sulphuric acid $= 369$ units.
(3) Heat evolved by combustion of an equivalent of copper ($= \cdot 9727$ grm.) in oxygen to form $1 \cdot 221$ grms. of copper oxide $= 588 \cdot 6$ units.

(4) Heat evolved by the combination of 1·221 grms. of copper oxide with dilute sulphuric acid = 293 units.

Therefore, for each gram of zinc consumed in a cell we have $1301 + 369 - (588 \cdot 6 + 293) = 788 \cdot 4$ thermal units available for external work.

The decomposition of an equivalent weight of water (·277 grm.) will require about 1060 thermal units for its decomposition. Hence a Daniell cell cannot decompose water; but a Grove cell, whose E.M.F. is about 1·9 of a Daniell, can perform the decomposition of water, as also can a battery of two Daniell's cells in series.

136. Hypothesis of Molecular Electrification.—

Seeing that in every electrolytic decomposition we have two ions, and for every electro-chemical equivalent of one ion which collects at the cathode a certain definite quantity of positive electricity has passed to the cathode, and for every equivalent of the other ion the same definite amount of negative electricity has passed to the anode, it is impossible not to think of the charges of electricity as bound up in the molecules of the two ions, and bound up with them in definite proportions, so that the same absolute quantity of electricity is associated with the electro-chemical equivalent of every ion, this charge being positive for a cation and negative for an anion. In this way electrolysis may be compared to an electrical convection in which each molecule of each ion with its own specific charge of electricity is constantly being transferred from and towards the opposite electrodes.

That this hypothesis is not an ultimate molecular law may be seen by noticing numerous exceptions to the rules cited above. Thus iodine in some compounds is an anion and in others a cation, and, as we have noticed, two chlorides of copper (Cu_2Cl_2 and $CuCl_2$) may be decomposed by electrolysis, the same amount of chlorine being yielded by both, but twice as much copper by the former as by the latter.

137. Grotthüs' Hypothesis.—The appearance of the separate ions at the electrodes without their appearance in a free state in the intervening liquid is generally explained by Grotthüs' Hypothesis.

This assumes that throughout the liquid there is a series of decompositions, and recompositions in the direction determined by the E.M.F. active at the electrodes.

Thus in the decomposition of water each element (hydrogen and oxygen) in the compound molecule retains its electrical affinity. The hydrogen being + is turned in each molecule towards the cathode, and the oxygen towards the anode. The series of *polarised* molecules may be represented thus (*a*, Fig. 127) :—

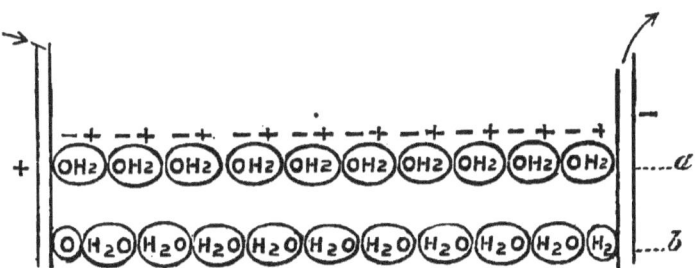

Fig. 127.

The discharge consists in the neutralisation of the electricity in each H_2 with the O of the next molecule at the same instant that these two elements unite to make a new water molecule. Thus, after discharge, the arrangement is represented by *b*.

After discharge the polarised state is instantly restored, and the series of polarisations and discharges succeed each other so rapidly that they present to our means of observation the appearance of a continuous current.

Exactly the same series of decompositions and recompositions takes place in the battery itself, the only difference being that the oxygen set free attacks the zinc, forming with it zinc oxide. We assume here that in the typical cell water is the electrolyte; but since sulphuric acid is always present, there is some doubt whether this is not really the electrolyte, the oxygen being a product of secondary action, as in every sulphate. It is at least remarkable that the quantity of acid present does not affect the E.M.F. of the cell.

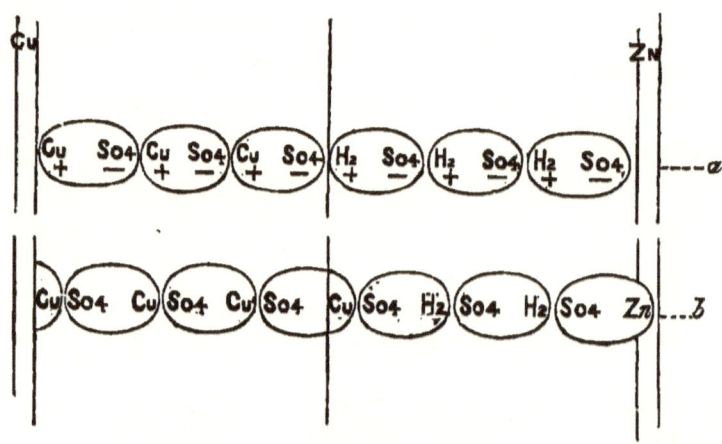

Fig. 128.

In the case of the two fluid cells it will easily be understood that a similar series of decompositions and recompositions takes place. Thus, in a Daniell cell, we should have the series of polarised molecules shown in Fig. 128 (a), and, after discharge, the series of Fig. 128 (b).

138. Polarisation of Electrodes.—After passing a current between electrodes, we find a backward E.M.F. which is called *Polarisation*. To exhibit it, arrange (Fig. 129) a battery (*A*) and a voltameter (*B*) in one branch of a contact breaker (*C*), and the same voltameter with a galvanometer (*G*) in the other branch. This can be arranged as shown (Fig. 129), where, when the moveable tongue is to the left, the battery is in circuit, but the galvanometer out; and when to the right, the

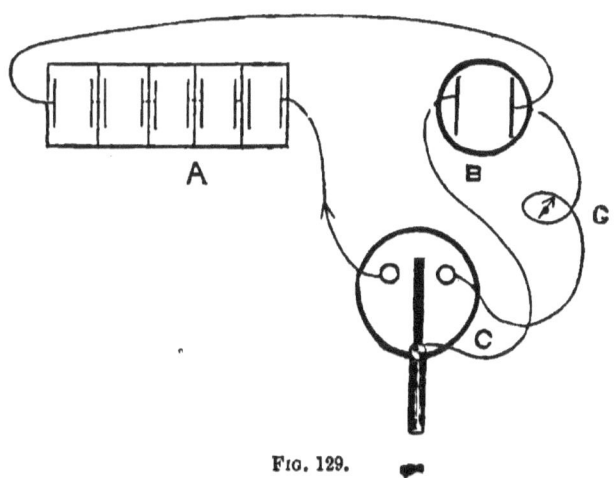

Fig. 129.

battery is excluded, and the galvanometer included. A mercury cup may be substituted for the contact breaker, putting in the battery and galvanometer wires alternately.

After passing the current for a short time with evolution of gas in the voltameter, turn the contact breaker; a current will pass through the galvanometer showing a current in the voltameter opposite in direction to the battery current.

139. Grove's Gas Battery, and Ritter's Secondary Pile.—This principle is used both in Grove's Gas Battery and Ritter's Secondary Pile. In Grove's Gas Battery (Fig. 130) each cell consists of two tubes, each containing a platinum plate, to which platinum wires are attached, which are fused through the glass tube, and terminate in binding screws or mercury cups. On passing the battery current, oxygen and hydrogen are liberated and collected. If the process be

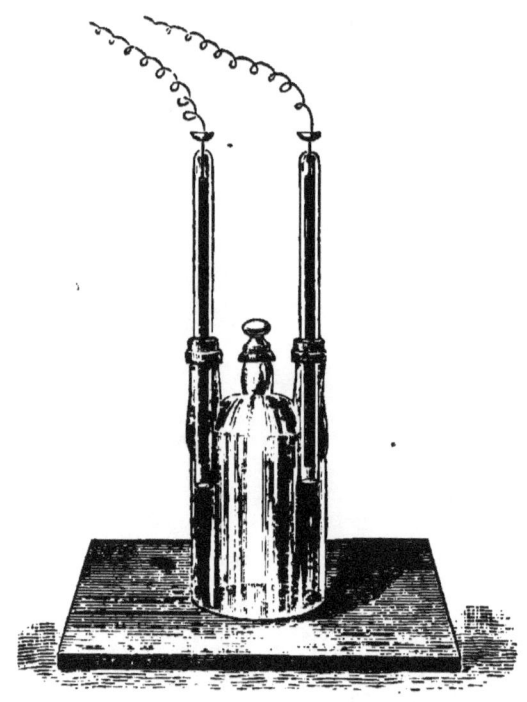

FIG. 130.

stopped, a current will be found to flow from the plate in the hydrogen to that in the oxygen, decomposing water, and setting free oxygen against the hydrogen plate, and hydrogen against the oxygen plate; these combine with the occluded hydrogen and oxygen to form water again. The E.M.F. of this battery is low, four cells being required to decompose water.

In Ritter's Secondary Pile, the plates of platinum are large, and it has been used as a condenser for storing large quantities of electricity.

140. Polarisation the test of an Electrolyte.—Clerk-Maxwell has pointed out that the existence of the polarisation current is the best test whether a given substance is an electrolyte, and may be applied where the quantities of the products of decomposition are too small to be detected by chemical means. Faraday has laid down the general law that no solid is ever an electrolyte, but it can be easily proved that glass, even at a temperature below 100° C., and while perfectly hard, is an electrolyte. Put mercury in a test-tube, and sink the test-tube in another vessel (a larger test-tube will do) containing mercury, and surrounded by a steam bath. Dip two wires in the mercury, one inside and the other outside the inner tube, and connect with a battery and galvanometer. As the temperature rises, a current begins to pass before the mercury is at 100° C., and on detaching the battery, and leaving the galvanometer alone in circuit, a polarisation current is seen to pass in the opposite direction, proving that the glass has been decomposed by the current.

141. Planté's and Faure's Cells.—In the practical use of electricity, it is probable that storage batteries on the principle of the Secondary Pile will play an important part. The form to which attention has most been directed was invented by Planté, and improved by Faure and others. Planté's idea was to immerse two lead plates in dilute sulphuric acid, and by a series of actions, partly electrolytic and partly chemical, to obtain a deposit of lead peroxide (PbO_2) on the anode, and pure lead in a spongy condition on the cathode.

In the cell, while discharge is taking place, the spongy lead acts as the zincode, and the lead coated with lead peroxide as the platinode. The preparation of Planté's plates requires a long time, as the current has to be sent through the cell several times with long periods of rest between. These intervals of rest are necessary, as during them both chemical and local actions take place between the lead and the products of electrolytic decomposition. When the plates are once brought to a proper condition, a single passage of the current for a few hours is sufficient to restore the cell after each discharge. The ultimate product of the discharge seems to be a deposit of sulphate of lead on both plates, and this is removed by electrolysis on repassing the current, that on the zincode (which in electrolysis is the cathode) being converted into spongy lead, and that on the platinode (or anode) into lead peroxide. The improvement introduced by Faure was designed to hasten the preparation of the lead plates. He coats both the plates at first with minium or red-lead (Pb_3O_4), which, after chemical and electrolytic action, in a relatively short time gives the plates the same condition as in Planté's cell. The E.M.F. of the cell, when in good condition, is about two volts.

142. Electro-metallurgy.—A very important application of electrolysis in the arts is the deposit of metals (especially copper, gold, and silver) from the solution of their salts, called electrotyping or electroplating.

The deposit of copper is very easily accomplished by using a cell containing a concentrated solution of copper sulphate, a strip of copper being suspended in it as the anode, and the body to be coated with copper as the cathode, with a single

Daniell's cell, or, for large plates, three or four Daniell's cells, as battery. The body to be coated with copper is often an impress or cast taken from a seal, coin, or other object, in wax, plaster, or gutta-percha. These moulds are non-conductors, but on being evenly coated with plumbago or black-lead they become conductors. The prepared mould is suspended by a copper wire in the electrolytic cell. An even coat of copper is thus deposited upon it, and after it has acquired a suitable thickness it can be removed from the wax mould, and will be found to give an exact copy of the engraved marks or stamp on the original seal or medal.

In some arrangements the conducting mould is made to take the place of the copper plate in the Daniell's cell itself.

Flowers and leaves can be coated with copper and afterwards silver-plated by making their surfaces conducting. The best method of accomplishing this is by immersing the object in a weak solution of phosphorus in carbon disulphide, and then allowing the solvent to evaporate, leaving a thin deposit of phosphorus. On immersing the object in a bath of silver nitrate, the silver becomes reduced as a thin superficial film. This is sufficient to make the surface conducting, and it can be coated with copper in the manner described above.

Copies of engraved copper plates can be made by immersing the original in the copper sulphate bath (having first rubbed its back over with a varnish, to prevent a deposit taking place on it). The deposit of copper will adhere to the surface, but after a sufficiently thick deposit has been made, it can be easily separated and will give a reverse of the engraving. On repeating this process with the reverse any number of copies of the original engraving can be obtained. It is now more usual to coat the original engraving with a very thin coat of steel in a specially prepared bath, which, after half an hour's immersion, gives a surface of extreme hardness, exhibiting every mark on the original plate. From this a great number of copies can be taken, and, if necessary, the steel coating can be removed by dilute nitric acid, and a fresh deposit made without injury to the original engraved plate.

The deposit of silver can best be made on a previously prepared surface of copper, nickel, brass, or gilding metal, which is a variety of brass rich in copper. Articles to be plated are first cleansed from grease by boiling in a weak solution of soda or potash, and then dipped into diluted nitric acid to remove any film of oxide. They are then brushed with a hard brush and sand, rinsed from any adhering impurities, and separately attached to clean copper wires. After this they are once more dipped in dilute nitric acid, washed, and while wet immersed in the silvering bath.

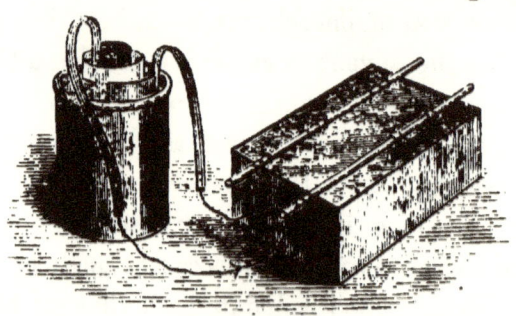

FIG. 131.

The silvering bath consists of a solution of silver cyanide, in potassium cyanide and water (one part of silver cyanide and one part of potassium cyanide in 125 parts of water), which should be gently warmed while the deposit is taking place. The objects to be silvered are suspended in the bath from copper rods and form the cathode of the cell, the anode being formed by a strip of silver also suspended in the liquid to prevent the solution from becoming weakened. The battery may be either Daniell's, Bunsen's, or Smee's; the number of cells employed depending on the size and number of objects to be plated. The diagram (Fig. 131) shows the arrangement for silvering with one Bunsen's cell.

The process of electro-gilding is very similar, except that the objects are first "pickled" in a bath of mixed dilute nitric and sulphuric acids. The gilding bath is usually a solution of potassio-gold cyanide, but many other baths can be employed with success.

143. Nobili's Rings.—These are obtained very easily by placing a drop of copper sulphate on a silver or platinum plate, and touching the plate with one end of a bent strip of zinc, whose other end dips into the copper sulphate. These form together a minute voltaic cell, and copper is deposited from the solution on to the platinum plate. The film of copper is thickest immediately under the zinc point, and diminishes pretty regularly, giving rings of varied colours. By using a solution of lead oxide in potash, and connecting the supporting plate with the platinode of a battery of several Grove cells, while the zincode is connected with a platinum wire which dips in the liquid, a deposit of lead peroxide is made, which exhibits very bright iridescent colours.

144. The Lead Tree.—To Electrolysis (partially, at any rate) we may refer the formation of the lead and silver trees. If we place a zinc and a copper rod in contact with each other in a flask which contains a solution of lead acetate, the zinc replaces the lead in the salt, forming zinc acetate, and the lead becomes deposited on the copper. Under these conditions the lead appears in bright branching crystals growing out from the copper, to which the name Lead Tree, or *Arbor Saturni*, has been given. The replacement of the lead by the more oxidisable zinc is a chemical action, but the peculiar form which the ramifications of the lead take is due to the electrolytic deposit.

CHAPTER III.

OHM'S LAW.

145. Ohm's Law.—This most important law, discovered by Ohm, states that with any given conductor, of which two parts are kept at different potentials, there is a constant ratio between the numerical measure of the potential difference, and of the strength of the current which traverses the conductor. This constant ratio depends only on the form, material, and temperature of the conductor, and is usually called its Resistance. Different conductors may be compared numerically, in respect of resistance, just as in respect of mass, capacity for heat, or any other physical property. By choosing suitable units of potential difference, current strength, and resistance, we may express Ohm's law numerically thus: Let V be the potential difference, I the current strength, and R the resistance of the conductor, all measured in these units, then $\frac{V}{I} = R$, or $V = IR$.

In the case of a battery cell, V will denote the difference of potential between the terminals when open, and R will be the total resistance made up of the internal resistance of the liquid part of the cell, and the external resistance of conductors, solid or liquid, outside the cell. If we denote the former of these by r and the latter by R, and if E denote the E.M.F. of the cell, we shall have $E = C(R + r)$,

or $C = \dfrac{E}{R + r}.$

146. Measurement of Resistance.—To measure a resistance we have to compare it with a certain standard resistance, which we will assume to be that of a certain measured length of standard wire at a certain temperature. This resistance is called the Ohm, and is universally used as the standard to which resistances are referred. We will assume at present that we have a series of these resistances made by taking

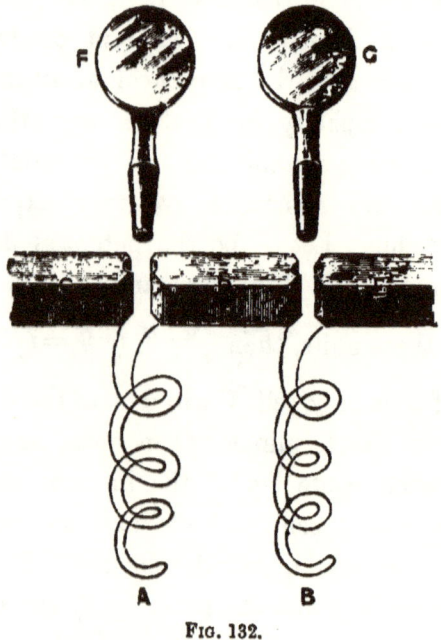

Fig. 132.

multiples of the length of the standard wire which gives one ohm resistance. These are issued in boxes of what are called Resistance Coils. Each coil is made of carefully insulated wire, folded in the middle and coiled round double, as shown in A and B, Fig. 132. The terminals of each wire are soldered to the stout brass rods—A to C and D, B to D and E, which are separated by small air spaces, the air space being formed of a conical hole, into which brass plugs (*F*, *G*) fit. When the plugs are in position, the current passes across the plug; but when the plug is withdrawn, the current goes through the corresponding wire. The coils are fitted up in boxes (Fig. 133), the numbers of ohms in successive coils being 1, 2, 3, 4, from which, by means of addition, all numbers up to 10 can be obtained. Then follow 10, 20, 30, 40, taking us up to 100; and then 100, 200, 300, 400, taking us up to 1000, and so on to any required extent.

Fig. 133.

We may observe that the ohm is about equal to the resistance of a yard of fine galvanometer copper wire (B. W. G. No. 48).

*147. **Potential Gradient.**—Our first illustration of Ohm's law consists of the construction of potential gradients. Take a battery of three or four Daniell's cells (*A*, Fig. 134), and introduce a set of resistances, of 100, 200, 300, 400 ohms respectively between the terminals *BF*. Also connect *B* with one terminal of a quadrant electrometer, the other terminal being connected with a loose wire, which can be applied to either of the brass pieces C, D, E, F.

The deflection of the electrometer shows the difference of potential between B and C, B and D, B and E, and B and F respectively.

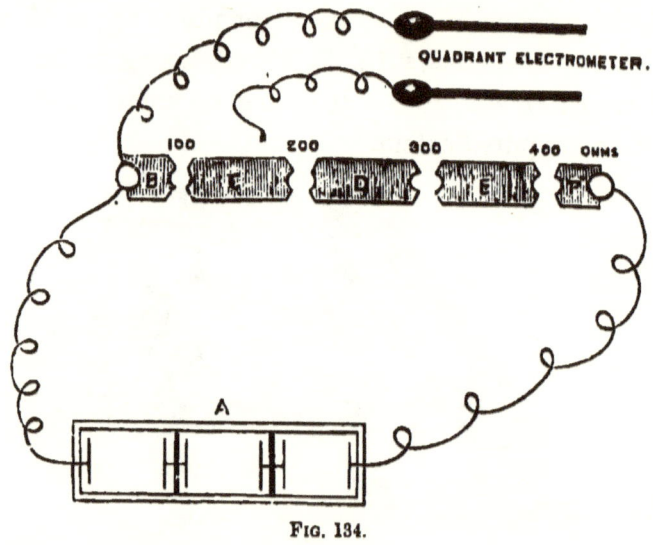

FIG. 134.

Taking a particular experiment, the number of scale degrees read off from the screen were—

    For B and C ... 9 scale divisions.
    ,, B and D ... 28 ,,
    ,, B and E ... 52 ,,
    ,, B and F ... 87 ,,

The numbers 9, 28, 52, 87 are sufficiently nearly in the ratios of 100, 300, 600, 1000 to suggest to us the rule that the fall in potential is simply proportional to the resistance.

If now we set off on a horizontal line distances proportional to the resistance, so that (Fig. 135) BC, CD, DE, EF represent on any scale the resistance in the previous figure (Fig 134), and set up at C, D, E, F, ordinates or perpendiculars

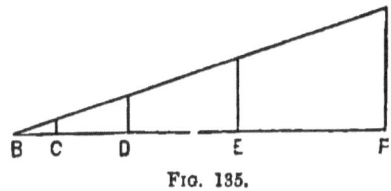

FIG. 135.

proportional to the observed potential differences, the extremities of these ordinates will be in a straight line, and that straight line may be taken as giving graphically the potential gradient in the conductor. The potential at any point may be found by simply drawing a perpendicular to meet the gradient line from the corresponding part of the line of resistances.

We may notice that this, in connection with the law of Ohm, gives us an independent proof of the constancy of the current in all parts of a circuit; the ratio between the potential difference and the resistance being the measure of the current strength. This measure is, in fact, the tangent of the angle at B, or of the inclination of the potential gradient.

When any amount of resistance is introduced between the terminals of the cell, the difference of potential becomes less than the total E.M.F. observed when the circuit is open. Assuming the current to consist of a series of polarisations and discharges, the chemical affinities or contacts must call up the difference of potential representing the whole E.M.F. after each discharge. The remaining part of the E.M.F. is really present in the liquid of the cell, which offers resistance to the current, and in it the potential follows exactly the same laws as in the solid part of the circuit. To illustrate this, let us take a single cell, and complete the diagram by setting off a horizontal line ABC, in which AB represents the resistance of the cell, BC the resistance of the connecting arc, and AD a vertical line representing the E.M.F. Then the line DC will give us the potential at every point in the circuit.

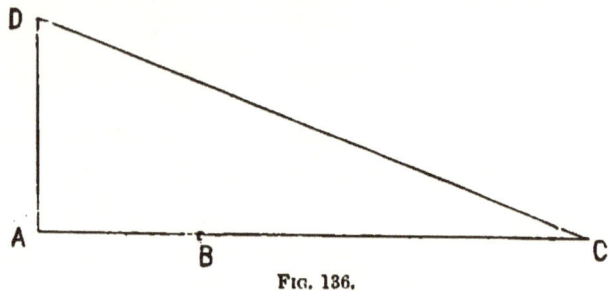

Fig. 136.

If there are several cells in compound circuit, AB represents the total resistance, and AD the total E.M.F. of the battery. The line of potential will not then be DC, but a broken line which rises at each cell. Thus, supposing we have three cells, the line of potential will be given by E, F, G, H, K, C.

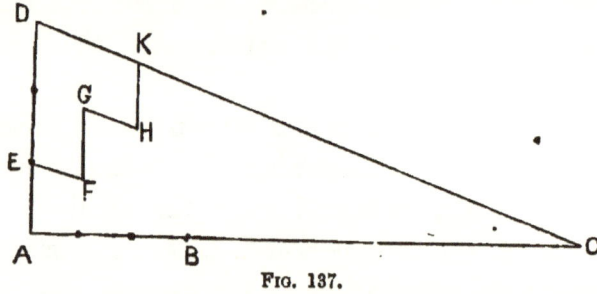

Fig. 137.

The potential gradient gives us only potential differences, and not the absolute potential at any point. If the cell and circuit be all insulated, the potential at some parts will be +, and at other parts —, depending on the capacity of the various parts of the circuit. If we connect the circuit with earth at any one point, we have only to draw a line parallel to the base line through the corresponding point on the gradient, and perpendiculars to this line will then give the absolute potential, positive when above and negative when below this line. The figures drawn would represent the potential, supposing the zinc plate brought to earth.

148. Oersted's Experiment — Galvanometers. — Oersted, a Danish philosopher, was the first who discovered the action of a conductor carrying a current on a magnet placed near to it. It can be shown by a stout wire bent in the form of Fig. 138, with a freely-pivoted magnet needle

FIG. 138.

within the circuit. ABC are three mercury cups for the purpose of introducing the battery wires. After placing the coil in the magnetic meridian, so that the wires are parallel to the magnet when no current is passing, and the north pole suppose towards B, place the battery terminals in A and B, so that the current passes under the magnet from A to B, and the north pole will be seen to deflect towards the east; on passing it from B to A it will deflect in the opposite direction; hence the direction in which the magnet deflects is reversed with the current. Next place the original B-terminal in C, so that the current passes above the magnet from A to C; the deflection will be to the west, or opposite to that which was seen when the current passed under the magnet from A to B. Hence we see that the deflection is in contrary directions, according as the current passes above or below the magnet. Lastly, put one terminal in B and the other in C, so that the current passes from B to A under the magnet, and from A to B above the magnet; these two parts of the current will conspire to deflect the north pole westwards.

The rule for the direction of motion of the magnet given by Oersted was: If a little figure swim in the current (which enters by his heels and leaves by his head), and look towards the magnet, the north pole will be driven to his left.

A rule identical with Oersted's, which will be greatly used afterwards, is: The direction of motion of the north pole is related to the direction of the current, as the direction of propulsion of any right-handed screw is related to the direction of the twist in the muscles of the wrist in driving it in. These two directions are said to be related in right-handed cyclical order. In Fig. 139 they are shown, the direction of the straight arrow being that in which a corkscrew is pushed in, and the arrows on the spiral being the direction of motion of the spiral or of the twist in

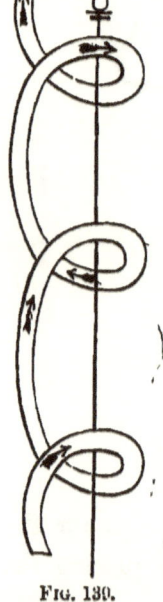

Fig. 139.

the muscles of the wrist when driving it in. The central arrow then shows the direction in which a free north pole would be urged by a current in the direction of the arrow circulating in the screw. Otherwise, if the current circulate with the hands of a watch, a north magnetic pole will be driven from the front towards the back of the watch.

A variety of instruments have been constructed on the principle of Oersted's phenomenon for detecting and measuring currents. To detect very weak currents, the effect on the magnet may be increased to a great extent by simply increasing the number of circuits round the magnet by winding the wire in a continuous coil, each coil producing its own effect on the magnet, and the sum of the effects of all the coils being added together. Such an arrangement is often called a current multiplier.

149. The Tangent Galvanometer.

—Where currents of considerable strength have to be measured, the most convenient instrument is that known as the Tangent Galvanometer (Fig. 140). It consists of one or several coils of stout wire on the edge of a narrow circular hoop (A), whose terminals are attached to the base. In the centre is pivoted a very short magnet (B) furnished with a pointer of aluminium, glass, or any non-magnetic substance. Under the needle is a graduated card for observing the deflection of the needle. The zero of the graduations is in the plane of the wire coil, and the instrument is capable of being turned on its base about a central axis to allow of the zero of graduation, and therefore the plane of the coils, being brought into the magnetic meridian before taking an observation.

Since a conductor carrying a current exerts force on a magnet pole near it, the current causes in the air around it a field of magnetic force, of which we may estimate the direction and intensity on the principles of Bk. I. We shall at present *assume* that the lines of magnetic force due to a plane circuit cut the plane at right angles, and that the strength of the field

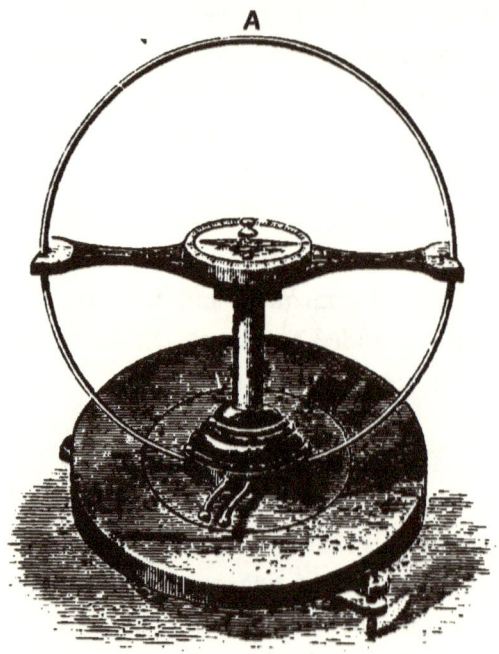

Fig. 140.

at each point is proportional to the current strength, but not the same for different points in the field. The movement of the needle will therefore generally bring its poles into parts of the field at which the strength is different. By making the needle very short compared with the diameter of the coils, the force urging each pole of the needle may be assumed in all positions sensibly the same as at its centre. This force is perpendicular to the plane of the coils, which we have made the plane of the meridian, and is proportional to the current strength. The method and construction of Art. 15 shows that the needle will rest at an inclination to the meridian, and that the force at right angles to the meridian is proportional to the tangent of the deflection. Thus, with the same instrument, the strength of the current traversing the coils will always be proportional to the tangent of the angle of deflection of the needle, and when we do not require currents in absolute measure it is sufficient to use the tangent of the angle as the measure of the current. A table of tangents for this purpose is given in Appendix II.

FIG. 141.

It is an improvement in construction to have two parallel coils (Fig. 141), with the current traversing them in the same direction, the magnet being suspended in the centre of the line joining their centres. By this arrangement, due to Helmholtz, the field round the magnet becomes much more nearly of uniform strength.

150. Sine Galvanometer.—In this galvanometer the reading is taken with the magnet poles always in the same position relatively to the coils, and the strength of the field therefore is strictly proportional to the current strength.

The tangent galvanometer can be used as a sine galvanometer by having a graduated circle attached to its base, and a pointer to the moveable framework which carries the coils. First bring the coils into the magnetic meridian, and observe the reading of the pointer on the fixed scale. On passing the current the magnet will deflect, but the coils can now be turned round so as to follow its deflection until (supposing the current not too strong) the magnet remains at rest in the plane of the coils. The fixed circle is again read, and the difference of the readings gives the angle through which the coils have been turned from the magnetic meridian. In this case the current strength is proportional to the sine of the angle of deflection, and for use with this form of galvanometer a table of sines is given in Appendix II.

The sine galvanometer can be made without any loss of accuracy in a portable form by making the coil long and flat, with a long needle suspended in its centre.

151. Astatic Galvanometer.—When we have to detect or to measure very weak currents, either the astatic galvano-

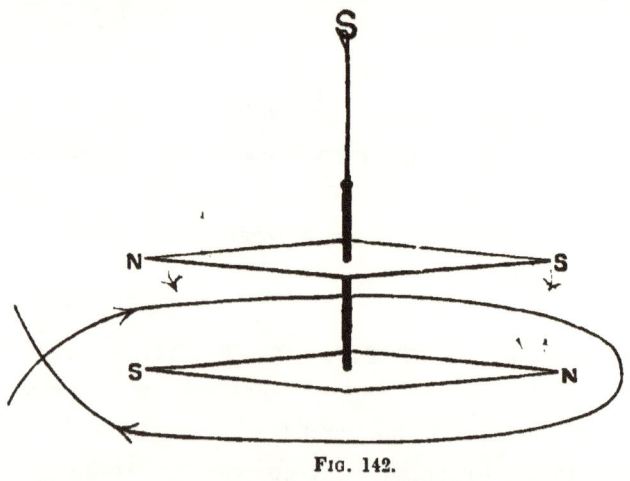

Fig. 142.

meter or Sir W. Thomson's mirror galvanometer may be used. The astatic galvanometer is named from the employment of an astatic needle. This consists of two exactly equal magnetic needles attached to a common axis, with their poles in opposite directions. Such a system will set equally in all directions under the action of the earth's magnetism—that is, it will be astatic. The magnets are very light, and the whole system is suspended by a single fibre of unspun silk. If a coil of wire carrying a current pass between the two magnets, and entirely surround the lower one, as in Fig. 142, Oersted's principle shows that the parts of the coil above and below the lower magnet conspire to deflect this magnet in the same direction; also that the part of the coil between the magnets, by its action on the upper magnet, tends to turn the magnetic system still in the same direction; while the lower part of the coil, by its action on the upper magnet alone, tends in the contrary direction. This effect will be much smaller than either of the other actions, owing to the greater distance between the magnet and the current. If the magnetic system were absolutely astatic, any current, however weak, would be shown by the magnets at once setting at right angles to the coils. In practice there is never an absolutely astatic system, but the earth's power is so much weakened that the very weak current becomes sensible by a deflection of the needle. In the best

Fig. 143.

instruments the set of the magnets is at right angles to the meridian. The general arrangement of the instrument is shown in Fig. 143. The upper needle moves over a graduated card to show the deflections, while the lower needle swings within the long flat coils shown below. The coils are capable of rotation so as to bring the needle to the zero of graduation, which is also in the plane of the coils, and the levelling screws on the base bring the suspension of the needle to the centre of the card. Since the magnets are long, and near to the coils, this instrument is only adapted to detect, and not to measure currents; it is rather a galvanoscope than a galvanometer.

152. The Mirror Galvanometer.

— In the reflecting or mirror galvanometer (Fig. 144), the magnet is very short and light, and attached to the back of a concave mirror (A) made of very thin glass, the mirror and needle not weighing more than a grain. This is suspended by a single fibre of silk in a cylinder of small diameter, round which is coiled the wire in a solid cylinder.

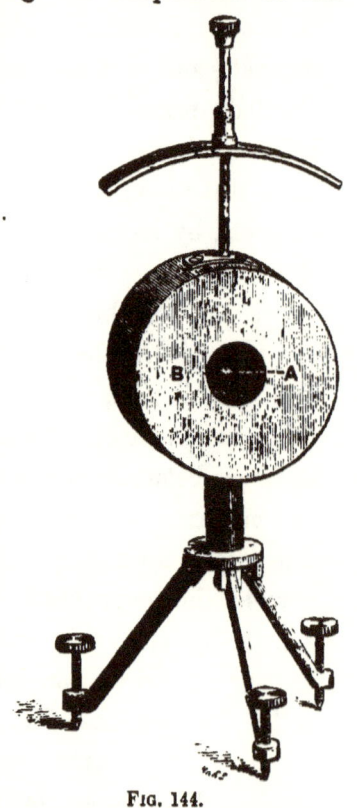

Fig. 144.

The length of the wire depends on the purpose for which the galvanometer is used, in some consisting of a few yards of stout wire, and in others of several miles of the very finest wire. The wire is carefully insulated by silk covering, and afterwards soaked in melted paraffin, which, on hardening, forms an excellent insulator. The reading of the instrument is accomplished by means of the lamp and screen, just as shown in the quadrant electrometer (Fig. 105). On the top of the coils is placed a permanent magnet, which controls the magnet in the galvanometer, bringing the spot of light initially to the zero on the screen. By proper adjustment it may be made to neutralise the earth's action on the needle, so that the magnet is almost astatic. This is really a tangent galvanometer, but as the deflections are always small, and the magnet is very short, the current is simply proportional to the deflection, the tangent being proportional to the angle, if the angle is small. (*See* table in Appendix II.)

153. Magnetic action of a Current in a Liquid.—
That Oersted's principle applies to currents in liquids, accom-

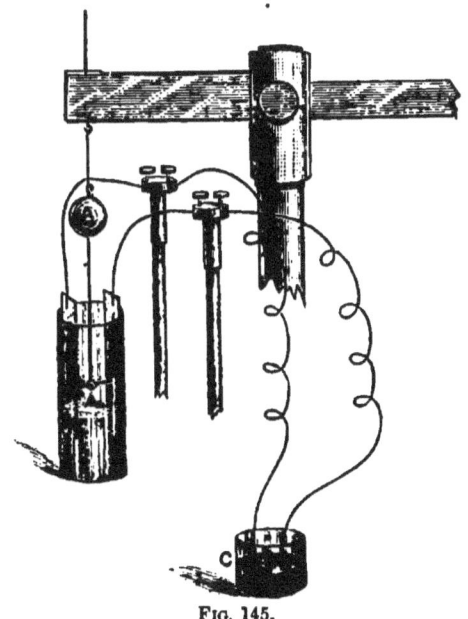

Fig. 145.

panied by electrolysis, as well as to currents in solids, can be shown by the arrangement represented in Fig. 145. The magnet (*A*) is suspended at right angles to the parallel zinc and copper plates of a simple unclosed zinc-copper couple, and immediately over the liquid. It is supported by a wire fixed to it, on which is cemented a mirror, and the whole is suspended by a single fibre of unspun silk. The movements of the needle are registered by the lamp and screen, as in a mirror galvanometer. On closing the circuit by means of the mercury-cup (*C*) the spot of light moves so as to indicate a current in the liquid from the zinc to the copper.

The deflection is much greater if, for the zinc and copper plates, we substitute two platinum plates, and send a current through the liquid (supposed to be acidulated water) from a battery of four or five Grove cells.

154. Units employed in Voltaic Electricity.—In every voltaic circuit there are three physical quantities concerned, E.M.F., Resistance, and Current Strength, connected together by Ohm's law. We have now described instruments by help of which these may be measured: E.M.F. by the Quadrant Electrometer, Resistance by a box of resistance coils, and Current Strength by a Voltameter or Galvanometer.

Before illustrating their use, it may be convenient to notice the units actually employed in practice, as they are different from those referred to in Frictional Electricity called absolute Electrostatic units. These are:

> For E.M.F., the theoretical unit of potential, which is the potential of a sphere of unit radius charged with unit quantity (Art. 80).
>
> For Current Strength, a current in which a unit of electricity passes per second.
>
> For Resistance (by Ohm's law), the resistance of a con-

ductor in which unit of potential difference would cause a unit of electricity to pass per second.

In Voltaic Electricity it has already been pointed out that these units are very inconvenient, since every E.M.F. would be represented by a very small fraction, and every current strength by a very large number. We consequently adopt a new and more convenient system, which will be fully explained later. For the present our units will be:

For E.M.F., the E.M.F. of a Daniell's cell of given construction (see Art. 124). This is called a *Volt*.

For Resistance, the resistance of a certain length of a certain wire at a given temperature. This is called an *Ohm*.

For Current Strength, that in a circuit in which the E.M.F. is one volt and the resistance is one ohm. This current strength is called an *Ampère*.

The quantity of electricity which flows per second in a current of one Ampère is called a *Coulomb*. It is our new unit of Electrical Quantity.

To connect these units with our units in electro-chemistry, the most natural assumption seems to be that the electro-chemical equivalents shall be the masses of the respective ions which appear to be associated with one coulomb of electricity. The results obtained by various experimenters seem to show that one coulomb of electricity sets free nearly ·0000105 gm. of hydrogen (*Numerical Tables and Constants*, by S. Lupton).

155. Illustrations of Ohm's Law.—The law as stated by Ohm can be illustrated by showing that in a battery (1) the E.M.F. is proportional to the current when the resistance is constant; (2) the E.M.F. is proportional to the resistance when the current is constant. It then follows on ordinary algebraical principles that the E.M.F. is proportional to the product of current strength and resistance where both vary.

(1) To prove that the E.M.F. is proportional to current strength with a constant resistance, use a series of Daniell's cells, all of equal E.M.F. If we interpose a very large resistance (5000 ohms say), the difference of potential at the terminals will be practically the whole E.M.F., the resistance of the battery being insensible compared with this large resistance. The current will then be so small that we must employ a Thomson's mirror galvanometer to detect it.

Fitting up the galvanometer and resistance with one cell, we get a certain deflection, 12·5 scale-degrees, suppose; with two cells the deflection becomes 24·6 divisions; with three cells, 37 divisions, and so on; hence proving the constancy of the ratio between the difference of potential and the current strength.

(2) To prove that the E.M.F. is proportional to the resistance when the current is constant.

Although we do not know the internal resistance of a cell of the battery, we may assume that when the battery is in compound circuit and the current passes through all the cells in succession, the total resistance is the sum of the resistances of each cell.

Fit up the battery and a set of resistance coils with a tangent galvanometer of no sensible resistance (or, at any rate, very low resistance compared to one cell). If we use one cell only, and introduce 10 ohms' additional resistance, the galvanometer will give a certain reading, say 20°. Next, use two cells and introduce 20 ohms' resistance, and the galvanometer reading is sensibly the same. And this reading will not alter if we introduce 3 cells and 30 ohms, or 4 cells and 40 ohms, and so on. Now in these cases the E.M.F.s have been in proportion of the numbers 1, 2, 3, 4, and so have the resistances, for if r be the resistance of one battery cell, the resistances have actually been $r+10$, $2r+20$, $3r+30$, $4r+40$.

Of course these two illustrations can only be taken as suggesting the soundness of the law. Like every great induction of science, its proof rests on an infinite series of observations which are constantly in progress. We can only add here that Ohm's law has borne the most rigorous tests of absolute accuracy that have been applied to it.

156. Experimental Determination of Battery Resistance.

—On account of the importance of Ohm's law we shall now, with a set of resistance coils, use it to determine certain resistances. These determinations are not susceptible of very great accuracy, and are not such as would be employed in practice. More accurate practical methods will form the subject of the next chapter.

To find the resistance of a cell or battery, fit it up with resistance coils (R) and a galvanometer (G) of small resistance (Fig. 146). Observe the deflection, and take the measure of the current from the table of tangents. Halve this measure and find the deflection which corresponds to half current. By introducing resistance, the current can be brought down to this reading. The resistance introduced will now be equal to the internal resistance. For if we halve the current, we double the resistance in the circuit, and since at first the only resistance was internal, the external resistance introduced must be equal to it. As an example, take the battery of four Daniell's cells used before, which, when fitted up with a galvanometer of small resistance, gives 73° deflection. Now tan $73° = 3·270$, therefore $\frac{1}{2}$ tan $73° = 1·635 =$ tan $58°\ 30'$ nearly. On introducing 24 ohms' resistance, the deflection of the galvanometer falls to $58\frac{1}{2}°$. We infer that the resistance of the four cells and of the galvanometer equals 24 ohms, or that the resistance of each cell is 6 ohms, neglecting the galvanometer resistance.

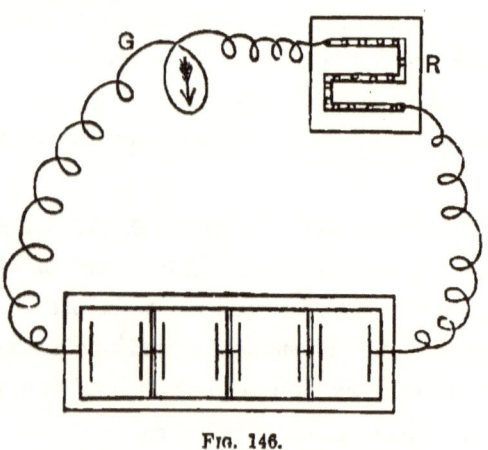

Fig. 146.

157. Resistance of the Galvanometer.—Fit up the galvanometer, whose resistance is supposed to be considerable, with resistance coils in the circuit of a battery or cell of known resistance, as in Fig. 146. Observe the reading with only the resistance of the battery and galvanometer ($r + G$ say). As before, introduce resistance till the current is halved, and then the introduced resistance will also equal $r + G$; whence r being known, G, the galvanometer resistance, becomes known. If necessary, resistance may be introduced at first to bring the galvanometer reading down if too high, since the reading should not be taken with a deflection above 75°, the change in the tangent becoming very large for each degree at higher angles.

158. To find the Resistance of a given Wire Coil.
—This can be done either by balancing the unknown against a known resistance, or by calculation.

(1) *By balancing.*—Fit up as in Fig. 147 a circuit consisting of a battery (A), a galvanometer (G), a box of resistance coils (R), and the unknown resistance (X), whose terminals are connected with the mercury cups (B, C). When the battery wire (P) dips into B, and the coil (X) is included, read the galvanometer. Next lift the wire (P) from B into C, thus excluding the coil. Introduce resistance in R till the galvanometer regains its former reading. The resistance introduced will then equal that of X, the unknown resistance.

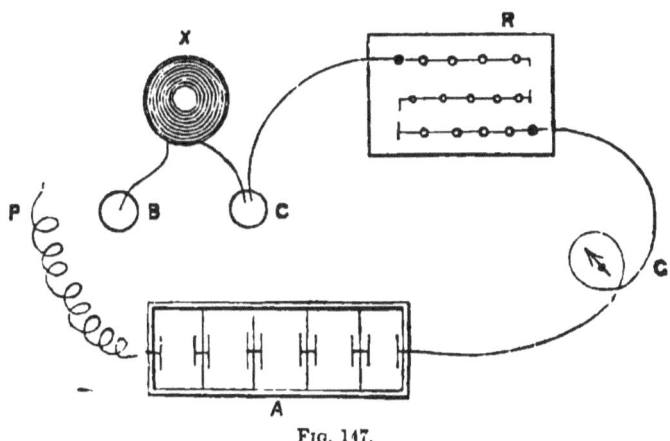

Fig. 147.

(2) *By calculation.*—Let E be the E.M.F., and r the internal resistance of the battery, g the galvanometer resistance, and x the unknown resistance.

Take out all resistance except that of the battery and galvanometer (when the battery is said to be short-circuited), and let the observed current be I_1. Then by Ohm's law

$$I_1 = \frac{E}{r+g} \quad \ldots \quad (1).$$

Introduce the unknown resistance x, and let the current be I_2

$$I_2 = \frac{E}{r+g+x} \quad \ldots \quad (2).$$

Introduce a known resistance n ohms, and let the current be I_3

$$\therefore \quad I_3 = \frac{E}{r+g+n} \quad \ldots \quad (3).$$

Dividing equations (2) and (1)

$$\frac{I_1}{I_2} = 1 + \frac{x}{r+g}.$$

Dividing equations (3) and (1)

$$\frac{I_1}{I_3} = 1 + \frac{n}{r+g}.$$

Hence we have, by eliminating $r+g$,

$$\frac{x}{n} = \frac{I_1 - I_2}{I_2} \times \frac{I_3}{I_1 - I_3}.$$

Since in this result only ratios of current strengths enter we may for the current strengths I_1, I_2, I_3, write the tangents of the observed deflections of the galvanometer, assuming it to be of the tangent form.

As a particular example, using the same battery of four Daniell's cells, and the galvanometer of small resistance, we find on short-circuiting the battery a deflection of 73°; on introducing the coil whose resistance is unknown, the deflection sinks to 37°, and on introducing 20 ohms, external resistance, the deflection is 61°.

We have from the tables (Appendix II.)

$\tan 73° = 3\cdot271$, $\tan 37° = \cdot756$, and $\tan 61° = 1\cdot784$.

Hence $3\cdot271 = \dfrac{E}{r+g}$: $\cdot756 = \dfrac{E}{r+g+x}$

$$1\cdot784 = \dfrac{E}{r+g+20}$$

$$\therefore \quad \dfrac{3\cdot271}{\cdot756} = 1 + \dfrac{x}{r+g} \quad \therefore \quad \dfrac{x}{r+g} = \dfrac{2\cdot515}{\cdot756}$$

$$\text{and} \quad \dfrac{3\cdot271}{1\cdot784} = 1 + \dfrac{20}{r+g} \quad \therefore \quad \dfrac{20}{r+g} = \dfrac{1\cdot487}{1\cdot784}$$

$$\therefore \quad r+g = \dfrac{1\cdot784}{1\cdot487} \times 20$$

$$\therefore \quad x = \dfrac{2\cdot515}{\cdot756} \times \dfrac{1\cdot784}{1\cdot487} \times 20 = 80 \text{ ohms nearly.}$$

The same equations give $r+g$, which, on working out, is found to be 24 ohms nearly.

159. Relation of Resistance to Dimension of a Conductor: Specific Resistance.

—We have seen that the resistance of a wire or of the liquid of a battery is proportional to the length which the current has to traverse; we may next inquire how it is related to the sectional area of the wire. The easiest way to do this is to take two equal lengths, cut from the same wire, and place them breast to breast (Fig. 148) as a single conductor, when we find the resistance to be exactly half that of either wire taken separately. Since the two wires are equal in all respects, they will behave exactly as if they were lying side by side, or in fact formed parts of a wire of twice the sectional area. Hence we infer that the resistance of a wire is inversely as its sectional area.

We may prove it roughly for the liquid in a battery by taking two equal cells, and after determining their resistances carefully (to see that they are nearly equal), fit them up in simple circuit, and it will be found that the resistance of the battery so formed will be half that of a single cell.

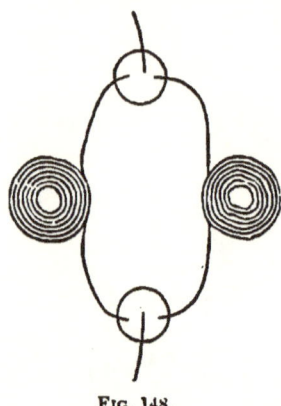

FIG. 148.

We learn that the resistances of wires of the same material are proportional to their length directly, and to their sectional area inversely. As the resistance also depends on the material, we may generally say that for any wire or liquid in a battery it

$$= \rho \times \frac{\text{length}}{\text{sectional area}},$$

where ρ depends only on the material, and is called its *specific resistance*. If we make the length and sectional area each unity, the resistance will then be simply ρ, the specific resistance. We may therefore define the specific resistance of any material as the resistance of a cube of that material whose edge is 1 cm.—the current being supposed to pass directly between two opposite faces.

The following are the specific resistances of the commonest metals at 0° C.[1] The unit is the millionth part of an ohm (or 10^{-6} ohm), called the microhm.

---

[1] See Lupton's *Numerical Tables and Constants*.

Silver, annealed,	1·521
Copper, hard drawn,	1·642
Platinum, annealed,	9·158
Iron, soft,	9·827
Mercury,	96·146
Bismuth,	132·65
German Silver,	21·17
Brass,	5·8

The specific resistances of liquids most commonly used are, according to the best determinations, in ohms,

Water at 4° C.,	$9·1 \times 10^6$
„ at 11° C.,	$3·4 \times 10^5$
Dilute hydrogen sulphate (5% acid) at 18° C.,	4·88
„ „ „ (20% acid) „	1·562
„ „ „ (30% acid) „	1·38
„ „ „ (40% acid) „	1·5
Hydrogen nitrate, at 18° C.,	1·61
Copper sulphate sat. solution at 10° C.,	29·3
Zinc sulphate sat. solution at 14° C.,	21·5
Sodium chloride sat. solution at 13° C.,	5·3

In all cases the resistance diminishes rapidly as temperature rises.

The specific resistances of the commonest insulators measured in megohms or 10^6 ohms.

Glass (crystal) below 40° C.,	infinite.
„ „ at 46° C.,	$6·182 \times 10^9$
„ „ at 105° C.,	$1·16 \times 10^7$
Paraffin, at 46° C.,	$3·4 \times 10^{10}$
Ebonite, at 46° C.,	$2·8 \times 10^{10}$

160. Application of Ohm's Law to a Simple Circuit.

—We can now compute the current obtained from a battery in simple circuit. The E.M.F. we have seen to be the same as for a single cell, and if we have n cells, each of resistance r, the total internal resistance becomes $\frac{r}{n}$, and hence Ohm's formula becomes

$$I = \frac{E}{\frac{r}{n} + R} = \frac{nE}{r + nR}.$$

When $R=0$, or the external resistance vanishes, the current $= \frac{nE}{r}$, or n times the current from one cell. If the external resistance becomes large, so that r vanishes in comparison with nR, the current becomes $\frac{nE}{nR} = \frac{E}{R}$, or the same as for a single cell. This can be proved experimentally by introducing a resistance of say 10,000 ohms, and showing that the current is the same as for a single cell.

161. Application of Ohm's Law to a Compound Circuit.—In the compound series of n cells, the E.M.F. becomes nE and the internal resistance of the battery nr. Hence

$$I = \frac{nE}{nr + R}.$$

When R is very large compared to nr, the current is $\frac{nE}{R}$, and therefore proportional simply to the number of cells.

If R, on the other hand, be very small compared to r, the current becomes $\frac{nE}{nr} = \frac{E}{r}$, or the same as from a single cell.

162. Application of Ohm's Law to a Mixed Circuit.—We have seen that with a simple circuit, and small external resistance, the current is directly proportional to the number of cells, while with a compound circuit and small resistance it is the same as for one cell. When the resistance is moder-

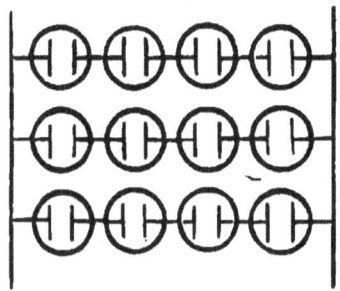

Fig. 149.

ately large, a better arrangement of the battery can be obtained by what is termed *Mixed Circuit*. In this a number of cells are compound-circuited, and placed in a row with other equal rows also compound-circuited abreast of them. Each row of q cells (each having E.M.F. $= E$, and resistance $= r$) will be equivalent to a single cell whose E.M.F. is qE, and resistance qr.

If we have p rows then we have p such cells in simple circuit, and we have for the current strength

$$I = \frac{qE}{\frac{qr}{p} + R} = \frac{pqE}{qr + pR}.$$

If we have n cells, then $pq = n$, and

$$I = \frac{nE}{qr + pR}.$$

*163. Arrangement of a Battery for the greatest Current.—This is to find the values of p and q which make I the greatest possible in the last expression.

We may write $I = \dfrac{nE}{(\sqrt{qr} - \sqrt{pR})^2 + 2\sqrt{nrR}}.$

This will be the greatest possible when the denominator is the least possible, and that is when the square it contains vanishes.

$$\therefore \sqrt{qr} - \sqrt{pR} = 0,$$

$$\text{or } R = \frac{qr}{p},$$

which gives the condition that the external and internal resistances shall be equal.

If the cells are in simple circuit the external resistance is $\frac{r}{n}$, and for this, or for any less external resistance, the simple circuit is the best. If the cells are in compound circuit, the internal resistance is nr, and for this, or any greater external resistance, the compound circuit is best. For intermediate values of R the best arrangement is found by solving the equations for p and q. For example, to find the best arrangement of 48 cells, each of resistance ·5 ohms to be used with an external resistance of 6 ohms. Here

$$pq = 48, \text{ and } 6 = \frac{q}{p} \times \cdot 5$$

$$\text{or } \frac{q}{p} = 12$$

$$\therefore q^2 = 576$$

$$q = 24$$

∴ best arrangement is 2 rows each of 24 cells.

If the external resistance had been 1 ohm, we should have had $\frac{q}{p} = 2$ and $pq = 48$,

$$\therefore q^2 = 96$$

∴ q is between 9 and 10.

Neither 9 nor 10 is a submultiple of 48; we must therefore

give to q either the value 8 or 12, and find which will give the greater current.

Substituting $q = 8$, gives $I = \dfrac{48E}{8 \times \cdot 5 + 6} = \dfrac{48}{10} E$ (Art. 162)

and $q = 12$, gives $I = \dfrac{48E}{12 \times \cdot 5 + 4} = \dfrac{48}{10} E$

or the currents are equal, and the best arrangement is either six rows each of eight cells, or four rows of twelve cells.

164. Method of changing rapidly the Battery arrangement.—For verifying these deductions from Ohm's law, it will be found useful to fit up a battery of six Daniell's cells, so that they can easily be changed from one arrangement to another. This can be done by placing the battery on a frame, one wire from each plate passing to a binding screw on the framework—all the zincs being in one straight line and all the coppers in another, so placed that the terminals

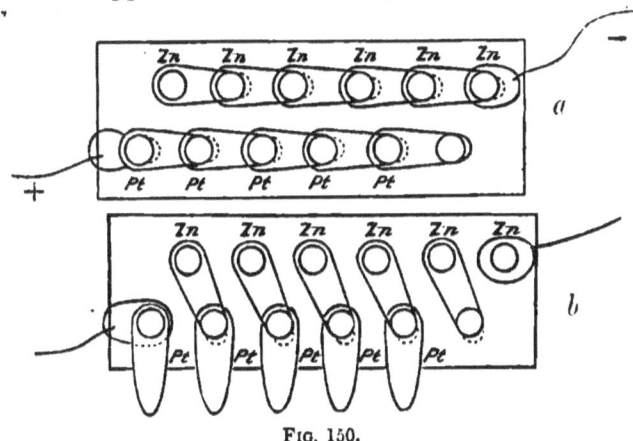

FIG. 150.

form a series of equilateral triangles. By brass or copper strips placed across the terminals, and screwed down by tightening the binding-screws, we can put the battery in simple circuit (*a*, Fig. 150), or in compound circuit (*b*, Fig. 150), or in any mixed circuit. Also, by a binding-screw which can be attached to any one brass strip, we can include as many cells as we please.

A caution must be here given against the use of the ordinary resistance coils with batteries of several cells, unless the resistance introduced be great, since strong currents are apt to heat and injure the resistance coils.

165. Measurement of E.M.F. by Galvanometer.—

Ohm's law gives us $I = \dfrac{E}{R+r}$, in which if r, the internal resistance, be made small compared with R (which can be made a large constant resistance), the current strength with different cells is in each simply proportional to its E.M.F. By using a sensitive mirror galvanometer and a very large external resistance (5000 ohms suppose), we may treat the total resistance as a constant with any battery we employ. The indications given by different cells or batteries are therefore proportional to their respective E.M.F.

Results obtained by this means may be compared with those obtained (Art. 117) by the quadrant electrometer, and will accord well for constant batteries, being smaller for all one-fluid cells owing to polarisation.

Instruments depending on this principle are called Potentiometers.

166. Laws of Divided Currents.—

We may here investigate experimentally some of the laws of divided currents. Suppose there are two conductors joining two points, the conductors being of different resistance, we shall find that the current in either branch is inversely as the resistance of that branch.

To show this we require two sets of resistance coils (*A* and *B* in Fig. 151) put breast to breast, in connection with mercury cups (*C*, *D*), into which the battery wires dip, and a galvanometer of small resistance compared to the resistances in *A* and *B*. In this case there will be no sensible alteration of the current in either branch by introducing the galvanometer. Take out resistances in *A* 20 and in *B* 30 ohms, the galvanometer resistance being a fraction of an ohm.

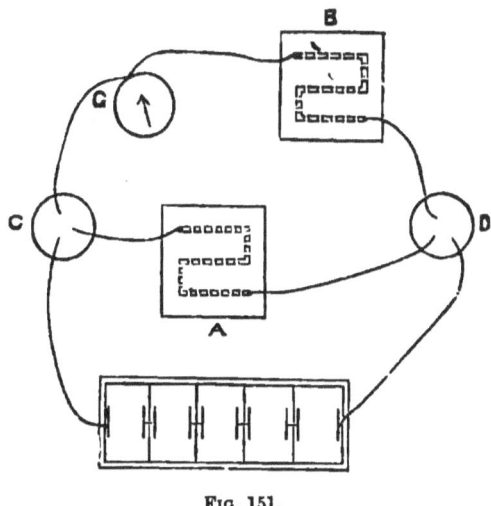

FIG. 151.

First include the galvanometer in the branch *BC*, the deflection is seen to be 30°. Next remove the galvanometer from the branch *BC*, and include it in *AC*; the reading then becomes 41°.

Referring to the table of tangents, we see that tan 30° = ·577, and tan 41° = ·865,

$$\text{and } \frac{865}{577} = \frac{30}{20} \text{ as nearly as may be.}$$

There will be apparently greater accuracy obtained by using

a coil of wire equal in resistance to the galvanometer, and placing it in the branches AC, BC alternately with the galvanometer.

Next, with the same arrangement, it is easy to prove that the total resistance of two branches of the divided circuit is given by the formula $\frac{1}{R} = \frac{1}{20} + \frac{1}{30} = \frac{1}{12}$, and therefore the resistance is 12 ohms.

The galvanometer must be placed in the battery branch, and its deflection observed when the coils are abreast. Remove the branch CAD, and take out in B 12 ohms' resistance, and it will be found that the galvanometer is at its former reading, showing that the 12 ohms' resistance just balances the two resistances, 20 and 30 ohms, when placed abreast.

167. Galvanometer Shunts.—For measuring strong currents a delicate galvanometer can be used by means of a *shunt* circuit. This generally consists of a short thick wire joining the galvanometer terminals, and having a resistance equal to $\frac{1}{9}$, $\frac{1}{99}$, or $\frac{1}{999}$ of the galvanometer. The current is therefore divided between the galvanometer and the shunt in the proportion of 1 to 9, 1 to 99, or 1 to 999. With the respective shunts $\frac{1}{10}$, $\frac{1}{100}$, or $\frac{1}{1000}$ of the current passes through the galvanometer. This method can only be applied when the total resistance in the circuit is large compared with the galvanometer resistance; otherwise, the introduction of the shunt of small resistance, by diminishing the total resistance, increases the total current in nearly the same proportion that the shunt diminishes the galvanometer current.

In the latter case the following modification may be employed :—Let the current pass through a stout wire (AB) of resistance, suppose 1 ohm. Arrange a branch circuit (AGB) containing the galvanometer (G) and a set of resistances, which, *with the galvanometer resistance*, will give respectively 99, 999, or 9999 ohms.

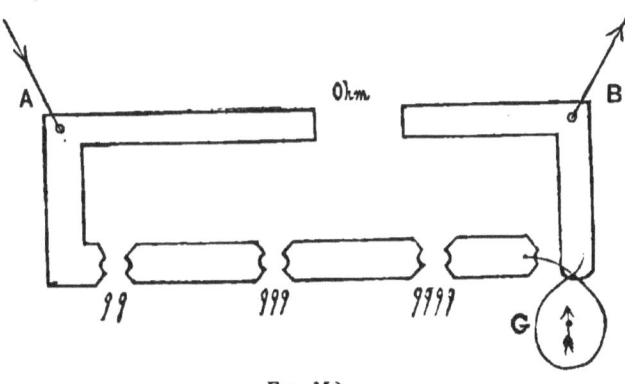

Fig. 152.

Let us, for example, put in the resistance numbered 999. The circuit is divided into two branches, whose resistances are 999 : 1. Therefore $\frac{1}{1000}$ of the current goes through the galvanometer, and $\frac{999}{1000}$ through the stout wire.

Again, the total resistance of main wire (AB) and shunt (AGB) is

$$\frac{1}{\frac{1}{1}+\frac{1}{999}} = \frac{999}{1000} = 1 \text{ very nearly,}$$

showing that the total resistance in the circuit is not altered by the shunt.

168. Thermal Effects of a Current in the Conductor.—The heating effect of a current in the conductor can

be shown by connecting the terminals of a battery of five or six Grove cells with platinum wires of various sections. The thicker the wire the smaller will be the rise in temperature; but with a very thin wire, such as is used for blowpipe experiments, 4 or 5 inches may be kept glowing at red heat. The shorter the wire, the more intensely it will glow, owing to the decrease in resistance, and therefore increase of current where the wire is shortened. It has been shown by experiment that the current which will keep an inch of wire at a given temperature would maintain a mile of the same wire at an equal temperature, but practically increasing the length of a conductor of considerable resistance diminishes the current, and fresh battery power must be supplied to maintain the same current.

The heating effect is closely analogous to the heating caused by passing a current of liquid through narrow tubes. The more rapidly the liquid flows, and the narrower the tube, the greater will be the frictional resistance.

The heating effect also depends on the nature of the material, being greater the greater its specific resistance. This is shown by having a chain, whose alternate links are of platinum and silver wires of about the same gauge. If the chain be placed between the terminals of the battery, the platinum will be found to glow with a red heat, while the silver remains dark and cold, though of course the current in all is the same. This is owing to the specific resistance of the platinum being about six times that of the silver.

*169. **Measure of Heating Effect.**—If we have a conductor whose extremities are at potential difference V, and a current I passes through it, that current represents a loss of energy represented by VI units of energy per second (Art. 143). Unless work is being done externally, that energy must be converted into heat in the conductor itself. Hence the heat given out per second will be the thermal equivalent of VI units of energy. If H be the number of thermal units given out, and J be Joule's mechanical equivalent of heat, we have

$$JH = VI = I^2 R$$ where R is the resistance, since $V = IR$ by Ohm's law.

Let now m be the mass, c the specific heat, and θ the rise in temperature, then $H = mc\theta$. Also let l be the length, a the sectional area, ρ the specific resistance, and D the density; then $m = laD$ and $R = \dfrac{\rho l}{a}$. Substituting, we have

$$JlaDc\theta = I^2 \frac{\rho l}{a}$$

$$\therefore \quad \theta = \frac{I^2 \rho}{JDc} \cdot \frac{1}{a^2}.$$

This will represent the rise in temperature per second, supposing no heat lost by radiation or otherwise.

This confirms our rule that the rise in temperature is independent of the length when the current is constant, and shows that the heating is inversely as the square of the section, or as the fourth power of the diameter when the section varies. This explains the enormous heat developed in a thin wire forming part of a circuit as in the incandescent lamp or fuze in mining.

The same general laws apply to the heating of the liquid parts of a circuit, the heat being simply proportional to the resistance in each section of the circuit. Thus on short-circuiting a battery, the cells are rapidly heated, and the stout wire remains cool. Here the energy of the current is wholly converted into heat in the battery itself. When a large resistance is interposed, the current is smaller, and only a small fraction of that heats the battery, the greater part heating the larger external resistance.

The formula $JH = I^2 Rt$ for the amount of heat given out in t seconds gives the result in gram-degrees, if we give J the value $4 \cdot 2 \times 10^7$ ergs, and measure I and R in absolute units of either the electrostatic or electromagnetic system. It can be proved (Art. 184) that if I be measured in ampères and R in ohms, the right-hand side must be multiplied by 10^7, which reduces the formula for the number of gram-degrees given off to

$$H = \frac{I^2 Rt}{4 \cdot 2}.$$

CHAPTER IV.

WHEATSTONE'S BRIDGE.

*170. **Theory of the Bridge.**—The measurements detailed in the last chapter depend on the use of a tangent galvanometer, an instrument which gives a good rough measure of a strong current, but is not very sensitive to small changes in current, nor capable of being read to a very great nicety. All the most accurate measurements are therefore made by extremely sensitive galvanometers of the astatic or mirror type, the adjustment of the apparatus requiring that the current through the galvanometer shall vanish.

The chief instrument used for measuring all resistances is Wheatstone's Bridge. The principle of this instrument is a divided circuit whose terminals are by a battery kept at a certain potential difference. Let the resistance be

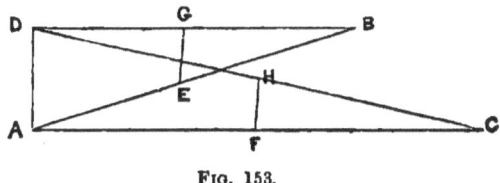

FIG. 153.

represented by the lines AB, AC in one plane, and the potential difference between A and B or C by a line AD perpendicular to the plane. The lines DB and DC will (Art. 147) give the potential-gradient. If two points E, F be taken in AB and AC respectively, so that $AE : EB :: AF : FC$

and EG, FH be drawn parallel to AD, then $EG=FH$ for $\frac{EG}{AD}=\frac{BE}{AB}$ and $\frac{FH}{AD}=\frac{CF}{AC}$, which shows E and F to be at the same potential. Hence a galvanometer placed in EF would be unaffected. This was put in practice by Wheatstone, who arranged a parallelogram into the sides of which resistances could be introduced. Let $AE\,BF$ be the parallelogram, the

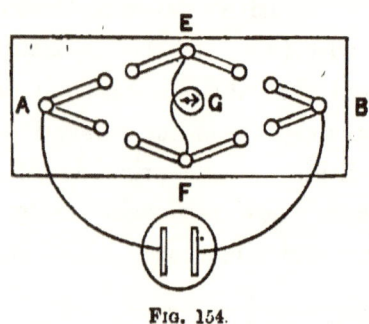

Fig. 154.

gaps in the sides being left for the resistances. In the diagonal AB is placed a battery, and in the other diagonal EF the galvanometer. Into one side he introduced the resistance to be measured, and into the others he put known resistances, which he varied till the galvanometer remained at zero. The unknown resistance was then given by the formula—

$$\frac{\text{Resistance in } AE}{\text{Resistance in } EB}=\frac{\text{Resistance in } AF}{\text{Resistance in } FB}.$$

*171. Use of the Bridge to find the Resistance of a Coil.—In modern instruments the form is altered, the fixed portions consisting of stout copper strips of no appreciable resistance (Fig. 155), the gaps in AE and EB being for the introduction of the unknown resistance, and a certain measured resistance. The branches AF and BF are formed by a single stout German silver wire, a metre in length, along which slides a key (F), by pressing down which contact can be made with the wire at any point. The key runs along a raised wooden

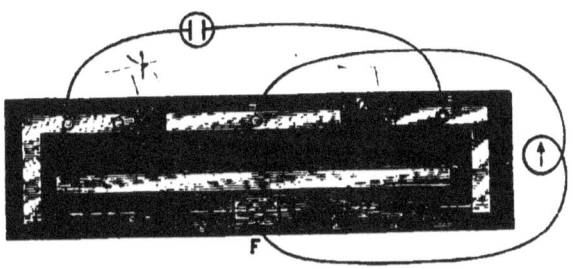

Fig. 155.

rod, whose upper surface is graduated carefully in millimetres, and read from both ends; so that the length of the two parts of the wire can be at once read off. This key is slid along the wire till the galvanometer remains at rest, whether the key is up or down, and in this position the reading is taken. If, then, p be the unknown resistance in AE, and q the known resistance in EB, and x, a the distances of F measured along the wire from A and B respectively, we have $\frac{x}{a} = \frac{p}{q}$, or $p = \frac{qx}{a}$.

In performing experiments it is often convenient to have two galvanometers—one a rough one, for getting an approximate adjustment, and finally a very sensitive one for getting an accurate adjustment.

Fig. 156 shows the arrangement actually made in finding the resistance of a coil of wire. Its terminals are placed in two mercury cups used for securing better contact, these being connected with the binding-screws by wide copper strips. The resistance-coils are connected with the other corresponding terminals. The battery consisting of a single

Daniell cell, and the galvanometer are in the two diagonal branches.

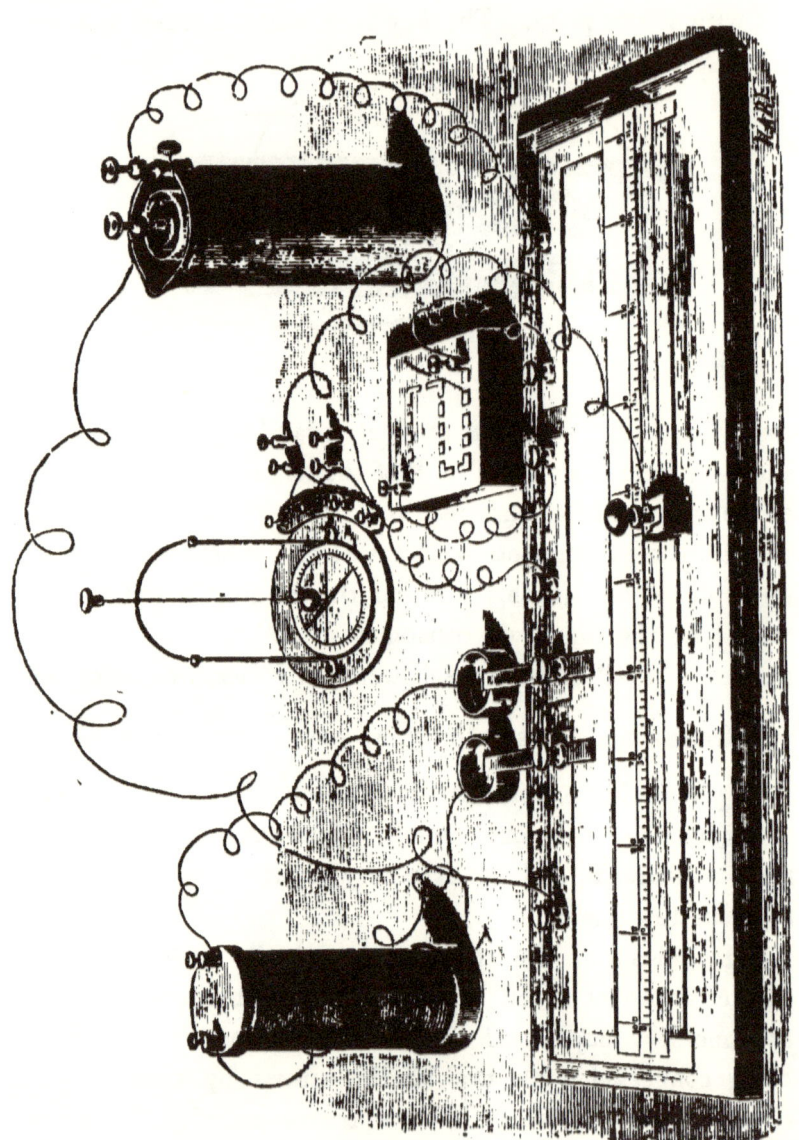

Fig. 156.

*172. Method of finding Galvanometer Resistance.

—The bridge may be used for finding the resistance of the galvanometer actually in use. The galvanometer is included in the branch AE (Fig. 155). Now it is clear that if E and F are at the same potential, the mere joining them by a wire will not alter the current in any branch. Hence if we put a contact breaker in the branch EF, and move the key till the galvanometer reading is not altered by depressing it, we may find the galvanometer resistance exactly as in the preceding case.

With a very sensitive galvanometer the current is often so strong as to deflect the needle through very nearly 90°, in which case the reading cannot be taken. To reduce the reading we must either introduce a very large resistance into the galvanometer branch EF, which can afterwards be subtracted from the final result, or we can, better, introduce a large resistance into the battery branch AB, so reducing the current in all parts of the bridge.

This method is due to Sir W. Thomson, and was suggested to him by Mance's method for finding internal resistance which follows.

*173. Method of finding Battery Resistance.

—To understand Mance's method, we must notice a further extension of the principle of the bridge, which appears from theory, namely, that so long as the relation $\dfrac{x}{a} = \dfrac{p}{q}$ holds between the resistances, whatever electromotive forces be introduced in the branches, the current in the branch circuit EF (Fig. 157) is independent of any E.M.F. or resistance in the branch circuit AB, while the current in AB is independent of E.M.F. and resistance in EF. Hence if we include the battery of unknown resistance in the branch AE, a galvanometer in AB,

256 *Electricity.* [Book III.

and a contact breaker in *EF*, we must shift the key till raising or lowering its button makes no difference in the galvanometer reading.

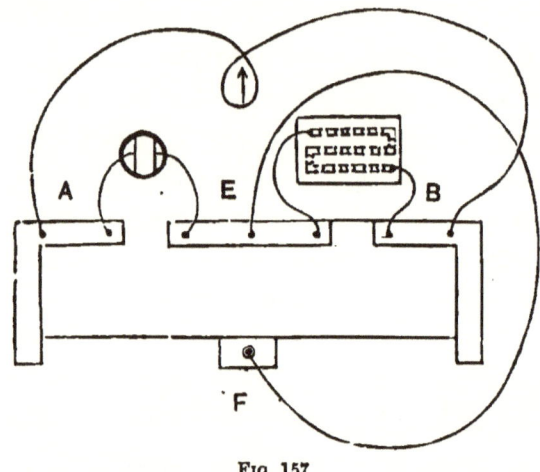

Fig. 157.

As in the last case if the current be too strong for the galvanometer, we can increase the resistance in the galvanometer branch.

*174. **Method of comparing the E.M.F. of Cells.**—We conclude this chapter with a method of comparing the E.M.F. of two constant cells by a method analogous to that of the Wheatstone Bridge.

Place the cell, whose E.M.F. we will denote by E, and a set of resistance-coils (A) in an open circuit which terminates in two mercury cups (*CD*). Also place the second cell, whose E.M.F. is E', with another set of resistance-coils (B) with its terminals in the same mercury cups, so placing the cells that they would send the current in opposite directions through a branch joining *CD*, and introduce a galvanometer in the branch *CD* (Fig. 158).

It then appears from theory that if r, r' be the internal resistances of the cells E, E' and R, R' the resistances intro-

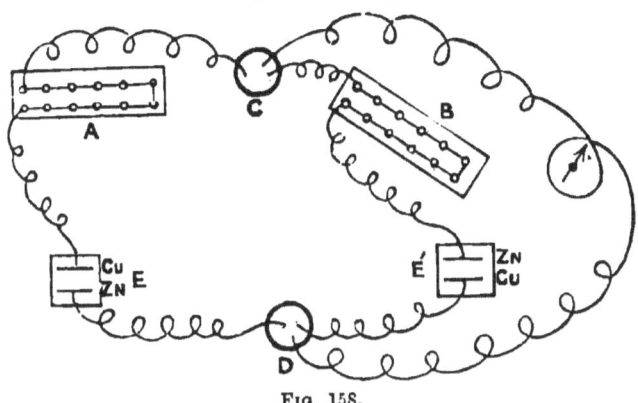

Fig. 158.

duced through the coils in A, B, there will be no current in the galvanometer branch if $\dfrac{E}{R+r} = \dfrac{E'}{R'+r'}$ . . . (1)

If one of the coils AB contain resistances which can be adjusted to small fractions (*e.g.* twentieths or hundredths) of an ohm, we can so arrange R, R' that the current in the galvanometer vanishes. If r, r' be known, this gives us the ratio of E to E'.

If r, r' be unknown, they may be eliminated by a second adjustment, for if we alter the resistance in A, B till there is again no current in the galvanometer, and if these resistances be now X, X', we shall have

$$\dfrac{E}{X+r} = \dfrac{E'}{X'+r'} \quad \ldots \quad (2)$$

which combined with (1) gives

$$\dfrac{E}{R-X} = \dfrac{E'}{R'-X'},$$

in which the internal resistances do not appear.

R

As a particular example we give the numbers obtained on comparing a Daniell and Leclanché cell. On taking out 40 ohms resistance in the Leclanché branch, and 31·5 in the Daniell branch, the galvanometer was at zero. Secondly, altering the resistance in the Leclanché branch to 70 ohms, that in the Daniell had to be adjusted to 54.

This gives

$$\text{Leclanché} : \text{Daniell} :: 70-40 :: 54-31\cdot5$$
$$:: 30 : 22\cdot5$$

Or Leclanché = 1·3 Daniell in respect of E.M.F.

CHAPTER V.

ELECTRO-MAGNETISM AND ELECTRO-DYNAMICS.

175. Bertins' Commutator.—In many of the experiments which form the subject of this chapter we require a convenient and rapid means of changing the direction of the current. This is done by a commutator, of which there

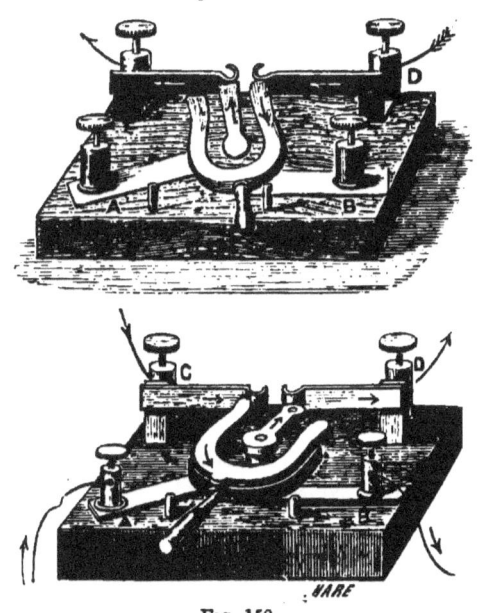

FIG. 159.

are many forms. That known as Bertins' is perhaps the simplest, as mere inspection of the instrument shows the direction in which the current is passing. On a fixed ebonite base (Fig. 159) are four binding-screws, two (AB) connected with the battery terminals, and two (*CD*) with the apparatus in use. On this base is a disc of ebonite carrying a brass horse-shoe, and a brass tongue within the horse-shoe, but insulated from it. These are separately connected with the battery terminals by metal strips and sliding contacts underneath. The other two binding-screws have metal springs attached to them, so that either end of the horse-shoe and the tongue may be simultaneously in contact with them. By turning the ebonite through a small angle, the tongue and horse-shoe come into contact with the springs in the reverse order, and so reverse the direction of the current. The diagrams show the commutator in the two positions, the direction of the current being shown by arrows.

176. Magnetic Field of a Straight Current.—

Oersted's experiment has taught us that a magnet pole placed near a current experiences force. Since this is the test of a magnetic field, it follows that a current of electricity possesses the properties of a distribution of magnetism in that it is surrounded by a magnetic field. To investigate this magnetic field we will take a straight wire, and place it so that it passes at right angles through a sheet of paper, on which we can sprinkle iron filings. On passing the current from five Grove cells in simple circuit, and tapping the paper, it will be seen that the iron filings arrange themselves in concentric circles round the wire. These are therefore the lines of force; and from Oersted's experiment, or by the use of a small magnet, we see that the direction of the lines of force is related to the direction of the current in right-handed cyclical order, as indicated by the arrows (Fig. 160). That is to say, if the direction of the current be the direction in which a corkscrew, or other right-handed screw, is propelled through the cork, the direction of the line of force is represented by the twist in the muscles of the wrist, by which it is driven in.

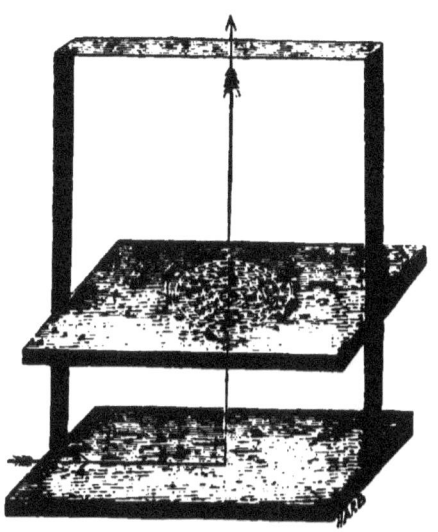

Fig. 160.

177. Rotation of a Magnet Pole round a Current.
—We infer from the last experiment that a magnet pole free to move will rotate round a current. The experiment was originally performed by Faraday by bringing the current to bear only on one half of the magnet, carrying it away again as soon as it reaches the centre. It is convenient to bend the magnet, so that it may be pivoted on its middle point, the current being brought to a mercury cup supported upon the revolving magnet, and carried away by a bent wire which dips into an annular cup of mercury, with which the battery wire is connected. On passing a strong current, the magnet pole rotates steadily, and on reversing the direction of the current, the direction of rotation is reversed (Fig. 161).

178. Rotation of a Current round a Magnet Pole.
—The third law of motion shows that whatever force a

Fig. 161.

current exerts on a pole, the pole must exert an exactly equal and opposite force on the current. Thus the system of forces between a magnet pole and a current consists of a couple, and the current, if free to move, will spin round the pole, having the same direction of rotation relatively to the pole that the pole has relatively to the current. These directions of rotation are shown by the dotted lines in Fig. 162.

The rotation of a current round a pole can be shown experimentally by pivoting a wire bent in the form of an inverted letter U on the top of a vertical magnet, the current being passed in through a mercury cup on the top of the wire, and leaving it again by an annular cup which surrounds the magnet lower down. If the magnet be of

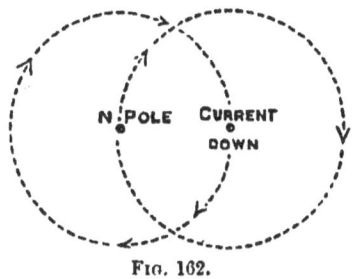

Fig. 162.

horse-shoe form, we may have two similar wires rotating in opposite directions round its two poles (Fig. 163). Instead of

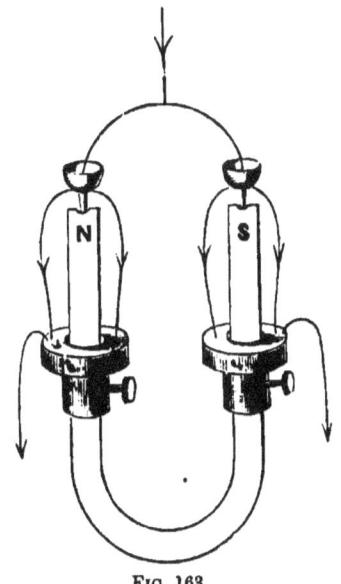

Fig. 163.

only one wire, we may have two or more soldered above, forming a cage round the pole, or we may have a single wire coiled in a spiral form, giving a pretty optical effect of continually screwing up or down; or we may vary the experiment by passing the current into one annular cup and out by the other, causing the wires to rotate in the same direction round the opposite poles.

179. Movement of Current in a Magnetic Field.— A little reflection will show that the motion of the current cannot depend on the mere magnet pole, but does depend on the field of force immediately around the current. The observed motion must, in fact, be the expression of a tendency on the part of any moveable current to cut lines of magnetic force at right angles, the direction of motion being reversed when either the direction of the lines of force or of the current is reversed.

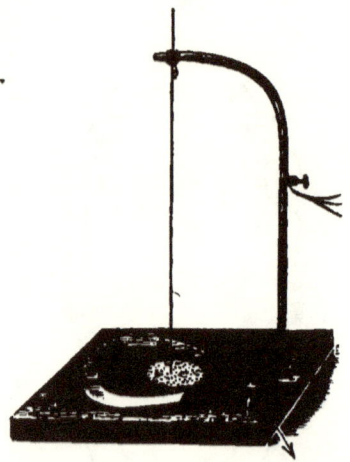

Fig. 164.

This is easily shown if we pass a current through a wire freely suspended above and dipping in a cup of mercury. If the poles of a strong horse-shoe magnet be brought near the wire, so that the wire lies between them, or in any way cuts

Chap. V.] *Electro-Magnetism and Dynamics.* 265

the lines of force, the wire moves through the mercury until contact is broken, falls back again, and so keeps up a vibrating movement (Fig. 164). The direction of motion can be altered by reversing the poles or the direction of the current. If the two poles be placed parallel to the wire, no effect is produced.

This principle is further illustrated by Barlow's wheel. The wheel consists of a brass wheel cut into a star with eight or ten points. The points, when they come in succession to their lowest position, dip into a mercury cup, and a current is sent from the axis down the vertical radius to the mercury, whence it returns to the battery. If now the poles of a magnet be placed on opposite sides of the wheel, the wheel begins to rotate, and by bringing the points successively into the mercury cup, keeps up a continuous rotation as long as the battery current continues. On reversing either the poles or the current, the direction of rotation is reversed (Fig. 165).

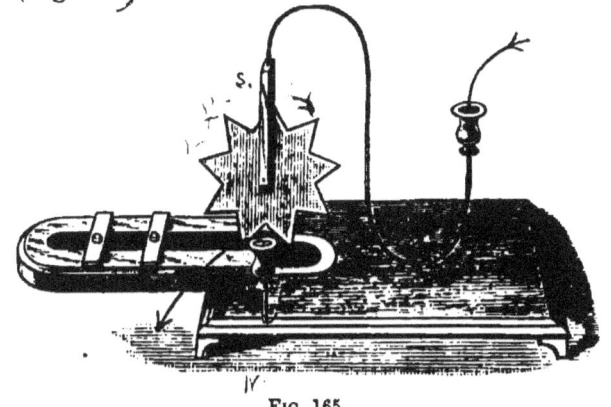

FIG. 165.

By means of this apparatus it is easy to study the direction of motion of a conductor in a magnetic field. The movement of the conductor is affected only by the lines of force which cut through it, and the direction in which it tends to move is at right angles to the plane containing the current and the lines of magnetic force which cut it. The effect is greatest when the current is placed so as to cut the lines of force at right angles. The following is a convenient *memoria technica* for remembering the relations of the three directions—current, lines of force, and movement of conductor:—*A figure swimming in the current, and looking along the lines of force, is carried to his left.* For example, a person standing erect carrying a current which flows from his heels to his head, and looking magnetic northwards, *i.e.* along the lines of the earth's horizontal force, is carried towards the west by the earth's horizontal magnetic field.

180. Methods of Suspending Currents.—To construct a circuit which shall be perfectly free to move, and yet be in connection with the terminals of a battery, presents a mechanical problem of some difficulty. Ampère overcame it by the invention of a stand which goes by his name, and some modification of which is still used. After many trials, the present writer has adopted the following method, which will give satisfactory results in all the experiments described with five Grove cells arranged for simple circuit, as in Art. 164. The axis of the central stem consists of a wire connected with one binding-screw, and terminating in a mercury cup. It is insulated by an ebonite cylinder from the outside, which consists of a brass tube, connected with the second binding-screw. On the brass tube slides an annular cup of mercury (Fig. 166). The wire frames of various forms are pivoted in the central mercury cup, and the other terminal dips slightly into

Chap. V.] *Electro- Magnetism and Dynamics.* 267

the mercury in the annular cup. The wires are so bent that the centre of gravity is brought below the cup. To diminish friction on the cup, the wire frame is also suspended by a few fibres of unspun silk, by which nearly its whole weight is . borne, (*see* Fig. 173), and the wire framework is left with remarkable freedom of motion. [The central stem is usually sold with a rather cumbrous arrangement for supporting the wire frames, whose movements are then very sluggish.]

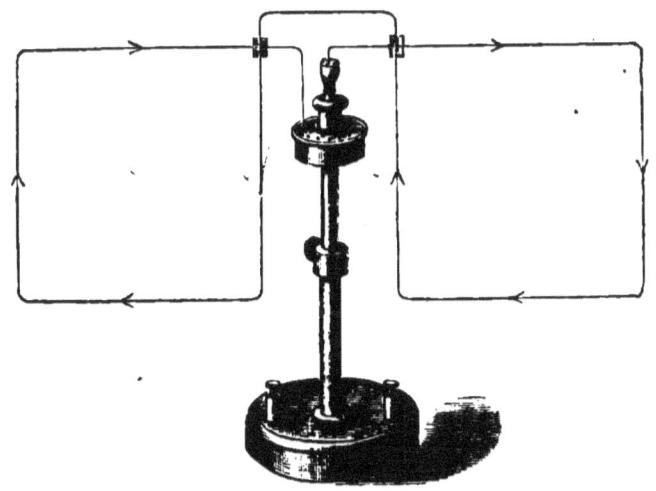

FIG. 166.

181. **Effects of Terrestrial Magnetism on Moveable Currents.**—By means of the double rectangle of Fig. 166, if the rectangles be made large enough (each not less than 10 in. by 8 in.), it will be found, on passing a current, that the framework sets as a magnet would, but with its plane at right angles to the magnetic meridian, the current ascending on the west and descending on the east side in each rectangle.

The same effect may be shown rather more simply by a coil of insulated wires (Fig. 167) wound ten or twelve times round, with its terminals dipping, one into a central mercury cup, and the other into an annulus surrounding it, from which cups wires go to the battery. The coil measures about 4 in. by 3 in., and is supported by a silk or cotton thread. On passing the current the setting is quite unmistakable, overcoming the torsion in the suspending thread.

In this case a little consideration shows that the figure swimming in the current and looking along the horizontal lines of magnetic force (which alone affect this experiment) is in all positions carried to his left as far as the mechanical arrangements permit, in accordance with Ampère's rule. If however we imagine, with Faraday, the lines of magnetic force as having a real physical existence, and distributed through the field of force in exceeding large but perfectly definite numbers, and in such a manner that the number of lines of force which cut unit area round any point in the field measures the strength of the field perpendicular to that area, we can then represent the behaviour of this circuit rather more simply. The current places itself at right angles to the lines of force (therefore including as many lines of force as possible), and its direction is related to that of the lines of force which it intercepts in right-handed cyclical order.

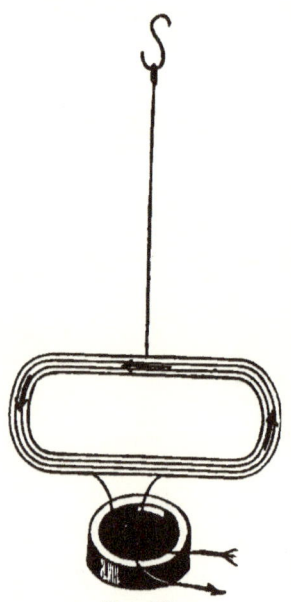

Fig. 167.

By supporting a wire framework, free to rotate about a horizontal axis at right angles to the magnetic meridian, and passing a strong current, it has been shown that it sets at right angles to the dipping needle.

By supporting a horizontal wire pivoted at one end, and with its other end just dipping into a mercury basin, on which it is supported by a cork float, it has been shown that on passing a current through the wire it rotates under the action of the vertical component of the earth's magnetism in accordance with Ampère's rule.

182. Magnetic Properties of a Closed Current.—If we take a wire bent in the form of Fig. 168, in which the current passes round the two equal rectangles (AB) in opposite directions—round A in a direction with the hands of a watch, and round B in the contrary direction—the whole system will be astatic with reference to the earth.

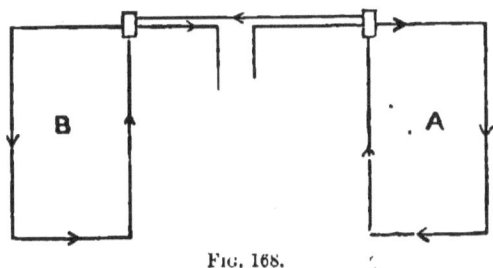

Fig. 168.

If we now take a magnet, and present its north pole to A, it will be found that A is attracted by it, and if we present the same pole to B it will be repelled. If we next present the north pole to the back of A it will be repelled, and the back of B will be attracted. If the south pole of the magnet be used, these attractions and repulsions will again be reversed.

This experiment teaches us that the action of A and B in the magnetic field are the same as if we were to substitute for A a thin sheet of steel magnetized normally to its surface and having south polar magnetism on the side facing us, and north polar magnetism on the opposite side, and for B a similar sheet, only with magnetisms reversed.

If we have a series of such circuits closely following each other, and parallel to each other, as we may have by bending a wire into circles separated by very short pieces of straight wire, or into a close helix, with the wires brought back inside

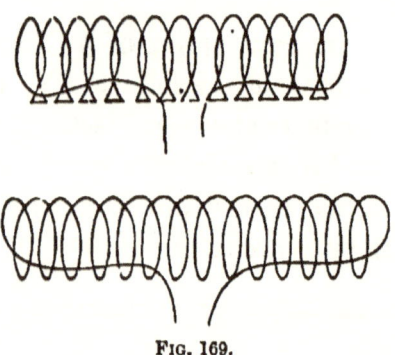

Fig. 169.

(Fig. 169), we shall have a series of magnetic shells magnetized normally, all in the same direction, which will therefore be equivalent to a series of slices cut from a bar magnet, and should behave collectively, just as a bar magnet. Such an arrangement is called a solenoid.

Place on the stand of Art. 180 a wire shaped as Fig. 170; then on presenting the north pole of a bar magnet we shall find that it attracts one end and repels the other.

The current will not be strong enough to show the directive action of the earth's magnetism or the repulsion and attraction between two similar solenoids, but if a coil of wire

Chap. V.] *Electro-Magnetism and Dynamics.* 271

be formed by closely coiling stout insulated wire from end to end of a cylinder 6 inches long, and bringing the wire through the cylinder, and again repeating the close coiling till four or five layers have been obtained, this will be found to act precisely as a weak magnet when presented to the ends of the solenoid, the pairs of poles attracting and repelling just as they would for two bar magnets.

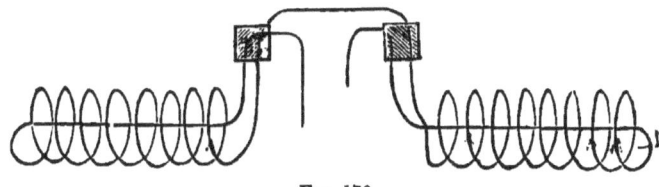

FIG. 170.

The rules for the north and south poles of the solenoid will be in accordance with what we said before; that will be the south pole in which the current, to an observer looking down upon it, goes with the hands of a watch, and a north pole in which the current goes against the hands of a watch (see Fig. 171).

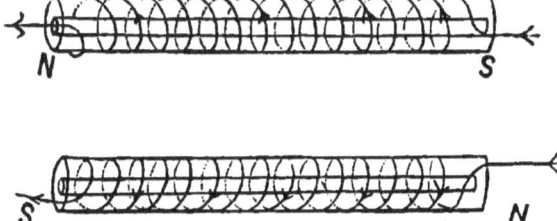

FIG. 171.

The behaviour of currents under magnetic force is sometimes illustrated by the floating battery of De La Rive. This is a simple zinc-copper couple, connected by several turns of insulated copper wire. The plates are mounted on the under-side of a cork float, and put on a vessel of acidulated water, which acts as the liquid of the cell (Fig. 172). By this means the behaviour of a closed circuit under a magnet can easily be exhibited.

Fig. 172.

By experiments, of which the above may be taken as types, and others depending on quantitative measures, Ampère was able to lay down as an experimental law that every closed voltaic circuit carrying a current is identical in its behaviour with a magnetic shell, magnetized normally, the current following the direction of the hands of a watch to an observer looking down on the south polar face. The strength of the equivalent current is directly proportional to the strength of the magnetic shell, or to its magnetic moment per unit area.

*183. **Distinction between a Voltaic Circuit and a Magnetic Shell.**—There is a very important difference between the shell and the circuit. For if P, Q be two points on the north and south side of a magnetized shell, a north pole placed at P will be repelled by the action of the shell, and carried round the edge to Q, where it will stop by impact against the shell. If a small aperture were made in the shell, though too small to affect the force on a pole at any external point, still in passing through this aperture the magnet pole would experience a retarding force, against which the work done by the pole between Q and P would just balance the work done on it by the accelerating force it had experienced up to Q, and it would reach P again with neither gain nor loss of energy. This is no more than the assumption that magnetic forces among fixed magnets obey the law of conservation of energy. If, on the other hand, we have a voltaic circuit, and P, Q be the corresponding points on opposite sides of its plane, the pole passes freely from Q to P without experiencing any retarding force, and reaches P again with an increase of energy. This energy is of course derived, as we shall see presently, from the current energy which has its source in the chemical energy of the battery.

*184. Absolute Electro-magnetic Units.—This experiment of Ampère is the key to the absolute electro-magnetic system of measurement alluded to in Art. 154.

We define in this system the unit current of electricity, as that current which, traversing any closed circuit, gives rise to an electro-magnetic field identical in all respects with the magnetic field due to a magnetic shell of unit strength, whose edge coincides with the circuit. This is called the absolute unit of current strength.

The absolute unit of quantity is the quantity of electricity which passes per second in a current of unit strength.

The absolute unit of E.M.F. or potential difference is the potential difference between two points such that unit work is done in carrying the absolute unit of quantity from one point to the other.

The absolute unit of capacity is the capacity of a conductor which, when charged with unit quantity of electricity, is at unit potential.

The absolute unit of resistance is the resistance in a circuit in which the E.M.F. is the absolute unit of potential and the current is the absolute unit of current.

These are not the units referred to above in Art. 154, as some would be inconveniently large, and others inconveniently small.

The *Coulomb*, or practical unit of quantity, is $\frac{1}{10}$ of the absolute unit.

The *Volt*, or unit of potential, is equal to 10^8, or one hundred million absolute units of potential.

The *Ampère*, or practical unit of current, is $\frac{1}{10}$ of the absolute unit.

The *Ohm*, or unit of resistance, is 10^9, or one thousand million absolute units.

The *Farad*, or unit of capacity, is 10^{-9}, or one thousand-millionth of the absolute unit. The *micro-farad*, more commonly employed, is the millionth part of the farad, and therefore 10^{-15}, or one thousand-billionth of the absolute unit.

185. Attractions and Repulsions of Parallel and Inclined Currents (Electro-Dynamics).—To investigate the action of one current upon another, the best form of apparatus is that of Fig. 173, in which the current in the two rectangles is astatic under the earth's magnetism. If the battery wires be parallel and very near to the extreme vertical currents, it will be found that the moveable wire shows attraction where the currents run in the same direction, but repulsion when in opposite directions. These

[Chap. V.] *Electro-Magnetism and Dynamics.* 275

actions will be made more visible if, instead of a single wire, we use a current multiplier, or a coil of several circuits, each rectangular in form, shown in Fig. 167. On presenting the opposite sides of the multiplier, in which the currents are in opposite directions, to one of the vertical wires on the stand, the attraction and repulsion are more strongly marked.

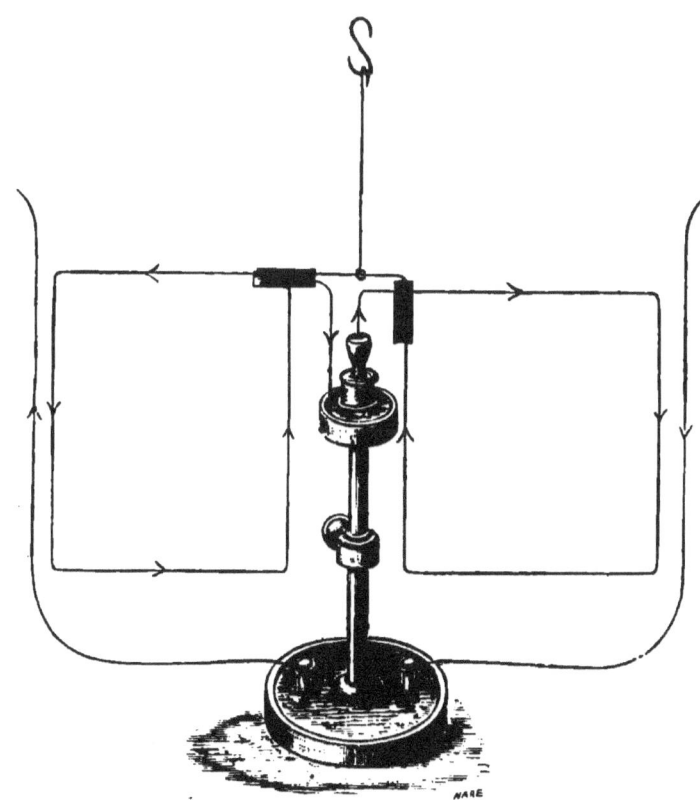

FIG. 173.

By the same arrangement it can be shown that when two finite currents are inclined to each other without crossing, they attract when both run towards or both run away

276 · *Electricity.* [Book III.

from the common apex, but repel when one runs towards and the other away from the apex.

The attraction and repulsion of parallel currents are admirably shown by the arrangement of Fig. 174, which consists of two flat spirals, each suspended by two wires, through which the current is carried. On the base is a

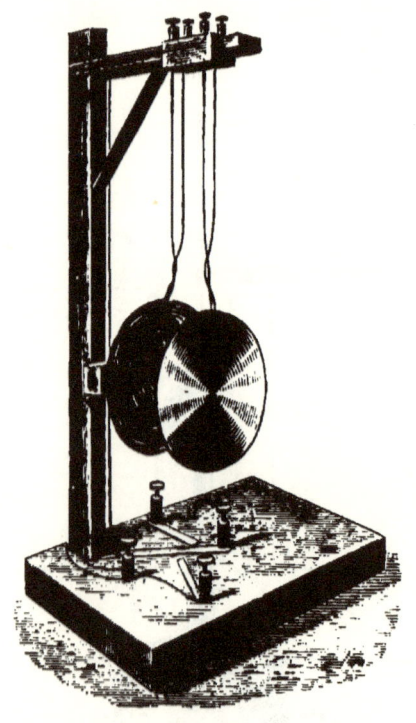

Fig. 174.

simple form of contact breaker and commutator. On causing the spirals to hang in parallel planes a short distance apart, and passing the current so that it shall run in parallel directions round both spirals, they are attracted towards each other. On hanging the spirals initially in contact, or nearly

Chap. V.] *Electro-Magnetism and Dynamics.* 277

so, and passing the current so as to traverse them in opposite directions, there will be a very marked repulsion.

The attraction of parallel currents is well illustrated by the vibrating spiral. This consists of a spiral of moderately thin copper wire suspended at its upper end and dipping at its lower end into a basin of mercury (Fig. 175). On passing a current, the successive turns of the spiral attract each other, draw the point out of the mercury, and break the contact; when the lower end of the spiral falls back again into the mercury cup. A vibratory motion is thus kept up as long as the battery connection lasts.

These actions are easily explained in accordance with the principles we have laid down, by regarding the parallel

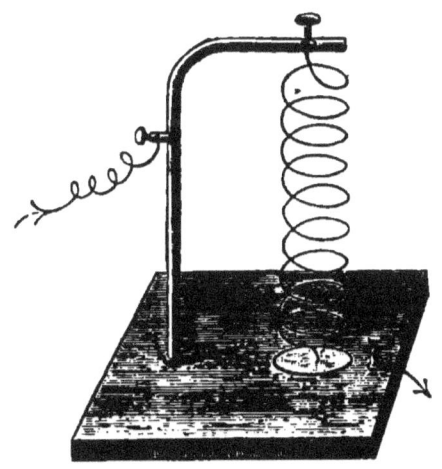

FIG. 175.

currents as edges of two magnetic shells which face each other. When the currents are in the same direction, the surfaces oppositely magnetized will be directly opposed, and therefore attraction ensues. If the currents are in opposite directions, the surfaces similarly magnetized will oppose, and therefore repel each other.

The same result will be arrived at also by considering either current in the field of force due to the other. For if A be a current, its lines of force will be more or less nearly circles round it, and those circles will rise out of the paper on one side and sink into it on the opposite (Fig. 176). If another wire carrying a current be placed on the paper below A, the figure swimming in the current and looking downwards will be carried to his left, *i.e.* towards A; and if the other current be above A, the figure swimming in the current and looking upwards will be carried to his left, that is, towards A also. Thus on both sides, A will attract a current running parallel to itself and in the same direction.

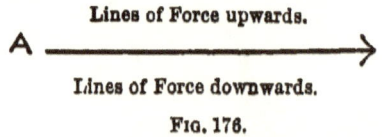

Fig. 176.

The laws of inclined currents can be explained by taking the equivalent magnetic shells, or by considering the resolved part of the field of force of one current perpendicular to the other.

186. Action of an Infinite Current on another wholly on one side.—If ABC represent a current, and DE another at right angles to it (Fig. 177), then, applying the principle of inclined currents, we see that the current in AB runs towards the apex, and that in DE runs away from it, and therefore AB and DE repel each other; while those in BC and DE both run away from the apex, and therefore attract each other. Hence, on the whole, DE, if

Chap. V.] *Electro-Magnetism and Dynamics.* 279

free to move, will move parallel to ABC, and with the current in ABC.

The same result is obtained if we consider DE as a current in the field of magnetic force due to ABC.

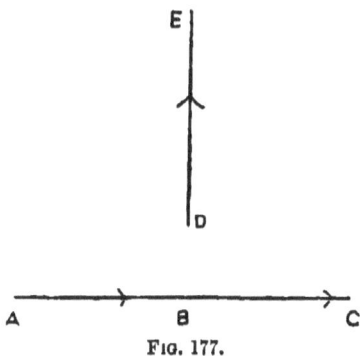

Fig. 177.

This can be illustrated by a copper vessel (A), containing copper sulphate, round which are coiled several strands of wire (not shown in the figure), which constitute the continuous current (Fig. 178). In the centre is an insulating stem which

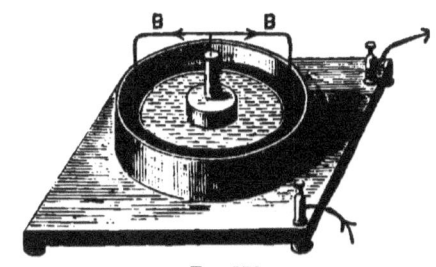

Fig. 178.

bears a mercury cup on its top. On this is pivoted a wire, which, extending horizontally both ways, is bent down at right angles and reaches the copper sulphate near the circumference of the vessel. Suspended by these two wires is a light copper ring, which dips into the copper sulphate. The current, after traversing the coil round the copper vessel, passes up the centre to the mercury cup, divides and descends by the two wires to the copper sulphate, whence it returns to the battery. The action of the continuous current on both the horizontal and vertical parts of the current in the poised wire causes it to rotate steadily, carrying with it the copper ring which steadies the motion.

187. Equivalence of a Sinuous and Straight Current.—Ampère laid down the rule that a sinuous current is equivalent to a straight current passing through it. This can be shown by making a compound solenoid in which the wire, coiled outside a tube in a helix, is carried through the tube in a straight line, and this is done four or five times, as described in Art. 182. We thus have an exterior sinuous current of about 24 yards, and an internal straight current in the opposite direction, whose length is about half a yard. On placing this arrangement parallel to one of the vertical wires in the suspended rectangle of Art. 185, and passing the current through them both, we shall find they are quite neutral to each other, the straight part just balancing the effect of the sinuous part.

If, on the other hand, the compound coil be approached endwise to the current, its action is seen to be similar to that of a bar magnet.

*188. The Magnetic Field inside a Solenoid.—One of the most remarkable things about a solenoid carrying a current is the great strength of the magnetic field inside it. To explain this, we may notice that the lines of force due to a straight current are circles, having their centre in the axis of the current. If we have a large number of straight currents parallel to each other in a plane, to find the strength of field at any given point, we must compound, according to the parallelogram law, the strength of field due to each current separately. This requires a mathematical investigation, but we can easily see the general effect. Let the line of dots AB (Fig. 179) denote the section of the paper by the currents which pass down perpendicularly through the paper, and extend indefinitely right and left. Let P be a point at which we want to construct the line of force. The force due to the current at A will be at right angles to AP, and right-handed to the current; we denote it by F. We can generally choose a current (B) such that $PA=PB$, and B

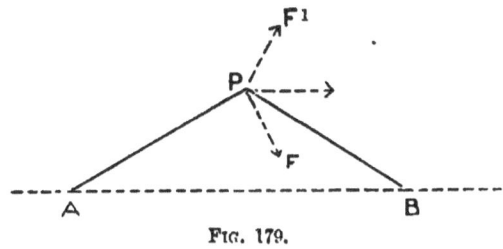

Fig. 179.

will give at P a force at right angles to BP equal to the force due to A; we denote it by F^1. Now F, F^1 are equal, and equally inclined to AB, and will therefore have a resultant parallel to AB. The same will be true of each pair of currents equally distant from P. The line of force at P will therefore be parallel to AB, and the strength of field will be somewhat increased by each single current. Of course, practically, the remote currents will produce little effect, and if the currents be finite with P near the middle, we may assume that the lines of force are parallel to AB, that is to say, in the system we have assumed the lines of force will cross the currents at right angles. Suppose, now, one of the wires bent into a circle or closed figure.

The lines of force will no longer be circles, but will be closed curves, being crowded together in the closed curve, and spread out outside it, somewhat as in the drawing (Fig. 180), in which we represent the curves obtained when we pass a current down one and up the other of two parallel wires near together.

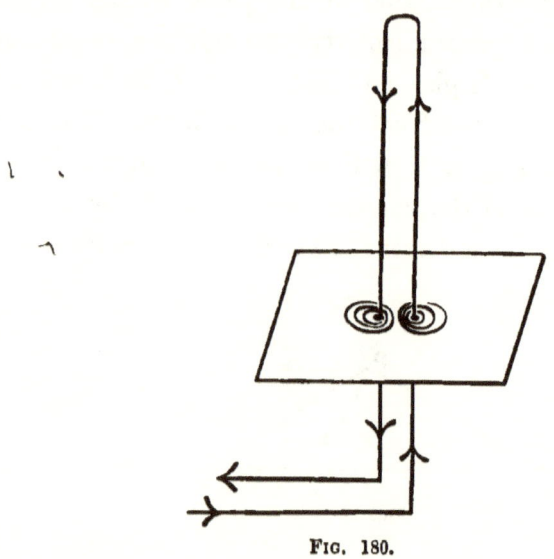

FIG. 180.

Now, suppose each of the circles forming the band of currents we considered just now to be bent into a circle, and we have the solenoidal arrangement. The lines of force must now be a series of closed curves linked with the cylinder, formed of the solenoid, entering by its south and leaving by its north polar end. Externally the lines will be the same as for a bar magnet (Art. 12), and the reasoning we used above shows that all the circles conspire to give at all internal points, except near the ends, a field whose lines of force are parallel to the axis of the cylinder. These lines, moreover, are very crowded, since all the lines pass through the cylinder, but are spread through the whole field outside it. The crowding together of the lines explains on Faraday's hypothesis (Art. 181) the great relative strength of the field within the solenoid. In Fig. 181 a diagram of the lines of force is shown, the two rows of circles being the section by the paper of the solenoid wire.

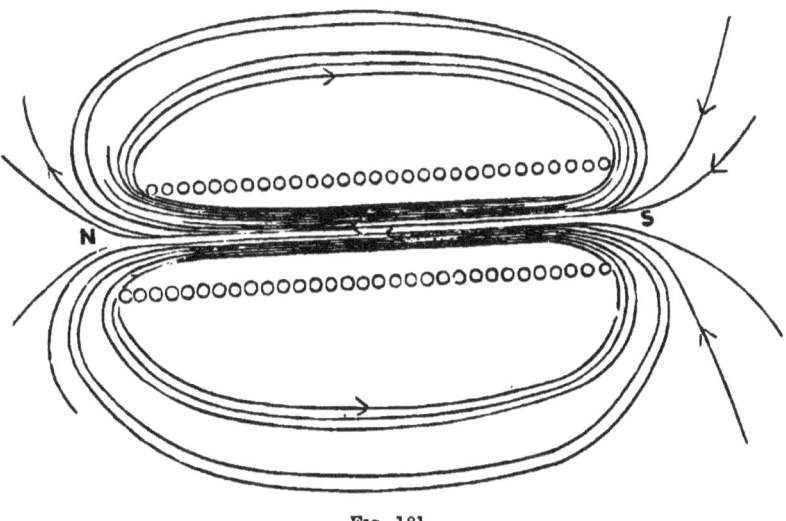

FIG. 181.

This explains why a soft iron wire placed outside will be magnetized very feebly and in the opposite direction to the magnetization of the solenoid, while a wire inside will be very strongly magnetized in the same direction.

189. **Electro-Magnets.**—Temporary magnets of great power are made by placing soft iron bars within helices of wire, through which a current is transmitted. The soft iron, while the current is passing, becomes a very strong magnet, but instantly loses its magnetism when the circuit is broken. This is easily seen by putting a stout soft iron wire

through a helix of insulated copper wire, when, on passing the current through the helix, the iron wire will acquire the power of picking up large quantities of brads or iron fragments, dropping them again the moment that contact with the battery is broken.

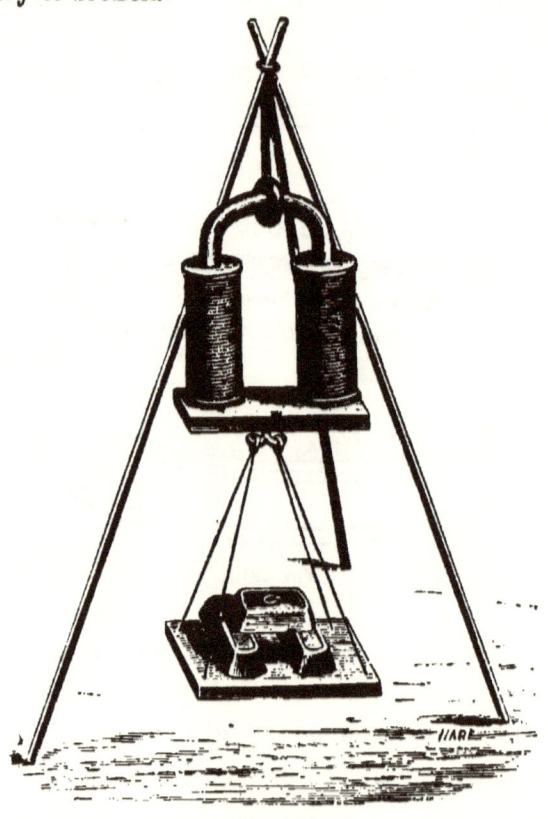

Fig. 182.

If a horse-shoe is made in soft iron, and a few dozen strands of wire are coiled in opposite directions round the two ends, on passing a current through the wire, a very powerful electro-magnet is made, capable of supporting very heavy weights when suspended from a soft iron armature joining its poles (Fig. 182).

If a bar of steel be placed within the helix, the magnetism induced is less strong than for an iron bar of the same size, but is largely retained after the current is broken. Small bars can be easily magnetized to saturation by placing them in a helix and giving smart blows with a hammer while the current is passing.

By the method just indicated temporary magnets can be made of vast power compared even with the strongest permanent magnets. To obtain the best effects very nice adjustments have to be made between the dimensions of the soft iron core and the coils of wire which surround it. If the core be too thick, only the outer parts are magnetized, while the inner part contributes nothing to the strength of the pole. There is again great difficulty in obtaining thick iron rods which are well annealed throughout, without which the iron is not *soft*. The core is therefore often made of a number of thin rods of soft iron. By these means, with proper precautions, magnets of vast power have been made.

190. Paramagnetic and Diamagnetic Substances.

—By means of the powerful electro-magnet possessed by the Royal Institution, Faraday showed that almost all substances were more or less susceptible to magnetic influence. He also discovered two classes of substances very different in their behaviour when under magnetic influence. The first class he called *paramagnetics*, which in their properties are similar to iron, nickel, and cobalt, so that when a bar of one of these substances is suspended in the strong magnetic field between the poles of the magnet, the bar sets with its length along the lines of force, or, as he termed it, *axially*. The other class he called *diamagnetics*, of which bismuth is a type. When a bar of such a substance is suspended between the poles of the magnet, it sets at right angles to the lines of force, or *equatorially*. This is illustrated in Fig. 183. He also discovered that, while a small particle of a paramagnetic substance is attracted by a magnetic pole, a small fragment of a diamagnetic substance is repelled. On testing the polarity of a

Fig. 183.

diamagnetic substance placed in the magnetic field, he found that the induced poles showed opposite polarity to those of a paramagnetic, a pole of like name being next to either inducing pole.

Faraday discovered that liquids and gases are, some para- and others dia-magnetic. To show the action of magnetism on liquids, he placed a drop of the liquid in a very thin watch-glass supported between the poles of the electro-magnet. On making contact with the battery, the shape of the drop was altered. If a paramagnetic, the drop was flattened, being drawn along the lines of force; if a diamagnetic, the drop was heaped up by the repulsion of the poles and made more convex (see Fig. 184).

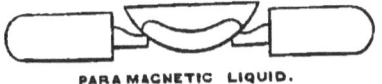
PARAMAGNETIC LIQUID.

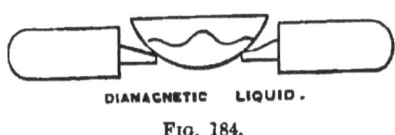
DIAMAGNETIC LIQUID.
Fig. 184.

To test the magnetism of a gas, he allowed it to escape from a fine circular orifice between the magnetic poles, and found that if paramagnetic it spread out like a fish-tail burner along the lines of force, and if diamagnetic it spread out across them.

A simple way of explaining the behaviour of diamagnetic bodies depends on the magnetism of the air surrounding them. Oxygen, at any rate, is a moderately strong paramagnetic, and any substance less strongly paramagnetic than oxygen, when immersed in it, would behave as a diamagnetic. For under the induction of the magnetic field we should have, at say the nominally north pole, a separation of north-polar magnetism on the solid, and at the same time a separation of south-polar magnetism in the oxygen in contact with it. If, then, the paramagnetism of the oxygen be the stronger, the south pole induced in the oxygen would overpower the north pole induced in the solid, and we should have effectively a south pole. In this way the general behaviour of diamagnetics can be explained.

All diamagnetics have only very feeble magnetic properties, and their demonstration requires a very strong electro-magnet. With a moderate magnet, it is possible to show that a bar of bismuth, carefully prepared without contact with iron tools, sets equatorially when freely suspended by a silk fibre between the poles of the electro-magnet, as in Fig. 183. A drop of chloride of iron, or any iron salt (all of which are for liquids powerfully paramagnetic), when placed in a watch-glass, and laid between the poles, can be seen slightly to alter its convexity when the current is passed. This is most easily observed by watching the reflection in the drop of a window bar or gas flame.

191. Electro-magnetic Toys.—On the property of electro-magnets suddenly acquiring, losing, or reversing their magnetic properties with changes of the current, many contrivances are made, some mere toys, and others very useful practical applications. One of the simplest depends on the earth's directive effect on a magnet. If an electro-magnet be pivoted on its centre, and a current transmitted, it will try to set north and south. If, immediately on passing the meridian, the current in the wire is reversed, the magnet will move onward, and try to set itself in the opposite direction; and if a similar reversal of current be made each half revolution, the rotation will be continuous. This is carried into practice by winding wire round a long thin iron rod, which is pivoted in the centre of a wooden cup, the terminals of the wire projecting downwards into the cup. The cup is divided

Electro-Magnetism and Dynamics.

into two halves by a wooden partition, shown in plan in Fig. 186, of which each half is filled with mercury, the convexity of the surface causing it to stand at a higher level than the wooden partition. These two halves are connected with the poles of a battery of one or two cells. When the partition is in the magnetic meridian, and the wires terminating the electro-magnetic coil, just dip into the mercury but pass over the partition, its change of polarity at each half rotation keeps up a constant rotation.

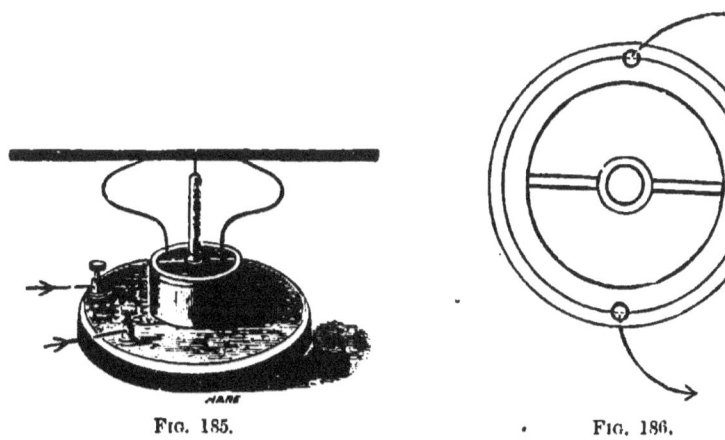

Fig. 185.   Fig. 186.

This commutator is used in a great number of electro-magnetic toys. On placing it axially between the poles of a permanent magnet, a short electro-magnet (Fig. 187, *a*), whose terminals dip into the commutator cup, can be made to rotate with great rapidity. If the partition be placed in the equator of the permanent magnet, a cage (Fig. 187, *b*) consisting of vertical wires pivoted on its middle, one half dipping into each half of the mercury cup, will keep up a constant rotation, as is easily seen by considering the motion of the conductor in the field of magnetic force, traversed by a current in one half

T

upwards, in the other downwards. Similarly a continuous coil of wire (Fig. 187, c) pivoted between the poles will rotate when the current is passed, this being an electro-magnet without a core.

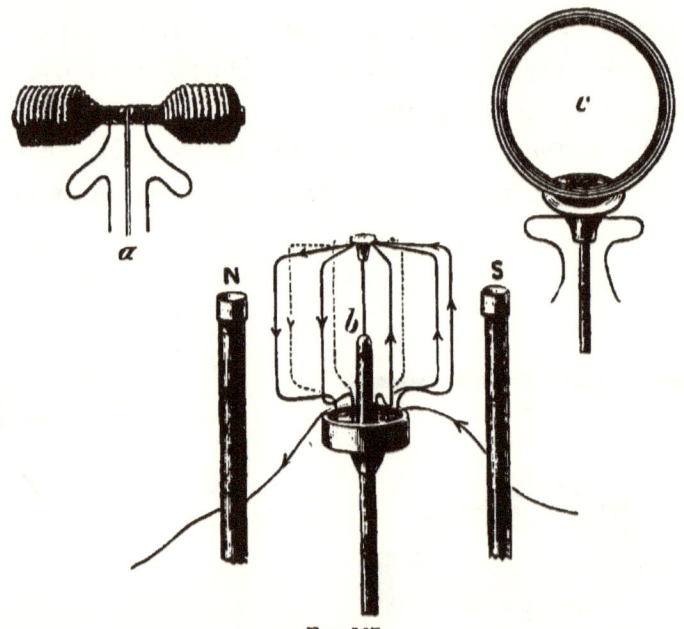

Fig. 187.

Sometimes the permanent magnet is replaced by an external coil of wire to carry the current, and we have the inner coil rotating continuously. This we may explain either by the electro-magnetic action of the two coils on each other, or by the attractions and repulsions of parallel and inclined currents on Ampère's principle. If the outer coil be free to move, but its terminals dip into a fixed central cup and annulus of mercury, in connection with the battery, while a commutating cup rotates with it, into which the terminals of the inner coil dip, the two coils will continue rotating rapidly in opposite directions. This arrangement is shown in Fig. 188.

Chap. V.] *Electro- Magnetism and Dynamics.* 291

192. Electromotors.—On similar principles have been constructed a great number of electromotors, intended by their

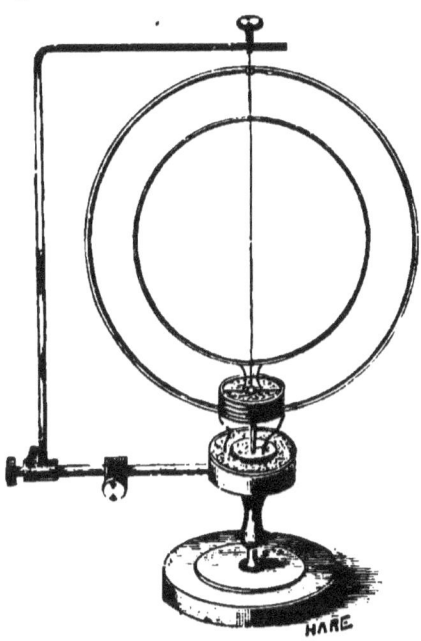

FIG. 188.

inventors to replace steam by electricity as prime motive power. None of them have as yet come into more than limited use, owing chiefly to their great expensiveness compared with steam-engines. Thus, weight for weight, zinc is fifty times as expensive as coal, and it appears that only about as much work can be obtained from a pound of zinc used through the medium of an electro-magnetic engine, as from a pound of coal used in a steam-engine. When electricity is generated by steam power, and either distributed by wires or stored in secondary batteries, it is probable that electromotors will be employed much more widely for a variety of domestic purposes, as well as for driving locomotives in underground railways, and doing work in places where the products of combustion of coal render the use of steam-engines unsuitable.

The first-made electromotors were obviously derived from the action of the piston in a steam-engine, masses of soft iron being attracted by electro-magnets, which were destroyed at the end of the stroke by automatic contact breakers; and the backwards and forwards motion so produced was converted into circular motion by the ordinary beam-and-crank arrangement. The short distance through which an electro-magnet exerts its power necessitated a very short stroke, introducing mechanical difficulties. Models on this principle are common.

Another form consists of masses of soft iron arranged on the circumference of a wheel, round which are arranged a number of fixed electro-magnets, having their poles very near its circumference. These electro-magnets are made when the piece of soft iron is approaching the magnet, and unmade when immediately opposite to it. Thus each mass of soft iron, when within about twenty degrees of an electro-magnet, and approaching it, receives a pull which is sufficient to send it on to within twenty degrees of the next magnet. To this class belong Froment's engine, of which the sketch (Fig. 189) represents a model. The arrangement for throwing the magnets alternately in and out of circuit consists of a wheel of eight projecting teeth revolving with the rotating wheel. Each projecting tooth, on coming in contact with a spring, makes contact in the battery circuit, and so makes the two electro-magnets.

Griscomb's Motor is a modern form of motor, weighing only two or three pounds, and capable, when worked with four or five Grove cells, of turning a sewing-machine, or a small saw.

Chap. V.] *Electro- Magnetism and Dynamics..* 293

Its principle is that of a moveable coil rotating within a fixed coil. The wires of each coil are wound on an iron framework, making a long narrow coil like Siemens' armature, the

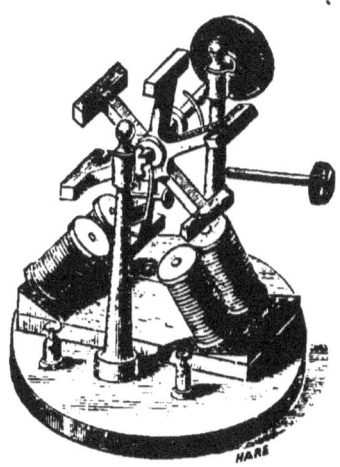

Fig. 189.

two opposite edges of the iron being north and south polar when the current is passing. The inner coil is furnished with a commutator, which reverses the current as soon as

Fig. 190.

opposite poles of the inner and outer coils are opposed. The general appearance of the machine is shown (Fig. 190), in which A represents the outer coil of wires, B one pole of the fixed electro-magnet made by them, and C the commutating arrangement by which the inner coil has the current reversed each half revolution. Fig. 191 (i) shows the inner coil (D), whose terminals are attached to the two halves of the spindle (E), which are carefully insulated from each other. In

Fig. 191.

Fig. 191 (ii) the commutator is shown in plan, the current being transmitted to the inner coil through the springs F and G, which carry the friction rollers, working on the commutator E.

The battery current enters at H, passes by F to E, through the inner coil back to the upper half of E, on by G to K, from

Chap. V.] Electro-Magnetism and Dynamics. 295

K through the outer coils to L, and from L back by a binding-screw to the battery.

193. The Electric Bell.—The next useful application of electro-magnetism is shown in the electric bell, now widely used for domestic and other purposes. The construction and working of the bell is easily understood from the diagram (Fig. 192). The bell is an ordinary metal dome-shaped bell (A), and

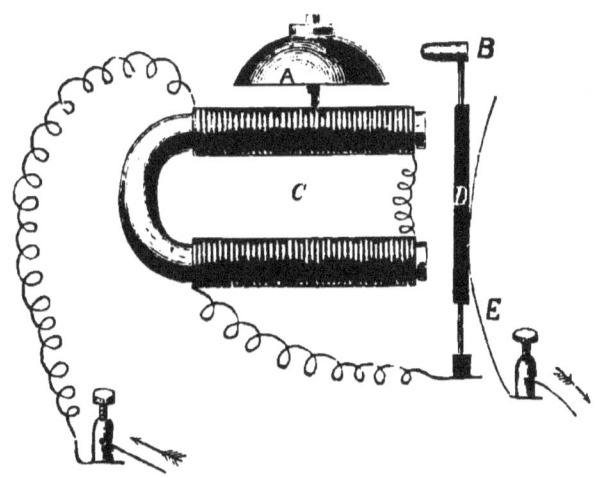

FIG. 192.

the clapper (B) is moved by the electro-magnet (C). The clapper is held by a spring, which has a piece of soft iron (D) attached to it, this piece of soft iron acting as the armature of the electro-magnet.[1] As soon as the current passes (in the direction shown by the arrows), the electro-magnet is made, and attracts the armature, which carries with it the clapper, causing it to strike the bell; the elasticity of the spring causes a recoil of the clapper and prevents a dead sound. The instant, however, that the armature is drawn forward, it ceases to press the spring (E), and contact is by that means

[1] In the instrument D is brought very near to the poles of the magnet.

broken, the magnet is unmade, and the elasticity of the spring carries the armature away from the magnet again, re-making contact with the battery, and setting up a vibratory motion in the clapper, which causes the bell to continue ringing.

The battery usually consists of two or three Leclanché cells, and contact is made at a distance by pushing a small button by which contact is made between two metal plates in the frame-work of the button.

194. The Electric Telegraph.—The most important application of these principles of electro-magnetism is found in the Electric Telegraph, which we must now briefly describe.

The earliest attempts at telegraphy consisted in organising a code of signals by the discharge of a Leyden jar through a circuit, which would cause a spark or series of sparks to be seen at the distant station. This was abandoned, because it was found impossible to secure insulation in the circuit in all weathers for electricity of high potential. Soon after Oersted's discovery of the deflection of a magnet by a current, it was seen that, by passing a current through a circuit, a magnet at a distant station might be deflected. At first it was proposed to use twenty-six wires and twenty-six magnets, each representing one letter of the alphabet. It was soon seen that by a properly arranged code of signals two wires and two magnets were sufficient—one to show deflections to the right, and another deflections to the left; and, still later, it was found that one needle, by reversing the current, was sufficient to supply all signals required.

Formerly each magnet used required two wires to make a complete circuit for the transmission of the current between two places, but now one of the two is replaced by the earth. The ends of the wire at both stations are simply connected with a metal plate sunk in permanently damp earth, which, with the line wire, completes the circuit.

The essential parts in any system of telegraph are therefore —(1) the line joining the two stations; (2) the battery; (3) the communicator; (4) the indicator—the last two at least being at both stations, and different in all the systems of telegraphy.

195. **The Line for Land or Marine Telegraph.**—The character of the line depends on the conditions under which it is to be used. If a land line, it may be either overhead or underground; but if it passes under the sea or a large river, some form of cable is used.

The overhead wires, seen in all parts of this country, are made of galvanised iron, $\frac{1}{6}$ inch in diameter (No. 8, B.W.G.). The iron is coated by electrolysis with a thin layer of zinc, which, being the more oxidisable metal, protects the iron from rust. The external zinc is coated by a rust or oxide, but since zinc-oxide is insoluble in water, it protects the interior from attack by the weather. In towns, where a large amount of sulphur is set free and brought down as acid in the rain, the oxide is soon destroyed, and the iron rusts away. To prevent this, wires in smoky neighbourhoods should be painted. This wire has to be insulated, and must therefore be kept free from all contact with buildings and trees. At intervals of from 90 to 100 yards, for a straight wire, it is supported on a larch pole 5 or 6 inches in diameter by porcelain or glass supports. These insulating supports, one form of which is seen in section (Fig. 193), consist of a double umbrella for throwing off the rain, and preventing surface leakage of electricity by interposing as great a distance as possible between the wire and the supporting post. When the wire has to be carried into buildings or under ground, it is carefully coated with a waterproof insulating material, generally gutta-percha.

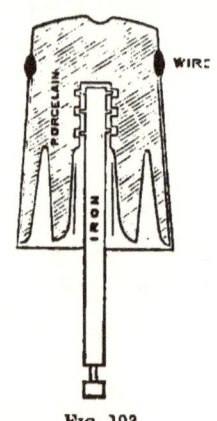

Fig. 193.

For marine telegraphy the conditions are very different. We need a very complete insulation, through which water under the enormous pressure at the bottom of deep sea will not force its way; and also great strength to withstand the strain brought on the wire in laying it down in deep water, and in lying, as it often must, on steep slopes on the sea bottom. The cables most commonly used consist, not of a single conducting wire, but of a spirally twisted strand of six or seven copper wires (Fig. 194), each about 1 mm. ($\frac{1}{30}$th inch) diameter. These are the core, and are surrounded by alternate layers of gutta-percha and Chatterton's compound (a mixture of tar, resin, and gutta-percha), which form the insulator proper. Round the insulator is a layer of hemp, and round this again a protecting sheath of about ten or twelve steel wires, each coated with hemp. Near the shore end the sheath of hemp and steel wire is made of very great thickness, as a protection against breakage by the force of the waves when in storm, but when the depth of about 100 fathoms is reached a much thinner cable may be used.

196. The Battery.—The battery most in use in this country is some form of Daniell's. They are fitted up in

Chap. V.] *Electro- Magnetism and Dynamics.* 299

troughs of about twenty cells, and will run for a considerable time without further attention than filling up with water when

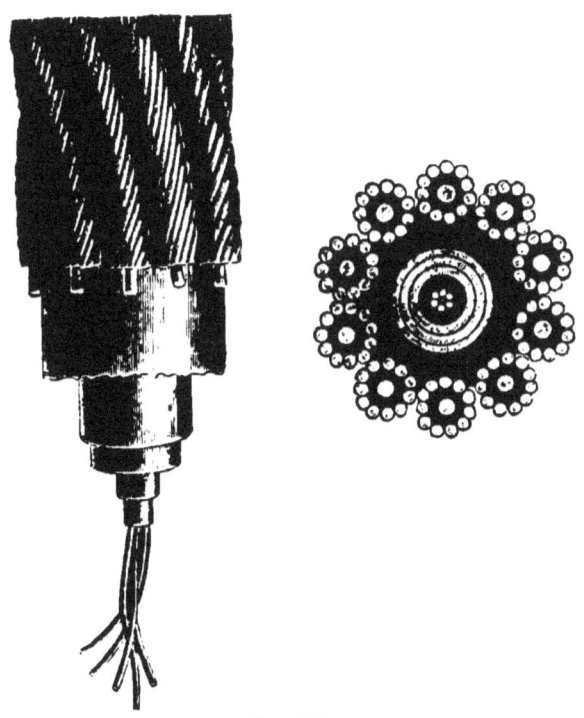

Fig. 194.

it has evaporated. They are the most constant of all cells, and therefore best suited for circuits where almost continuous work has to be done. On other circuits some variety of the simple zinc-copper cell is still used, and Leclanché's are gradually coming into use. In what was called the magneto-telegraph, the battery was replaced by some form of magneto-machine which generated the current.

197. The Single Needle Telegraph Communicator.—This consists of a commutator by which the current can be rapidly changed in direction or put out of circuit when no message is being sent, at the same time allowing a current to pass through it from the distant end of the line.

Fig. 195.

The diagram (Fig. 195) shows such a commutator. It consists of two brass springs, having ivory buttons on their ends. When at rest they press upwards against two metal

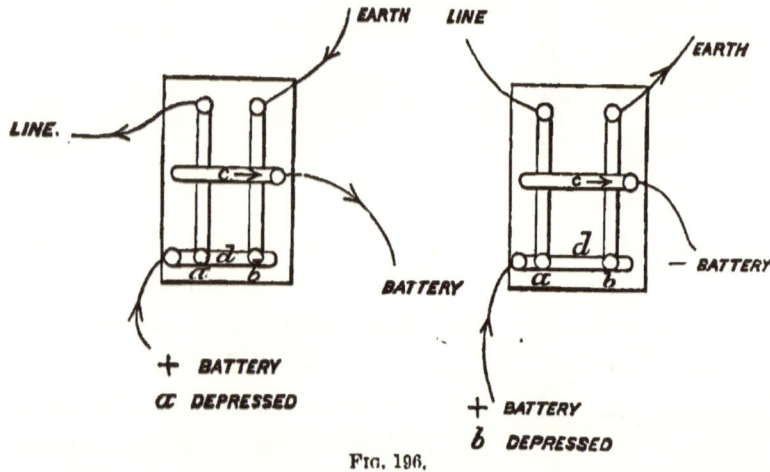

Fig. 196.

studs in the metal cross-piece. When either is depressed, it is released from contact with this cross-piece, but presses on one of the two metal studs on another metal cross-piece, which passes under the ivory knobs. This throws the battery into circuit, and, examining the arrows in the two figures (Fig. 196), it will be seen that the current runs in opposite directions through the line, according as a or b is depressed.

When a is pushed down, the current goes in order: battery — a — line — earth — b — c — battery.

When b is pushed down, the current goes in order: battery — b — earth — line — a — c — battery.

When neither a nor b is depressed, a message will enter from the line, and follow the course: line — a — c — b — earth, or *vice versa*.

Fig. 197.

198. The Single Needle Indicator.—This consists of a coil of wire (A, Fig. 197) similar to that used for an astatic galvanometer. Its resistance is made proportional to the line resistance, consisting, for a short line, of a few turns of moderately stout wire, and, for a long line, of numerous turns of very thin wire. The coils are placed vertically, and within them hangs a magnetic needle, also having its axis vertical. This needle (B) is deflected right or left according to the direction of the current, and its movement is shown by a long pointer (C) attached to it by a horizontal rod which passes through the coil and registers the movements of the needle on a dial outside. The motion of the pointer is usually checked by two stops on the dial. (The dial is not shown in the figure, being on the front of the instrument.)

199. Arrangement of Apparatus at Telegraph Station.—The arrangement of these parts at each station can be understood from the diagram (Fig. 198), which shows either the sending or receiving station.

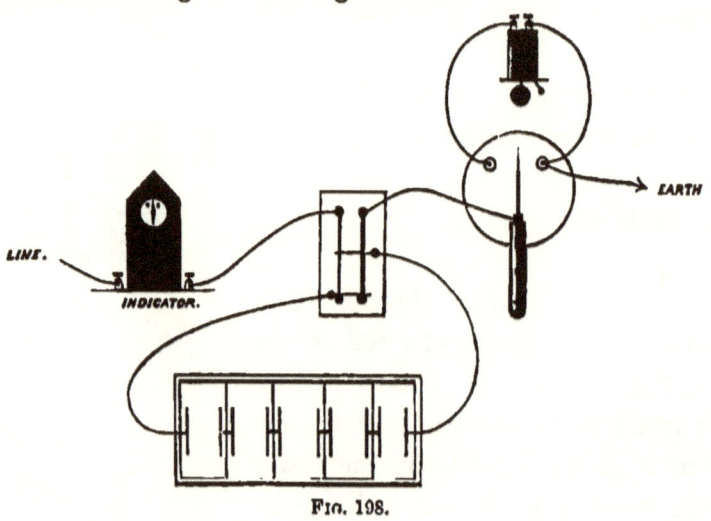

Fig. 198.

In addition to the essential parts described, there is usually an electric bell at each station to call the attention of the clerk when a message is to be sent. This can easily be done by a contact breaker, one branch of which contains the bell, placed at any part of the line, between the communicator and the earth, as shown in diagram (Fig. 198). The clerk, when he leaves the telegraph-room, turns on his bell, and any signal made by the clerk at the further end will then cause the bell to ring.

200. Codes of Telegraph Signals.—The code of

signals consists in denoting each letter, numeral, or sign by a certain number of deflections of the needle to the right, and a certain number to the left, those letters which occur most frequently being denoted by the fewest strokes. In the printing telegraph, which we consider next, the same code is used, the stroke to the left being denoted by a dot (·), and the stroke to the right by a dash (—). The alphabet on the two systems is given side by side :—

	Single Needle.	Morse's System.		Single Needle.	Morse's System.
A	╲╱	· —	N	╱╲	— ·
B	╱╲╲╲	— · · ·	O	╱╱╱	— — —
C	╱╲╱╲	— · — ·	P	╲╱╱╲	· — — ·
D	╱╲╲	— · ·	Q	╱╱╲╱	— — · —
E	╲	·	R	╲╱╲	· — ·
F	╲╲╱╲	· · — ·	S	╲╲╲	· · ·
G	╱╱╲	— — ·	T	╱	—
H	╲╲╲╲	· · · ·	U	╲╲╱	· · —
I	╲╲	· ·	V	╲╲╲╱	· · · —
J	╲╱╱╱	· — — —	W	╲╱╱	· — —
K	╱╲╱	— · —	X	╱╲╲╱	— · · —
L	╲╱╲╲	· — · ·	Y	╱╲╱╱	— · — —
M	╱╱	— —	Z	╱╱╲╲	— — · ·

For figures the following code is used :—

	Single Needle.	Morse.
0	╱╱╱╱╱	— — — — —
1	╲╱╱╱╱	· — — — —
2	╲╲╱╱╱	· · — — —
3	╲╲╲╱╱	· · · — —

	Single Needle.	Morse.
4	\\\\/	. . . . — —
5	\\\\	. . . . .
6	/\\\	— . . . .
7	//\\	— — . . .
8	///\	— — — . .
9	////	— — — — .

This code will well repay the trouble involved in learning. Depending on two signals of great simplicity, it has already received various applications, and bids fair to become the universal alphabet in cases where an ordinary written alphabet is unsuitable. It can be made either visible by the movements of a single finger, or audible by the use of two sounds of different pitch, the longer movements or deeper sounds representing the dashes, and the shorter movements or higher sounds the dots. These considerations point to it, amongst other things, as likely to supersede the deaf and dumb alphabet at present in use.

*201. **The Morse Key.**—In Morse's printing telegraph the message is written at the receiving station either by a style indenting a paper strip, like a tape, or actually printed in ink on the tape by contact with a narrow inked roller.

The communicator is a simple contact breaker, called the Morse key. It consists of a brass lever (A) working on a fulcrum in the middle, with a metal stud towards one end, and an adjustable screw (D) at the other end. On depressing the alternate ends of the lever, contact is made with two metal studs (B and C) on the base (Fig. 199). When the ivory knob attached to A is not depressed a spring holds D constantly in contact with C. E and F are binding screws connected with the fulcrum and the stud C, and there is a similar one on the opposite side connected with the stud B. By means of these screws, B is connected with the local battery, E with the line, and F with the indicator.

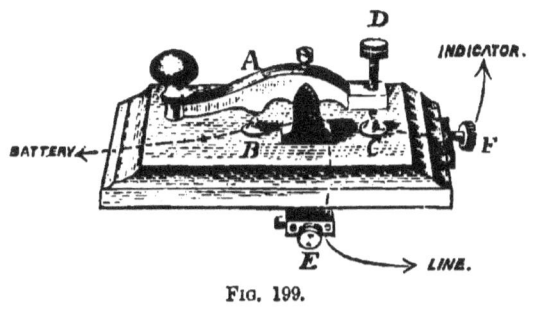

Fig. 199.

In receiving a message from the distant station, the key is left alone, the current passing from the line through $E-A-C-$ indicator – earth.

In sending a message A is depressed, breaking contact with the home indicator at C, and introducing the battery current at B, which now proceeds by the course, battery $-B-A-E-$line, to the distant indicator, and makes on the indicator a dot or dash according to the length of time during which the key is held depressed.

*202. **The Morse Indicator.**—The Morse indicator is made in a variety of forms, but consists essentially of two parts,—a train of clockwork, by which the paper tape is payed out between two friction rollers from a large horizontal or vertical wheel, on which it is coiled, and an electro-magnetic arrangement by which dots and dashes are made on the strip as it passes, according to the will of the distant operator (Fig. 200). The coil of paper on the vertical wheel is shown at *A*, and *B*, *C* are the friction rollers between which it passes by the action of the clockwork in the case (*D*), which can be started or stopped at will by removing or applying a detent. *F* is an electro-magnet round which the current from the line passes. It has a soft iron core, and is wound with numerous turns of fine wire, having a resistance which varies

Fig. 200.

from 50 to 500 ohms, according to the conditions of the circuit. Opposite the poles of the electro-magnet is a soft iron armature carried on a brass lever, which turns round a pivot, and has its motion upwards checked by a screw (*a*), against which it is held when no current is passing by a spring (*b*). The lever carries on its further end a steel style, pointing towards the tape, and so adjusted that when the soft iron armature is attracted by the electro-magnet, the style presses gently on the paper and makes an indentation as long as the current is passing. In modern instruments the style is replaced by a narrow roller, which turns in a vessel containing printers' ink, and, when drawn up by the magnet, marks with its edge the paper passing in front of it, thus permanently printing the message sent.

*203. **The Morse Relay.**—In long land lines the current becomes much weakened by leakage, due to imperfect insulation, and it is not strong enough to work the Morse indicator. In this case there is used what is called a relay, which at each make or break of contact in the line circuit makes or breaks contact in a new battery circuit, in which the indicator is included.

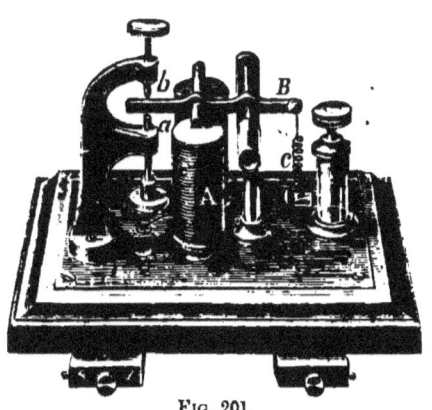

FIG. 201.

In the diagram (Fig. 201), A is an electro-magnet through the coils of which the original current passes to earth. The soft iron armature is carried by a brass arm which is lightly suspended on a pivot (B), and has its motion controlled by the two screws, a, b, of which b is insulated by having its point of ivory. When no current is passing, the arm is held by the weak spiral spring c, in contact with b. On passing the current the armature is attracted and brought into con-

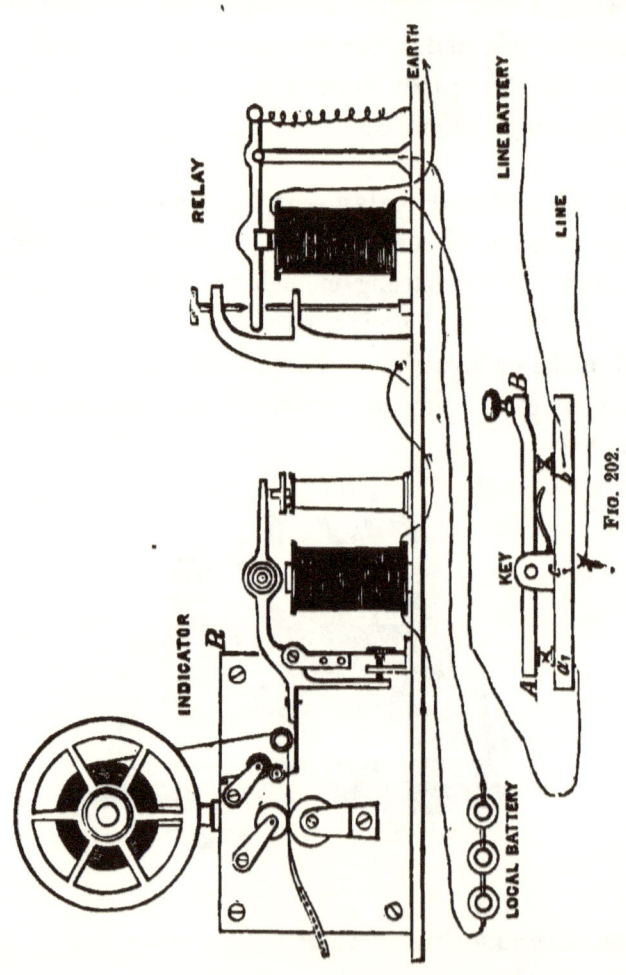

Fig. 202.

tact with a, thus completing the circuit in the local battery, in which circuit the indicator is included. Each time that the current from the line passes through the relay, the local battery transmits a current through the electro-magnet of the indicator, the two working therefore completely in sympathy.

In the case of long land lines there are a series of "relay stations" where the message is not received and retransmitted, but passed on with renewed energy by means of a relay. One terminal of the local battery is to earth, and the other is connected through the relay with the continued line. By this means there is a continuous telegraph, without retransmission by hand between London and Teheran, there being five relay stations on the road.

The arrangement at each station of key, relay, and indicator can be understood from the diagram (Fig. 202), remembering that the same must be repeated at each end of the line.

*204. **Morse Sounder.**—The peculiar click made by the armature either of the indicator or relay against its stops enables an expert clerk to take down the message by ear as it passes, only comparing afterwards with the tape to insure accuracy. This depends on a slight difference in the click, according as it is made by a momentary contact (for a dot), or a prolonged contact (for a dash). On this principle is constructed the Morse Sounder, which is identical with the relay in construction, but much smaller, and is used for military telegraphy, or under conditions where economy of apparatus is important.

*205. **Electrostatic Induction in Cables.**—As soon as marine cables of great length came into use it was found that signals transmitted by them suffered a remarkable retardation, the making contact with the battery for an instant at one end causing at the other a gradual rising and sinking again of the current, occupying several seconds. This would make the rate of signalling very slow were it necessary to wait till each signal had completely died away before transmitting the next.

The retardation is easily explained if we remember that the core of the cable forms the inner coat of a Leyden jar of enormous capacity, of which the conducting sea-water is the outer coat. The effect of contact with the battery terminal is to bring the core of the cable to a potential which near the battery, nearly equals the potential of the battery terminal. This can only be done by charging the Leyden jar. In the case of a long cable this charging takes a finite time, and on breaking contact, the Leyden jar is discharged through the receiving galvanometer, and this again occupies about the same time.

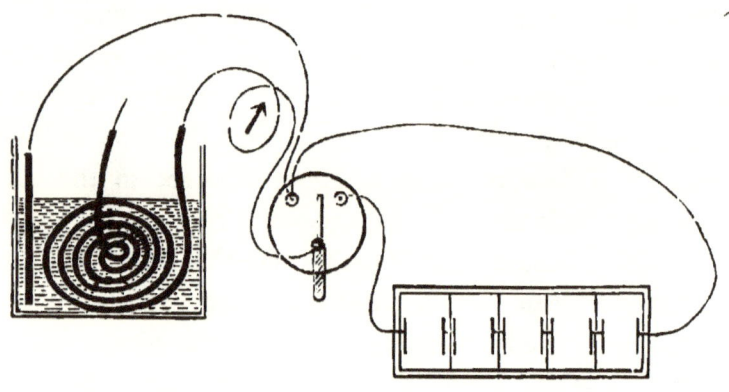

Fig. 203.

The effect can be illustrated by the apparatus of Fig. 203, which consists of a coil of cotton-covered wire, 20 or 30 yards long, and about a tenth of an inch in diameter, coiled into a solid coil, and afterwards dipped in melted paraffin to perfect insulation. This represents the cable, and is placed in a vessel of water, with one terminal exposed and insulated.

The other terminal is connected through a galvanometer with the contact breaker. Of the other two terminals of the contact breaker, one is connected both with a battery terminal and with a strip of metal sunk in the water, which represents the *Earth* of the telegraph battery, and also with one terminal of a battery. The other terminal of the battery is connected simply with the third terminal of the contact breaker. On turning the contact breaker handle to the left, so as to bring the tongue into contact with the right-hand terminal, the battery will charge the core of the wire coil, and will cause a momentary deflection in the delicate galvanometer. This is of interest, showing us that the magnetic effects of a current are not confined to cases where the electricity has a complete circuit in the ordinary sense, but accompany any displacement whatever of the electricity. Quite instantaneously the charging current will cease, and the galvanometer return to its zero. On turning the handle to the right, the battery is thrown out, but the galvanometer is deflected for an instant in the opposite direction to the deflection on charging, showing that the Leyden jar formed by the core is being discharged through it.

The effect on the galvanometer is very much increased by using, in place of the wire coils and water, a condenser made of several hundred sheets of tinfoil, separated by paper immersed in melted paraffin and pressed together when hot. The alternate sheets are brought together by projecting flaps, and connected with the two terminals of the condenser. By means of a large number of such condensers an artificial cable can be made, and all the effects of a real cable exactly reproduced.

*206. Thomson's Marine Galvanometer.—To overcome the difficulty presented by the very slow rate of cable signalling, Sir W. Thomson invented his Marine Galvanometer, a variety of the reflecting galvanometer, in which the oscillations of the needle are damped, the needle simply deflecting right or left when a current is transmitted, and returning to its zero without making oscillations about it, as in the common form of the instrument. This of course does not obviate the retardation of the signals noticed above, but enables the clerks by practice to interpret the indications of the galvanometer without waiting for each signal to die away before another is transmitted, each observation depending not only on the signal last sent, but on the twenty or thirty preceding it.

*207. Thomson's Syphon Recorder.—This is an instrument by which the messages sent through a cable are made self-recording. It consists of a tape payed out vertically, much as in the Morse Indicator. Opposite the tape is a fine capillary glass tube bent somewhat in the form of the letter S, whose upper end hangs in a vessel containing ink, and whose lower end is opposite the middle of the tape. The ink vessel is electrified by a small frictional machine, worked by the clockwork which pays out the tape; and, according to the principle of the electrical watering-pot (Art. 93), the ink will spurt out from the tube on to the tape, making a straight line along it if the syphon remain stationary. The syphon tube is attached by fine silk threads to a peculiar kind of galvanometer, by which it is deflected right or left according to the direction and magnitude of the current sent through the cable. This galvanometer consists of a coil of fine wire, through which the cable current is sent, and which hangs suspended between the poles of a powerful permanent magnet. This coil, owing to its magnetic properties when traversed by a current, is deflected in one direction or the other, according to the direction of the currents, and to an amount directly proportional to the current strength. By means of the attached silk threads, the movement of the syphon tube is made proportional to the movement of the galvanometer coil, and the syphon recorder therefore gives a permanent register of every change in strength or direction of the line current.

*208. **Step by Step, or ABC Telegraph.**—There is a great variety of other telegraph machines used in various parts of the world, including some in which the message is actually printed in ordinary type. These depend on more

Fig. 204.

complex machinery, but involve no new principle in electricity. The only other form we shall refer to here is the ABC telegraph, specially adapted for the use of persons who are not familiar with any telegraphic code. The message is received on a dial marked with the twenty-six letters of the alphabet, a needle rotating always in the same direction, and pausing at each letter which the distant operator wishes to transmit. This, and all other "step by step" telegraphs, require two parts,—a *manipulator* at the sending station, and an *indicator* at the receiving station, with, of course, the usual line and battery.

The Manipulator (Fig. 204) consists of a dial marked with the letters of the alphabet and two additional spaces, which can be used to denote the beginning and ending of a sentence. Over the letters moves an arm, rotating about the centre of the dial, having attached to it behind the dial a toothed wheel, the number of teeth being half the number of letter and other spaces round the dial. The teeth, by pressing a spring, make contact in the line battery, when the arm is opposite each *alternate* letter.

The indicator (Fig. 205) contains an electro-magnet, furnished with a soft iron armature. This armature carries a long arm, whose end is formed to act as an escapement against a toothed wheel having the same number of teeth as the wheel in the manipulator. The toothed wheel carries an index hand, which moves over a dial whose divisions correspond to those in the manipulator. Each time the current passes the armature is attracted, and the detent (Fig. 205, *a*) by its wedge-like action pushes on one tooth of the wheel, and, on breaking, retains the next against the flat end of the wedge. Thus in the making and breaking, the index hand passes over two letters, just as in the manipulator.

To call attention to the instrument, a bell is attached to the indicator (not shown in drawing), which can be put in or out of circuit by a simple contact breaker.

There is also on the indicator a small button moving a lever, by which the index hand can be moved over the letters successively without employment of the current, by which the manipulator and indicator can be brought to the same letter initially.

Fig. 205.

To send a message, the operator turns the manipulator arm till it is opposite the letter he wishes to transmit, at which he makes a pause. Each letter he passes over will be passed over by the index hand in the indicator, which will also pause at the letter over which he causes the manipulator to make a pause, and so a message, letter by letter, can be spelt out. The process is very slow, as it is often necessary to turn the manipulator round nearly a whole circumference between two letters, B and A, for instance, as it will only work in one direction. The manipulator, again, must be moved very slowly, as otherwise it will often pass over two letters before the detent in the indicator has had time to set more than one free, throwing the two parts of the instrument out of correspondence.

*209. **Ampère's Theory of Magnetism.**—On observing the intimate connection between a solenoid and a magnet, Ampère introduced a hypothetical theory of the construction of a magnet. He assumes that each molecule of magnetic matter has an electric current constantly circulating round it. When the body is unmagnetized these currents are in all directions, and neutralise each other's effect on external magnetism. The act of magnetization consists in setting the currents round all the molecules in parallel planes and in the same rotational direction. Thus any section across a magnet shows a series of currents rotating round the molecules (Fig. 206). Assuming these currents all of the same strength, the current in two consecutive molecules will be equal and opposite along the faces in contact, and therefore will neutralise each other, while the currents in the outermost molecules being in contact with the air are not neutralised, but give a continuous current, or series of currents, round the outside of the magnet. These currents constitute a solenoid of which the successive turns are infinitely near together, and are, according to Ampère, the source of its magnetic properties,—the Ampèrian currents being right-handed, or in direction of the hands of a watch to an observer looking down on the south pole, and left-handed to an observer looking down on the north pole.

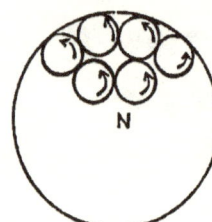

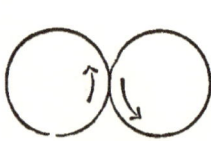

Fig. 206.

Chap. V.] *Electro-Magnetism and Dynamics.* 317

All the relations between a magnet and electric currents can, by means of the Ampèrian hypothesis, be reduced to the actions of currents on each other, but they can be easily explained by actions in the magnetic fields of the magnets, demonstrable by experiment, while the Ampèrian currents are only hypothetical.

210. Reiss' Telephone.—That the magnetization of a bar is accompanied by some molecular movement is proved by the magnetic tick which accompanies its magnetization and demagnetization. The sound can be easily heard by

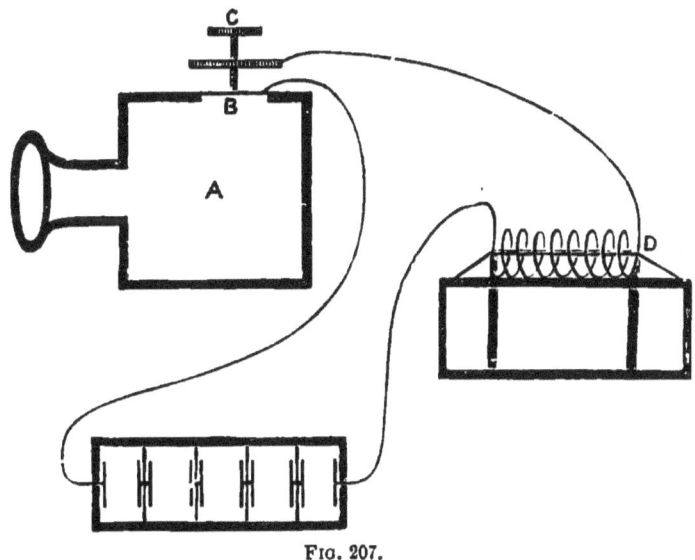

FIG. 207.

stretching a soft iron wire, about 1 metre long and a millimetre in diameter, over a sounding-board (Fig. 207 *D*, shows a section), and surrounding the wire, through nearly its whole length by a narrow glass tube, which is supported out of contact with the wire. Round the glass tube is closely wound moderately stout insulated copper wire two or three layers in depth. On connecting the ends of the copper wire with the terminals of a battery of four or five Grove cells, and placing any contact breaker in the circuit, a sound is heard from the wire each time that contact is made or broken.

On this principle Reiss has constructed a telephone capable of transmitting musical notes, but not the tones of the human voice. The notes are sung or sounded through a mouthpiece into a box (A), whose upper surface is closed by a thin sheet of metal (B) stretched tightly. Near its centre is adjusted a screw (C) whose point all but touches the metal membrane, and does touch it at each vibration of the membrane, when a note is sounded into the mouthpiece. The note depends simply on the number of vibrations per second, and each of these vibrations makes and breaks contact in a voltaic circuit. This circuit includes the electro-magnet D, which gives the magnetic tick for each make and break of contact, and reproduces the note sounded.

CHAPTER VI.

CURRENT INDUCTION.

211. Work done in the Electro-magnetic Field at Expense of the Current.—In the experiments of the last chapter, where movements of conductors or magnets take place under electro-magnetic force, it appears from theory that the work done during the movement is accompanied by a diminution of the current while the movement lasts. This falling off in most cases is so small, compared to the total current passing, that it is rather difficult to show either by including a rough galvanometer in the main circuit, or a delicate one in a branch circuit. It can be shown by passing the current from five Grove cells continuously through two electro-magnets of horse-shoe form, and placing a delicate galvanometer in a branch circuit, the galvanometer of course being at considerable distance from the magnets. If the electro-magnets be now held, one immediately above the other, with contrary poles opposed at a distance of 1 or 2 inches, and the upper be allowed to fall on to the lower, a movement of the galvanometer will be noted, showing a slight momentary falling off of the current. On lifting up suddenly the upper magnet, and separating it from the lower, there will in the same way be seen a slight increase of the current.

*212. **Theoretical Explanation of foregoing Experiment.**—It will be worth while considering how the fall in the current is a source of energy. Let I be the current when the machine is at rest, and I' the current when the same machine is in motion. Let also E be E.M.F. of the battery, and R the resistance, which is the same in both cases. The energy given out from the battery is in the two cases EI and EI' (Art. 169), and the heat generated measured in mechanical work is RI^2 and RI'^2 (Art. 169) each per second. If T be the time in which a gram of zinc is consumed in the battery with current I, it will require a longer time, namely, $\frac{I}{I'}T$, when the current is I'. Hence the heat given out per gram of zinc consumed will be in the two cases RI^2T and $RI'^2 \times \frac{I}{I'}T$, and this latter is equal to $RII'T$, which is necessarily less than RI^2T, if I' is less than I. But the energy given out from the battery must in both cases be the same, since equal amounts of zinc are dissolved. Hence, when the machine is in motion there is less energy given out in heat than that abstracted from the battery by $R(I^2-II')T$ per gram of zinc used. This energy then does the work in the machine.

When work is done against electro-magnetic forces, the current is increased, the work done on the system being evolved from it as increased heat in the circuit.

213. **Induced Currents.**—Returning to the apparatus of Arts. 177 and 178, in which we have the movement of a magnet pole in the electro-magnetic field of a current, and of a current in the magnetic field of a magnet, we will replace the battery by a sensitive galvanometer, of course re-

moved to a distance from the magnet (Fig. 208). On rotating the magnet pole or the current by hand, the galvanometer shows a current, and the direction of the current changes with a change in the direction of rotation. We shall notice, if we examine the direction of the current, that it is opposite to the current which would have caused the actual rotation. These are called induced currents; they correspond with the falling off in the current noticed above, and may in fact be regarded in an algebraical sense as a falling off in the current, when that current is zero.

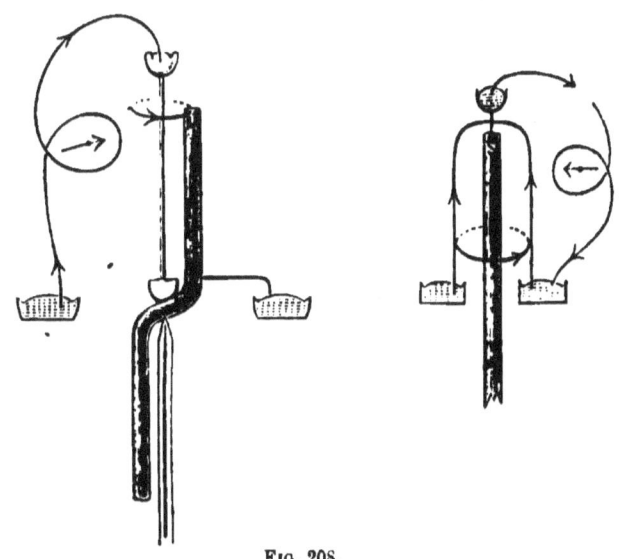

Fig. 208.

Since the induced current is opposite in direction to the current which would have caused the motion, it is clear that the electro-magnetic effect of the induced current is to oppose the motion taking place in the field. This is one case of Lenz's law, of which we will now give illustrations, by performing backwards some of the experiments of last chapter.

x

214. Current induced in a Coil by a Moving Pole.—Fit up in a circuit a coil of wire and a distant galvanometer, but no battery. On moving the pole of a bar magnet near the coil, a current is induced. The direction of the current is shown in Fig. 209 for a north pole approaching the coil. The current is seen to make the face of the coil towards the magnet north polar. Thus again the electro-magnetic effect of the current is seen to be such as would oppose the motion. On reversing either the direction of motion or the sign of the pole the current is reversed.

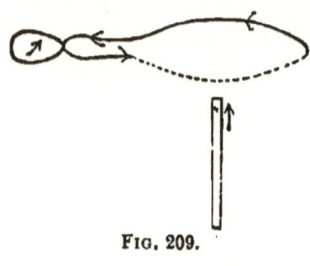

Fig. 209.

If the north pole be passed on through the coil, in retreating from its upper face it will induce a current, in the same direction as while approaching the lower face. This will continue as long as the influence of the north pole preponderates over that of the south—that is, until the middle of the bar has reached the coil. At this instant the current ceases momentarily, and then, if the movement be still continued, is reversed.

These principles explain the damping action noted above (Art. 206) in Thomson's Marine Galvanometer. The movement of the poles of the magnet, as it swings inside the coils, calls up a current which opposes the motion, and therefore "damps" the swing. By sufficiently increasing the number of turns in the galvanometer, the damping is so great as to cause the needle, when deflected from equilibrium, slowly to return to its zero without oscillating about it.

Current Induction.

215. Induced Current in Barlow's Wheel.—If in Barlow's wheel (Art. 179) the battery be replaced by a galvanometer (Fig. 210), and the wheel made to rotate, there will be a current induced in the circuit, the directions of rotation and of the current being shown by arrows. This current, if acting independently, would cause the wheel to rotate in the opposite direction.

FIG. 210.

216. Currents induced by Terrestrial Magnetism. —Delezenne's Circle (Fig. 211) is adapted to show the current induced in a wire coil under the induction of the earth's magnetism. It will be remembered that a coil carrying a current tends to set itself at right angles to the dip. A coil capable of rotation about a diameter, which is placed at right angles to the dip, will on continuous rotation be traversed by an induced current, whose direction is changed each time it reaches the position of equilibrium. If, then, by means of the spring commutator (Fig. 211, *a*), we change the direction of the current in the galvanometer relatively to its direction in the coils at each half revolution, we have a continuous current in the galvanometer, whose amount depends on the rapidity of rotation. We can by the mechanical arrangement shown set the instrument so that the axis of rotation is horizontal, vertical, or in any other position, in which cases the effective part of the earth's magnetism is the component at right angles to the axis of rotation; the induced current vanishing when the axis of rotation is parallel to the dip.

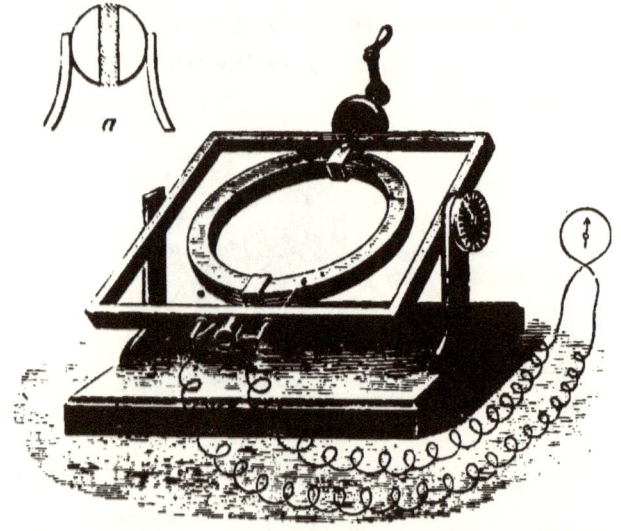

Fig. 211.

If we compare Delezenne's Circle with the coil of Fig. 187, *c*, placed in the magnetic field, we can see that the induced current is such as would cause the coil to rotate in the opposite direction. The expression of this result may be modified by adopting Faraday's conception of a finite number of lines of magnetic force. In the position of equilibrium the circuit contains the greatest number of lines of force (Art. 181), and as we rotate the circuit up towards that position, the number of lines of force enclosed by the circuit is increasing, and after passing it the number is diminishing. When the number of the earth's lines of force is increasing, the current will be found left-handed to the lines of force, and, when diminishing right-handed.

217. Current induced by moving Parallel Conductors.

—We have observed that parallel currents attract each other when in the same direction, and repel each other when in opposite directions. To show that these movements cause induced currents, take the pair of flat spirals of Art. 185, and connect one with the battery while the other hangs parallel to it, with its terminals attached to a galvanometer. On moving either spiral towards the other, or from the other, currents are induced in opposite directions, concurrent with the battery current when the spirals recede from each other, and opposite to it when they approach each other.

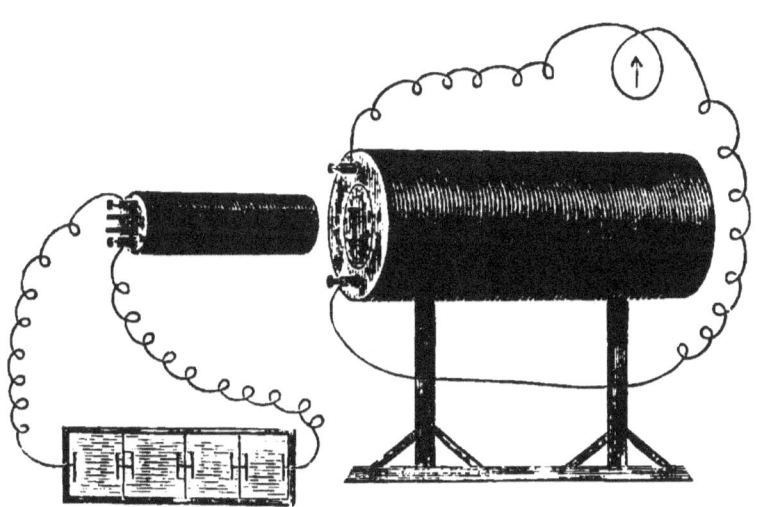

Fig. 212.

The same thing may be illustrated by thrusting a coil of wire (Fig. 212) carrying a current inside a hollow coil consisting of very many turns of fine wire with which a galvanometer alone is connected. When the spirals are approaching each other, the induced will be inverse or opposite to the battery current, but on withdrawing one from the other, the current will be direct or in the same direction as the battery current.

The effect is much increased if the inner coil has a soft iron core, making it an electro-magnet, since this enormously increases the strength of the magnetic field in which the movements are made.

218. Currents induced by changes in strength of the Magnetic Field.

—We will first show that an induced current passes through neighbouring conductors when a magnetic field is made or destroyed, by making or breaking contact in a battery circuit. Using the apparatus of the last experiment (Fig. 212), and placing the electro-magnet within the wire coil, it will be seen that a current passes in the galvanometer when contact is made or broken in the battery circuit. On making contact, the current is inverse, and on breaking it is direct.

These effects are also much increased by enclosing a soft iron core in the battery coil.

We may, with the same apparatus, illustrate changes in the strength of the magnetic field. For by short-circuiting the battery current we can leave the electro-magnet in a branch circuit of great or small resistance, and allow any part of the current we please to traverse the electro-magnet. Induced currents will be produced in the external coil whose directions will be similar to those just named.

In all the foregoing experiments we notice that the induced current tends, by its electro-magnetic effect, to oppose the change taking place in the field, for the direct induced current tends to strengthen the field when it is being weakened by the falling off of the battery current, and the inverse induced current tends to weaken the field when it is being strengthened by a rise in the battery current.

219. Currents induced in Electromotors.—On the same principles, it is clear that any form of electromotor may be used to generate a current by means of movements of the machinery brought about mechanically. This will even be true in motors such as Froment's and Griscomb's, where the movements depend entirely on electro-magnets; the residual magnetism in the soft iron cores being always sufficient to start a current, which then rises in compound interest ratio as the rotation continues. This is the principle of all the dynamo-machines now used for generating electricity for lighting and other purposes.

220. The Extra Current or Galvanic Spark.—On making and breaking the battery circuit, a bright spark is noticed to pass between the terminals at the instant of making and breaking. This cannot be due to the battery current, as it only occurs momentarily when that current is made or broken, and we shall find it has a much higher E.M.F. than the battery current itself. On including a large coil of wire or an electro-magnet in the circuit, the intensity of the spark is very much increased, causing a brilliant flash if contact be broken in a mercury cup.

This is no doubt the effect of an induced current in the conductor itself, which behaves in this respect just like any other conductor in the field, experiencing an induced inverse current on closing, and an induced direct current on breaking the battery current.

These currents were discovered by Faraday, and by him were called the inverse and direct extra current respectively.

To exhibit their direction by the galvanometer is not easy, as they occur with the battery current, in the same conductor. Faraday showed the direct extra current by arranging a circuit containing a battery and an electro-magnet (C in Fig. 213), and placing a galvanometer in a branch circuit AGB (by means of the mercury cups A and B),

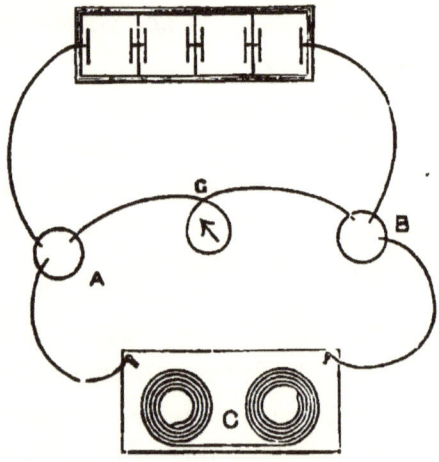

Fig. 213.

which was therefore traversed by a certain fraction of the battery current, causing the needle to deflect. By laying a piece of cork or a brass weight on the galvanometer card he blocked the needle, retaining the needle at zero, while the battery current was passing. Contact was broken by lifting the battery wire out of the mercury cup A or B, and the direct extra current passed round the closed circuit $ACBG$. Assuming the battery current to pass through the electromagnet in the direction ACB, and through the galvanometer in the direction AGB, the direct induced current traverses the galvanometer in the opposite direction to the battery current. On breaking contact, therefore, the needle swings away from its stop, thus proving the existence of the extra current.

The high E.M.F. of the extra current may be shown in a variety of ways. Thus, if the galvanometer in Fig. 213 be replaced by the two hands of the operator, one finger being placed on each cup, a sharp pricking sensation is felt whenever contact with the battery is made or broken in the mercury cups. This sensation is increased by rapidly making and breaking contact, as by rubbing the end of the battery wire over the surface of a file, one end of which is held in the mercury cup. That these effects are not due to the direct battery current is shown by passing it through the body, when no sensation whatever is produced. Next, replace the galvanometer by a voltameter. The battery must be reduced, if necessary, till no evolution of gas is caused in the branch circuit by the steady battery current. If, now, the contact be rapidly made and broken, small quantities of gas will be given off continuously from both plates.

The direct extra current has always much higher E.M.F. than the inverse, though the same amount of electricity must pass in both. This is why the spark on breaking is always much brighter than on making contact with the battery.

221. **Lenz's Law.**—All induced currents, such as we have been experimenting upon, obey the Law of Lenz, to which we have already alluded. It may be stated thus: *If either a conductor forming part of a closed circuit be moved in the magnetic field, or the field in which the conductor is placed undergo any change of strength, during the movement or change the conductor is traversed by a current, whose electro-magnetic effect is to oppose the movement of the conductor or the change in the field.*

The following are but cases of the general law, which we have already illustrated by experiment :—

(1) If a north pole approach a closed circuit, the induced current makes the face, opposite to the north pole, also north-polar, so as to resist the advance of the pole (Art. 214).

(2) If a linear conductor forming part of a closed circuit be moved across the lines of force, so that a figure in the conductor looking along the lines of force is carried by the motion to its left, the induced current will enter by its head and leave by its heels (Art. 215).

(3) If a closed conductor carrying a current approach towards a closed conductor not carrying a current, a current will be induced in the latter conductor in opposite direction to the battery current (Art. 217).

(4) If a conductor be moved so as to include fewer lines of magnetic force, there will be a right-handed induced current whose electro-magnetic effect is to increase the number of lines of force (Art. 216).

(5) If the strength of a current, or the magnetism of a magnet, be diminished, every conductor in its field will experience a current right-handed to the lines of force (Art. 218).

(6) If the current be established in a conducting circuit, an inverse extra current will be developed in the circuit itself (Art. 220).

It is almost superfluous to remark that in each case a reversal of the direction of motion or of the change also reverses the direction of the induced current.

222. Currents induced in Solid Conductors moved in the Magnetic Field.—For the development of induced

currents it is not necessary to have wires forming closed circuits, since induced currents occur whenever a conducting mass is moved through a magnetic field across the lines of force. This is easily shown by the resistance experienced in drawing a metal sheet between the poles of a strong electro-magnet. A piece of copper (usually shaped like a saw), on being drawn through air between the poles of the electro-magnet feels to the operator as if it were being drawn through some viscous fluid like honey or treacle. This is obviously due to the induced currents in the metal sheet which oppose the motion.

The same thing is often shown by suspending a copper cube by a fine string between the poles of the electro-magnet (Fig. 214). After putting torsion on the string, by rotating the cube

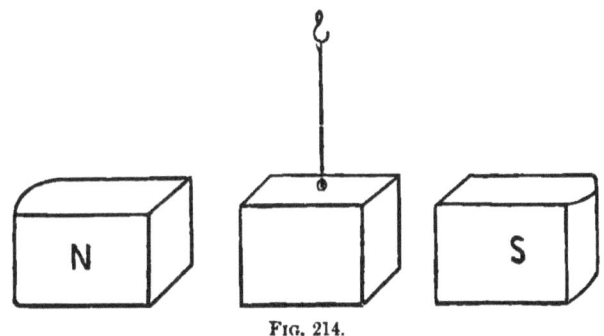

Fig. 214.

several times, it, when left to itself, with the magnet unmade, spins rapidly round, untwisting the string. If while the string is untwisting contact be made with the battery, the cube is rapidly pulled up, as if it were meeting with resistance in the air; but on breaking contact again it goes on spinning as before.

Before Faraday's discovery of induced currents, Arago had observed that if a horizontal copper disc be rotated rapidly, a magnet needle suspended by a fibre over its centre is deflected in the direction of rotation, and if the rotation is rapid enough, the magnet also spins round, following the motion of the disc.

223. Clarke's Magneto-Electric Machine or Dynamo.

—We proceed now to some practical applications of induced currents. We take first the magneto-electric machine or dynamo, all forms of which depend on the generation of electricity by the rapid movement of a conductor in a magnetic field. As in describing telegraphic apparatus, we shall confine ourselves to very few instruments.

Of these, Clarke's machine was one of the earliest; it is very simple in construction, and still continues more or less in use for medical purposes.

It consists (Fig. 215, *a*) of a single horse-shoe magnet, or a battery of three magnets, in front of the poles of which revolve on a spindle passing between them two bobbins of wire (*BC*) containing soft iron cores.

Suppose we are looking down on the bobbins, and consider the nature of the pole facing us. When opposite the north pole of the permanent magnet, this pole is a north pole by induction, and *vice versa*. Hence the pole of the bobbin *B* in half a revolution changes from north to south, that is, it will continually be losing north-polar magnetism. The current induced in the bobbin therefore opposes the change, and circulates round the coils in a direction against the hands of a watch. For exactly the same reason, the current in the bobbin *C*, which, in the same half revolution, goes from the south to the north pole of the permanent magnet, will be with the hands of a watch. The current in each bobbin is therefore reversed at each half revolution.

Chap. VI.]   *Current Induction.*   333

The arrangement of the bobbins is shown in section in

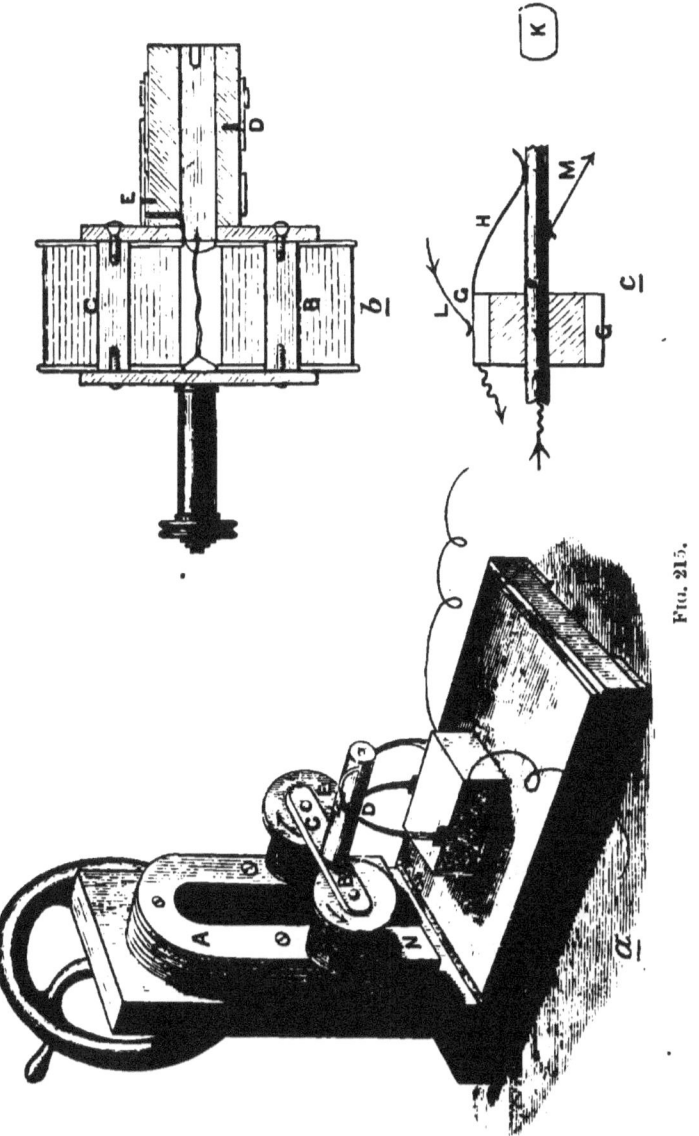

Fig. 215, *b*. The wires from the bobbins are brought to a pair of common terminals in such a manner that both bobbins tend to send a current in the same direction through the external circuit. One of these terminals is connected with the metal spindle, on which fits closely an ebonite cylinder carrying on its surface two metal ferrules whose arrangement depends on the use to which the machine is to be put; they are shown by D and E. One of them (D) should be connected by a screw which passes through the ebonite with the metal spindle, and thus with one terminal of the bobbins. The other terminal is insulated from the spindle but connected with the ferrule E. The current is carried away from the ferrules by metal springs which continuously press against them as they revolve (Fig. 215, a).

If the ferrules are complete circles running side by side round the ebonite cylinder, the machine gives alternating currents. If they are made the two halves of one ferrule insulated from each other so that the same spring which is in contact with D during one half its revolution is in contact with E during the other half revolution, it is a commutator reversing the current at each half revolution, and so making a continuous current in the external circuit; just as in Delezenne's Circle (Fig. 211).

For medical purposes, the principal current is short-circuited at each half revolution, thus bringing in the direct and inverse extra current in the external circuit, of which we have already noticed the high E.M.F. and remarkable physiological action. This is accomplished, where the two half ferrules D and E are separated by a spiral line, making D broad where E is narrow, and *vice versa*. The contact springs in part of the revolution press one on D and the other on E, the current then passing through the external circuit; at another part both at once press on D, when the current is short-circuited. At the opposite part both press on E, again short-circuiting the current.

The same effect is often obtained by simply connecting one terminal of the wire with the metal of the spindle (F, Fig. 215, c), the other being connected with an insulated ferrule (G) upon the spindle. A spring (H) in connection with this latter ferrule also presses against the spindle, and while it presses short-circuits the current. By filing away the opposite faces of the spindle to the form shown at K, the spring (H) ceases to touch the spindle for a moment at each half revolution, and the current suddenly passes through the external circuit (L—M). These changes are accompanied by strong extra currents.

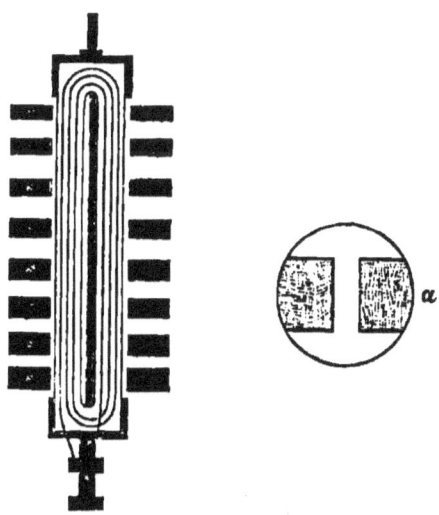

Fig. 216.

224. **Siemens' Dynamo.**—Much power is lost in Clarke's machine through the bobbins never being in the strongest part of the field, that is, between the magnet poles. To remedy this defect, Siemens' armature (Fig. 216) was

invented, consisting of a long iron framework (seen in section Fig. 216, *a*) with the wire coiled in a long flat coil. This, being narrow, can be made to rotate in a cylindrical cavity cut between a row of north and south poles of permanent magnets. Still further power was obtained by substituting electro- for permanent magnets. The electro-magnets were at first charged by an external machine or battery; but it was soon found that better results were obtained by diverting the whole or part of the current induced in the armatures through the electro-magnet coils. As was pointed out above, the residual magnetism starts the current, which then rises rapidly to its maximum for the given rate of rotation.

225. The Gramme Machine.—There is one other machine whose armature is so peculiar in construction as to deserve special notice, and it is the parent of a class of machines now very widely used. This is the Gramme machine. In it the armature revolves between the poles of a powerful permanent or electro-magnet (*M*). It consists of a cylindrical ring (Fig. 217, *a*) made of soft iron, upon which is coiled a continuous wire, forming in itself an unbroken circuit. This coil, at thirty-two points equally distributed along it, has wires soldered to it (*AB* . . .), which are in connection with thirty-two separate copper pieces (*C*), carefully insulated from each other by mica plates, and surrounding the spindle of the armature. Against this cylinder of separate copper pieces, above and below it, press two metal brush collectors, which are connected with the terminals (*FG*) of the machine.

To explain the action we will first consider it as an electro-motor. Taking the dissected diagram (Fig. 218), the current enters by the terminal (*A*), and, through the brush *C* enters

Fig. 217.

Y

the coils at *b*, where it is divided, part going through the coils on the semicircle *bca*, and part through those on the semicircle *bda*. These parts unite again at *a*, and pass by the brush *D* to the terminal *B*, by which the current returns to the battery.

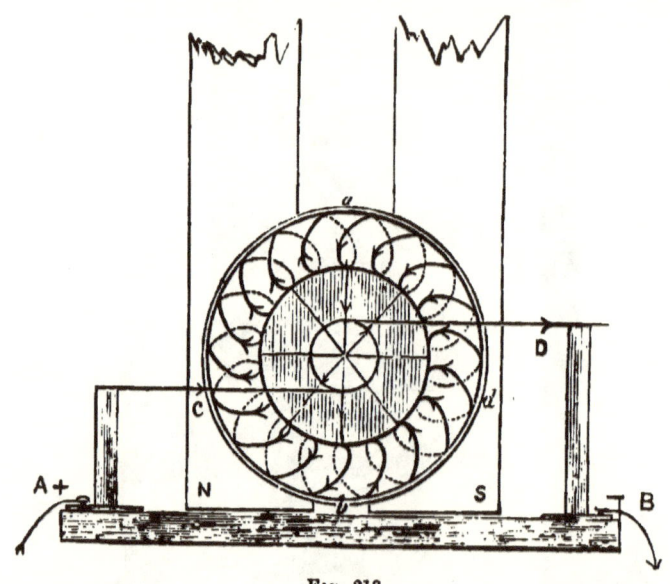

Fig. 218.

The wire coiled round the iron core of the semicircle *adb* tends to make it a magnet of horse-shoe type, having a south pole at *a*, and a north pole at *b*. In the same way, the current in coils round the iron core of *acb* being in the opposite direction, also make a south pole at *a* and a north pole at *b*. Thus the iron circular core has a double south pole at *a* and a double north pole at *b*. These will be repelled and attracted by the poles of the permanent magnet, *a* being driven in the direction *ac*, and *b* in the direction *bd*. This process is repeated as each successive portion of the coil comes in contact with the brush, and a continuous rotation is maintained in the direction $a-c-b-d$.[1]

Applying Lenz's law, we see that if we cause the armature to revolve, an induced current is developed in opposite direction to the battery current which would cause the rotation. This is the action of the machine when used as a dynamo.

In powerful machines electro-magnets are used for the field magnets, and these may be charged by diverting part or the whole of the current through them. But the power of the machine is seen in a small model, turned by hand, and weighing less than a hundredweight, by which 6 inches of thin platinum wire may be made red-hot, the phenomena of electro-dynamics and electro-magnetism exhibited, a series of small incandescent lamps lighted up well, and a small arc lamp (of Browning's pattern) lighted up as well as by eight or ten Grove cells.

226. The Incandescent Electric Lamp.

—One of the great uses for dynamo-machines in the future will probably be the generation of electricity for lighting purposes, and it will be convenient to say here a few words about this application. There are two distinct modes of lighting,—by incandescent or glow lamps, and by the arc lamp,—besides one or

[1] The present writer has lately made a model to illustrate the above action of the Gramme ring. A circular coil of iron wire is wound, as in the ring, with insulated copper wire, making a continuous coil. To this are soldered two wires at opposite extremities of a diameter. This is supported on a simple framework of wood, and pivoted, with its plane horizontal, between the poles of a horseshoe magnet, the two straight wires dipping in the commutator cup, which is placed axially between them, just as for the small electro-magnet of Fig. 187, a. On passing the current of one or two cells, the ring rotates rapidly.

two other methods which hold an intermediate place between these two.

All the incandescent lamps (Fig. 219) at present in use consist of one or more filaments of carbon (a), of horse-shoe form, attached at their ends to stout platinum wires b, c, which are fused through the glass of the small globe d. These globes are exhausted by a Sprengel mercury pump, and then hermetically sealed. By different inventors the whole vegetable kingdom has been ransacked to find the

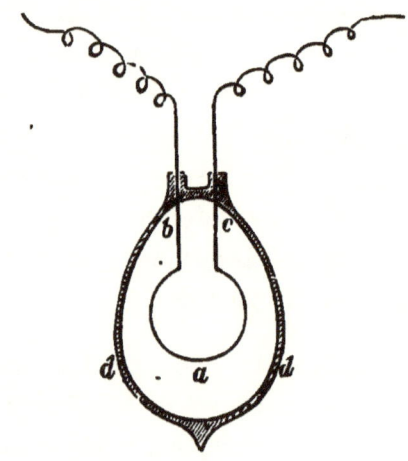

Fig. 219.

fibre which yields the most suitable carbon filament. These are heated (air being excluded) to expel water and gases, and then compressed in a mould. The chief difference between the lamps in use is the source and mode of preparation of the carbon filament, and the nature of the residual gas.

These lamps can now be constructed of very uniform resistance, and the most economical arrangement is that in multiple arc (Fig. 220), all the lamps being hung between two stout copper wires, which carry the battery current. In this way of arranging them, the greater the number of lamps the smaller the external resistance (Art. 166), the current being equally divided between them all. The same general principles as to external and internal resistance hold for dynamos as for batteries, and where the external resistance is very small, the best dynamo will be that of least resistance (Art. 163). Moreover, the E.M.F. required in the circuit is small, but the quantity of electricity very great. In this case we are forbidden to have our dynamo armatures coiled with great lengths of thin wire, as in that case the internal resistance becomes too large. Dynamos are therefore constructed with few coils of thick wire, or, by Mr. Edison, with copper rods instead of wire coils. In these cases the E.M.F. is very

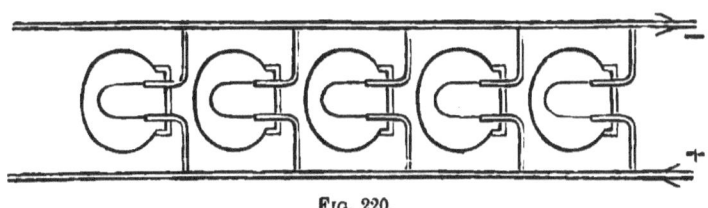

FIG. 220.

low, and the requisite quantity of electricity in the circuit is obtained by very high speed of revolution, which in some machines varies from 1500 to 2000 revolutions per minute, this speed being attained by a steam- or gas-engine.

Among the advantages these lamps offer for domestic illumination is the absence of the poisonous products of combustion, which make gas-lighted rooms absolutely fatal to plants, and, in the absence of perfect ventilation, deleterious to human health. The heating effect is small, since, although the carbon filament is at a very high temperature, its mass is so small that the quantity of heat given out never makes even the globe unpleasantly warm to the touch. The light can be placed in any position, as under water, or in contact with inflammable materials, even in mines, where the air itself forms an inflammable compound, without danger of fire. Even if the globe were accidentally broken, the carbon would be burnt up and the light extinguished instantaneously, before any material, however near (except an inflammable gas), could come in contact with its heated filament. Moreover, the low E.M.F. of the current makes insulation a matter of great ease, and removes the peculiar dangers incident to electrical apparatus of high potential when carelessly handled.

227. The Arc Lamp.—With arc lights, the light appears between the extremities of two carbon rods, which are kept at a slight distance apart in air. The carbons are both burnt away, though unequally, that forming the positive terminal the more rapidly. To prevent the reduction and extinction of the light by the consuming of the carbons, various forms of automatic regulator have been invented. The principle of them can be understood from the very simplest—

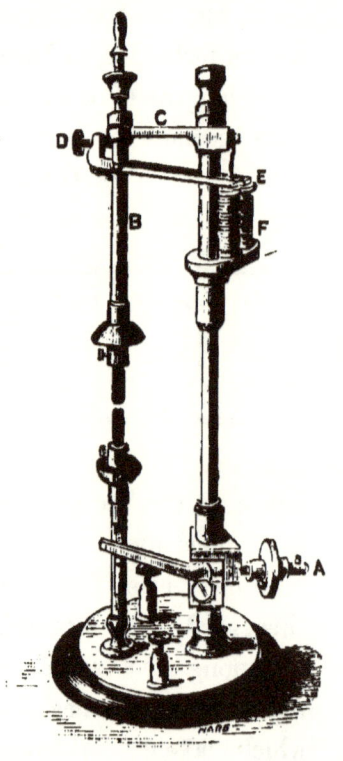

FIG. 221.

that of the Browning lamp (Fig. 221). Its simplicity depends chiefly on the fact that the lower carbon is fixed, but its position can be regulated by hand by means of the milled head (A), which, acting on a lever, raises or depresses the lower carbon, which should be negative. The upper carbon is held by a brass rod (B), which slides freely in the upper framework, and naturally slides down until it rests on the lower carbon. The sliding rod is pressed by a small detent (D) at the end of a lever, whose opposite end (E) forms the armature of a small electro-magnet (F). The current passes through this electro-magnet to the positive carbon, and across the arc to the negative. As soon as the current passes, the detent presses on the sliding rod, and by its friction prevents the carbon from falling; but as the carbons are consumed, the resistance grows greater, the current falls off, and the detent loses its hold, causing the carbon to slide down. In a properly regulated lamp, the friction of the detent and the strength of the electro-magnet are so well balanced always that the carbon falls regularly, with but small flickering of the light.

228. Source of the Voltaic Arc.—The carbons must be at first in contact. The current, encountering great resistance at the point of contact, heats the carbons red-hot, making the air round them also hot, and therefore rarer, and a better conductor. As the carbons burn away, the current is still maintained by a series of disruptive discharges through the hot air. These disruptive discharges are accompanied by a stream of particles of carbon in an incandescent state, which fly from the positive to the negative pole, as is proved by the fact that the positive burns away about twice as fast as the negative carbon, and by the form of the carbons, the positive being regularly pointed, but with a hollow extremity, and the negative irregularly convex (Fig. 222).

Fig. 222.

229. Arrangement of Arc Lamps.

—In arranging these lamps it is impossible to use "multiple arc," as the resistance in each changes so rapidly that we should have at each instant only the one offering least resistance alight, and all the others extinguished, because the current passing in each is inversely as the resistance (Art. 166). They must therefore be arranged in continuous series (Fig. 223).

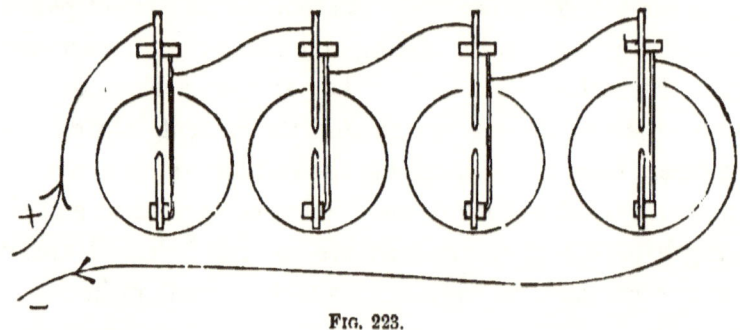

Fig. 223.

The current which will then light one will light any number, but it is obvious that the E.M.F. must be proportional to the number of lamps in circuit, to keep up the current against the increased resistance. In this case the external resistance is necessarily very great, and the dynamo or internal resistance comparatively insignificant. Hence in constructing dynamos for arc lamps, it is usual to make long coils of thin wire for the armature, and the speed of rotation can be made more moderate— about 400 revolutions per minute.

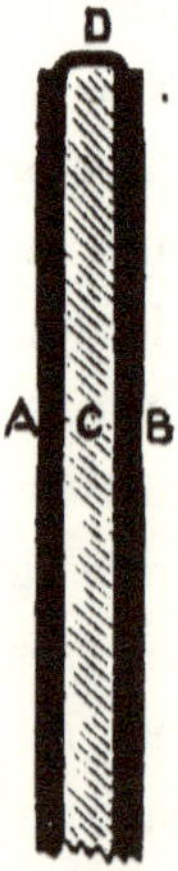

230. Jablokoff Candle.

—An intermediate form of lamp is the Jablokoff Candle (Fig. 224) used in Paris. This consists of two parallel carbon rods (AB) separated by a thin layer of kaolin or china clay (C), and crossed by carbon filament (D) at the top. The

Fig. 224.

voltaic arc is formed between the two carbons at first, and by its heat makes the kaolin incandescent, tending to make the light more steady. To secure an equal consumption of both carbons, a form of dynamo which gives alternate currents must be used. The principle will be understood from Clarke's machine (Art. 223).

231. **Induction Coils.**—We have already noticed the great E.M.F. possessed by certain induced currents, compared to that of the battery current by which they are induced. In the construction of an induction coil the aim is to heighten as far as possible the E.M.F., so as to give us results comparable with those obtained by statical electricity. The principle is this:—Make a primary circuit by a stout wire coiled a few times round a bundle of soft iron wires, so as to make the strongest electro-magnet possible for the dimensions. Round this place a secondary coil consisting of a vast number of turns of thin wire. If we rapidly make and break contact in the battery circuit, each time the electro-magnet is made or unmade, an inverse or direct current passes in the secondary coil. The E.M.F. of this current depends on (1) the strength of the magnetic field; (2) the number of turns in the wire of the secondary coil; (3) the rapidity with which the current in the primary is made and broken.

The parts in an induction coil (Fig. 225) are, in addition to the battery, (1) a commutator (A), by which the current is admitted, and by which its direction can be reversed; (2) a contact breaker (B), for alternately making and breaking contact in the primary; (3) a condenser (C), which makes the breaking of contact more sudden; (4) the primary coil and core; (5) the secondary coil, with insulated sliding terminals (GH).

The Commutator (Fig. 226).—This usually consists of a solid ebonite cylinder, having holes at either end for admitting a

Fig. 225.

spindle in two parts. Upon its surface are fastened two brass plates connected by wires with the two ends of the

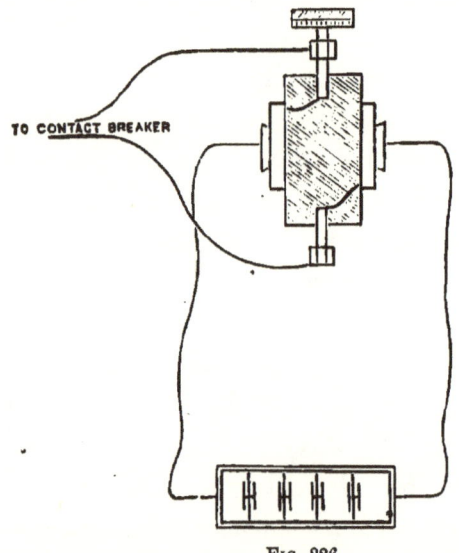

Fig. 226.

spindle; and against them press brass springs, which, by binding-screws, are connected with the battery. The two uprights in which the spindle works are insulated from each other, but connected with the contact breaker.

The Contact Breaker.—This in large coils is an independent engine, but in small coils is worked by the electromagnet of the primary coil. The end (*A*) (Fig. 227) of the core is a powerful magnet pole, and attracts the hammer-shaped piece of soft iron (*B*) which is carried by a stiff spring (*C*). On this stiff spring opposite to *B* is a

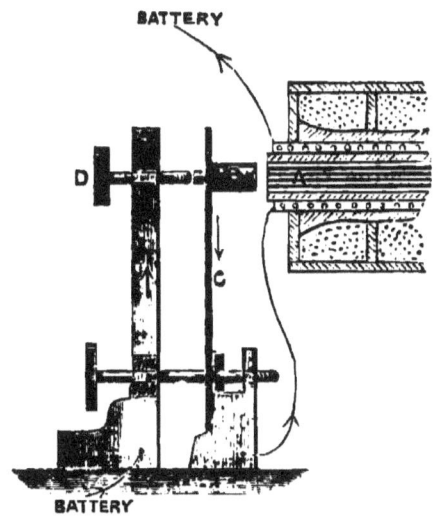

FIG. 227.

metal stud, which makes contact by pressing against the adjustable screw *D*. The passing of the current makes the electro-magnet, which attracts *B*, and breaks the circuit in doing so. *B* continues rapidly vibrating backwards and forwards. The opposed surfaces must be of platinum, as any other metal is rapidly oxidised, and the oxide acts as a non-conductor to the current.

The Condenser (Fig. 228).—This is made of sheets of tinfoil, separated by silk or stout paper soaked in paraffin; the alternate sheets are connected with the opposite terminals of the contact breaker. It is usually folded in a case, forming the

Fig. 228.

base of the instrument. The object of it is to reduce the direct extra spark in the primary coil induced by making and breaking contact. Without a condenser we have a bright spark between the screw and stud each time contact is broken, which, by prolonging the current, increases the time occupied in destroying the magnet, and thus diminishes the E.M.F. of the induced current. With a condenser the first effect of the extra spark is to charge the condenser, and its E.M.F. is thus rendered so low that hardly any spark passes, the condenser being discharged again by the extra spark on making, which is in the opposite direction.

Fig. 229.

The Primary Coil (Fig. 229).—This is composed of a few thicknesses of stout copper wire (B) surrounding a bundle of soft iron wires (A). The inner coil is connected with the battery through the contact breaker.

The Secondary Coil.—This (*C*) is coiled outside the primary coil, very great care being taken to secure good insulation on account of the high E.M.F. of the current passing through it. Each wire is separated from its neighbour by some hard insulator, and care taken that no two parts of the coil at a great difference of potential shall be near to each other. This is accomplished by dividing the secondary coil into compartments by partitions of vulcanite, the coils in successive compartments being connected in series, and the current passing from the inside to the outside of one compartment, and from the outside to the inside of the next. The length of wire on some secondary coils is as much as fifty miles. The ends of the wire of the secondary coil are connected to terminals which can be adjusted by a pair of insulated handles.

232. Experiments with the Induction Coil.—By large induction coils, sparks of length up to 2 feet have been obtained. They appear continuous, but their discontinuous character can be shown by rotating a coloured disk or a spoked wheel under the illumination of the spark, and it will be seen the colours or spokes do not blend, but stand separately, as they could not do were the light continuous. When the spark passes through a wide air space, the effect is probably due almost wholly to the direct induced current, as this, by its higher E.M.F., can break through a greater air space than the inverse. This is shown if we connect the terminals of a Leyden jar with the terminals of the secondary circuit, which, if there be a large break in the wire through which the spark has to pass, will be charged by the direct current, but without this break the direct and inverse current passing in equal quantities neutralise each other.

If we connect the platinum electrodes of a voltameter with the terminals, water will be decomposed, but mixed gases will be given off at both electrodes. If, however, we leave an air space across which the spark breaks, we shall find the gases, separated by the direct current only, collected at the electrodes.

The power of the secondary spark can be much increased by connecting the terminals with the inner and outer coats of a Leyden jar. This condenses the spark, making fewer and shorter sparks pass, but those sparks are of much increased intensity. By this means metals and other substances can be deflagrated for spectroscopic examination or other purposes.

Many chemical combinations can be made by the spark from an induction coil. Thus a minute spark is sufficient to cause hydrogen and oxygen to combine with explosive violence, forming water. The passage of the current through an hermetically sealed tube of air causes the oxygen and nitrogen to combine, forming nitrous oxide.

233. Discharge through rarefied Gas.—When the discharge takes place in air or any gas or vapour in a highly rarefied state, we obtain remarkable luminous appearances. A stream of coloured beams, formed of the gas in a state of incandescence, appears to flow from the positive to the negative terminal, and by examination with the spectroscope gives the spectrum of the gas. Frequently the stream of light has a stratified appearance, not yet well understood. The best way of observing these phenomena is by Geissler's tubes. These are made of glass tubes and bulbs (Fig. 230), in various shapes, with platinum wires fused through them at two points. After being filled with some gas, air, hydrogen, etc., they are exhausted by the mercury pump, and hermetically sealed. On connecting their terminals with the secondary coil, remarkable streams of light are observed, more like the play of the Aurora Borealis than any other natural phenomenon. In fact, it is more than probable that the Aurora Borealis is produced by a cause exactly analogous to these secondary discharges. We have noticed that it always accompanies a magnetic storm, during which the magnetic elements all over the earth show sudden changes, and earth currents appear in the earth, either as the cause or consequence of these magnetic changes. If we remember that air at a sufficient height must be, on account of its rarity, a conductor of electricity, we might expect currents to pass in this conducting envelope, induced by changes in the earth's magnetism.

Fig. 230.

234. Graham Bell's Telephone.—One of the most wonderful applications of induced currents in modern times is found in Professor Graham Bell's telephone, the first instrument capable of transmitting articulate language through hundreds of miles.

To understand the telephone, we will first show two experiments to prove the effect on which the telephone's action depends. Take a narrow bobbin (Fig. 231) of thin wire, and place it round the pole of a bar magnet, supported horizontally, including a sensitive galvanometer in the circuit. On taking a piece of thin plate iron, 2 or 3 inches in diameter, and moving it towards the pole, we have an induced current in one direction, and on moving it away from the pole, we have the induced current in the opposite direction. The origin of these currents is easily understood. The iron plate

Fig. 231

becomes a magnet under the induction of the permanent magnet, and on moving it towards the permanent magnet it acts inductively upon it, altering its magnetism, and therefore causing an induced current.

Remove now the galvanometer, and replace it by a similar magnet, also surrounded near one of its poles with a narrow bobbin of thin wire (Fig. 232). Opposite the pole of this magnet suspend an equal iron plate (B) with a long straw

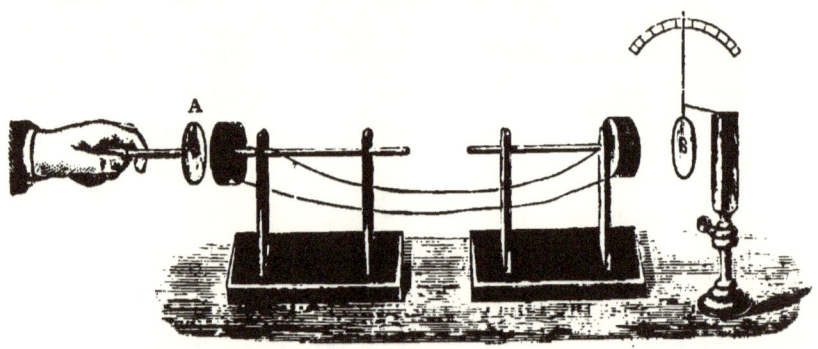

Fig. 232.

pointer attached (the suspension may be a pin passing through the straw), placed so as not to be drawn into contact with the magnet pole. If we now take the former iron plate (A), and move it about backwards and forwards with a regular vibratory motion, we shall soon see the suspended plate vibrating in sympathy with our movement of the first plate. This is an exaggerated model of a pair of Bell telephones, the first acting as transmitter, and the second as receiver.

To understand how sounds are transmitted by this apparatus we must remember that every sound consists of pulses communicated to the air, or the medium which conveys the sound, the number of these pulses per second defining the pitch of the note. It is clear, then, from the experiment, that if the plate A be made to vibrate at a certain definite rate, the plate B will vibrate at exactly the same rate, and therefore in unison with it. That is to say, the note given out from B will be of exactly the same pitch as the note sounded at A. This is equally true of Reiss's telephone (described Art. 210), and so far the Bell telephone is no improvement upon it. But the latter instrument does more, reproducing not only the pitch of the note, but also what musicians call the quality of the note, as well as the very complex modification and superposition of notes on which articulate speech depends. These produce on the transmitter a very complicated system of movements, which are by the induced currents absolutely copied at the receiver, the only difference being that the sound is very much weaker, and its quality is affected by the natural vibration of the metal plates, which gives the sound a peculiar nasal intonation.

The actual construction of the instrument, in which transmitter and receiver are identical, is shown in section, Fig. 233. A is a magnet about 4 inches long, and $\frac{1}{4}$ inch in diameter. Round one pole is wound a coil of wire (B), whose resistance is from 70 to 350 ohms. The magnet and coil are protected by a wooden case (*C*), of which the thin part serves for holding the instrument in the hand. At the broad end is the mouth-piece, consisting of a wooden ring, concave inwards, shaped like the mouth of a stethoscope, and immediately behind it a plate of ferrotype iron (*E*) (*i.e.* the iron plate used in the process known as ferrotype photography), loosely held by three screws, which leave it free to vibrate. At a very small distance behind this plate is the pole of the magnet, whose distance must be regulated by a screw (*F*), and carefully adjusted in each instrument. From the coil the wires are brought through the wooden case to two binding-screws.

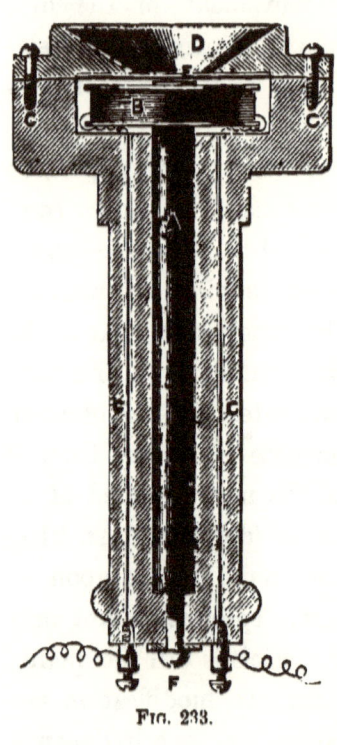

Fig. 233.

With two of these instruments at opposite ends of a circuit hundreds of miles in length, conversation can be carried on, but the sound given out is so feeble that it is inaudible unless the ear be placed in close proximity to the mouth of the receiver. The instrument is also peculiarly liable to disturbance from induction in the circuit; the make or break of contact in a telegraph wire, parallel to the telephone wire, but 20 feet distant, causing a harsh grating sound in the telephone, altogether overpowering the conversation. This is prevented by using a double wire, the return wire being united with the direct, though of course insulated from it.

It will easily be seen that the telephone of Graham Bell is a very sensitive galvanoscope, and may be substituted for a galvanometer in many cases where a delicate adjustment is required, as in Wheatstone's bridge, while it forms an essential feature in many pieces of apparatus required for special investigations, as the microphone, the induction balance of Professor Hughes, and the tasimeter of Mr. Edison, all of which followed rapidly on the invention of the telephone.

235. **The Microphone.**—The Microphone consists essentially of two pieces of carbon resting loosely one upon the other. A very simple form is that shown (Fig. 234), in which two square bars of gas carbon are fastened to an upright piece of wood, and joined by another square bar, also of gas carbon, tapering at its ends, which rest loosely in sockets sunk in the horizontal bars. On passing a battery current, great resistance is encountered at the loose contacts, and any vibration in the instrument makes rapid alterations in these contacts, therefore rapid alterations in the resistance, and therefore again rapid alterations in the current. These are easily observed by simply including a Graham Bell telephone in the circuit. If the wooden base of the microphone be scratched with the fingernail a very harsh grating sound is produced in the telephone, while the ticking of a watch is heard with remarkable loudness. In more sensitive forms of the instrument the walk of a fly over it is said to suggest the tramp of a regiment.

The forms of the microphone are infinite. A jar of cinders having electrodes sunk in it, resting on a vibrating plate, has been used with success, as also a heap of nails, or any conductors or semi-conductors piled loosely together.

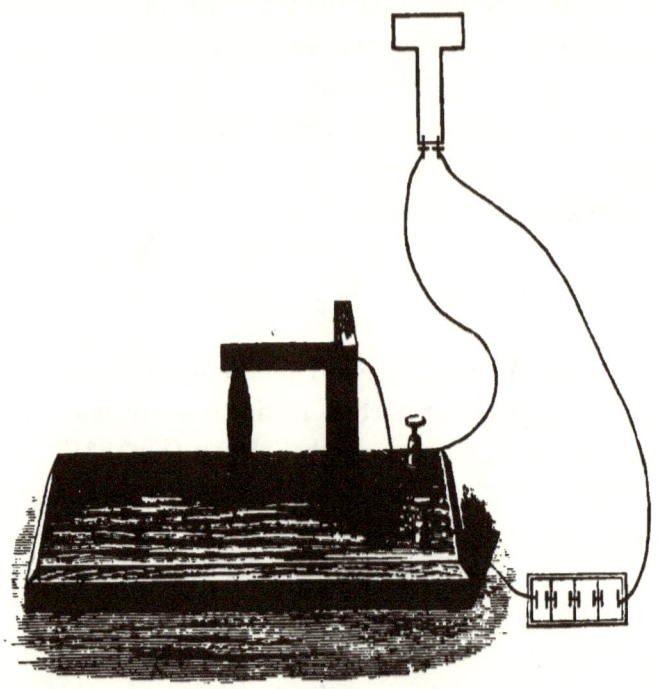

Fig. 234.

The invention of the microphone following rapidly on that of the telephone, led to attempts to use some form of the microphone as a transmitter, and the telephone as a receiver only. This idea has received its practical accomplishment in the loud-speaking Gower-Bell Telephone, used in the Telephone Exchange. The transmitter is a wooden plate, on the under-side of which is suspended a microphone (Fig. 235) of peculiar form. The transmitter also contains a small electro-magnet, which is included with the microphone in the battery circuit. This seems to act by heightening the extra current which accompanies each change in the main current. The receiver is a telephone of peculiar construction.

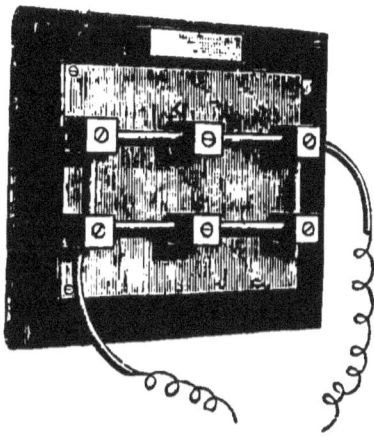

Fig. 235.

The inside is shown (Fig. 236, b), in which A is a strong permanent magnet, over whose poles are two coils of wire

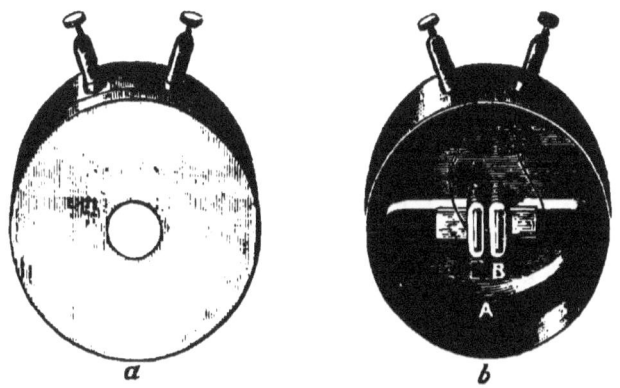

Fig. 236.

(B) with soft iron armatures. The varying strength of the current in the coils alters the magnetism of the cores, and causes vibration in the plate of thin sheet-iron, which is adjusted so as to be all but in contact with them. The plate is held in the outside case (Fig. 236, *a*), which has an aperture in the centre, through which the sound caused by the vibration of the plate escapes.

The sound from the Gower-Bell telephone is much louder than that obtained from the ordinary Bell telephone, but it can only be heard when the ear is placed within a few inches of the receiver.

QUESTIONS ON BOOK III.

Chapters I.—IV.

1. Given that one litre of hydrogen at normal temperature and pressure[1] weighs ·08957 grams: find what volume of hydrogen is given off for each gram of zinc consumed in each cell of the battery.

Ans.—·343 litre.

2. A litre of oxygen weighs 1·4298 grams. Find the weight of zinc consumed in each cell of a battery before 100 cub. cm. of oxygen have been collected in a voltameter.

Ans.—·581 gram.

3. In a decomposition of copper sulphate, it is found that ·59 gram of copper is separated. Find the amount of zinc consumed in each cell of the battery.

Ans.—·606 gram.

4. Four Grove cells in compound series are used to decompose hydrochloric acid. Find the total weight of zinc used in obtaining one gram of chlorine.

Ans.—3·66 gram.

---

[1] It will be assumed throughout this Exercise that gases are at normal temperature (0° C.) and pressure (760 mm. of mercury.)

Questions on Book III. 359

5. In the decomposition of hydrochloric acid find the volumes of hydrogen and chlorine respectively separated when one gram of zinc has been consumed in each cell of the battery. One litre of hydrogen weighs ·08957 gram.

Ans.—343 cub. cm. of each.

6. Draw the potential gradient for three cells in compound circuit and no external resistance. Show from the gradient that the current is the same as for a single cell.

7. Draw the potential gradient for three cells in compound circuit, each separated from the next by a wire whose resistance equals that of a single cell, a point midway between two cells being to earth.

8. Draw the potential gradient for one cell and for three cells in simple circuit having the same external resistance. Show that if the external resistance be large the current is nearly the same in both.

9. In a certain circuit the potential difference between the extremities of a resistance of 300 ohms is equal to 16 volts. Find the whole E.M.F. if the total resistance in the circuit is 2400 ohms.

10. Find the current strength in a circuit with E.M.F. of 9·8 volts and resistance 5 ohms.

Ans.—1·96 ampères.

11. Find the resistance in a circuit if an E.M.F. of 10 volts gives a current of 1·6 ampères.

Ans.—6·25 ohms.

12. Find the E.M.F. if the current strength in the circuit be 3·5 ampères, and the resistance 24 ohms.

Ans.—84 volts.

13. It is found experimentally that one coulomb of electricity sets free ·0000105 gm. of hydrogen. Find in ampères the strength of a current which has yielded ·035 grm. of hydrogen in two minutes.

Ans.—27·7 ampères.

14. Find the weights of silver, chlorine, and copper which will be set free by one coulomb of electricity.

Ans.—·001134 gram silver; ·0003727 gram chlorine; ·0003318 gram copper.

15. A current of two ampères passes for five minutes through a voltameter: find the total weight of water decomposed.

Ans.—·0567 grams.

Questions on Book III.

16. A battery of several cells is included in a circuit with a voltameter and tangent galvanometer. After passing the current for five minutes, ·098 grams of hydrogen were collected, and the average reading of the tangent galvanometer taken each ten seconds was 55°. Find the current in ampères, and find the constant multiplier required to convert the galvanometer indication into current measure in ampères.

ANS.—31·1 ampères: 21·8 nearly.

17. A battery of five cells when short-circuited with a galvanometer of no resistance gives a deflection of 9°. On introducing 20 ohms resistance the deflection sinks to 3°. Find the internal resistance of the battery.

ANS.—10 ohms.

18. A single cell when short-circuited gives in a galvanometer 45°, and when 2·5 ohms are introduced it falls to 26½°. Find the sum of the resistances of the battery and galvanometer, and calculate the galvanometer reading when five more ohms are introduced.

ANS.—2·5 ohms: 18½° nearly.

19. Using a sine galvanometer whose resistance is ·3 ohm, a battery gives 72° when short-circuited. On introducing 15 ohms resistance the deflection falls to 36°. Find the resistance of the battery.

ANS.—24 ohms.

20. A battery short-circuited gives 54° deflection to a sine galvanometer. Find the reading of the galvanometer when the total resistance is doubled.

ANS.—24° nearly.

21. A circuit, including battery and tangent galvanometer only, gives a deflection of 63°. On introducing 20 ohms additional resistance, the reading is 42°, and on introducing a coil of unknown resistance in place of the 20 ohms, the reading is 25°: find the resistance of the coil.

ANS.—54·5 ohms.

22. The resistance of the battery is known to be 24 ohms, and of the tangent galvanometer ·5 ohm. On short-circuiting the reading is 42°. On introducing a coil of wire the reading sinks to 25°. Find the resistance of the coil.

ANS.—22·8 ohms.

Questions on Book III. 361

23. A battery cell gives a resistance of 4·5 ohms, and the (tangent) galvanometer resistance is *nil*. On short-circuiting, the reading of the galvanometer is 14¼°. Find the reading on introducing 5 ohms resistance.

Ans.—7°.

24. Find the resistance of a silver wire one metre long, and sectional area ·0007791 sq. cm. (British Wire Gauge, No. 30).

Ans.—·195 ohm.

25. Find the sectional area of a copper wire of which one meter offers resistance 1 ohm.

Ans.—·0001642 sq. cm.

26. Find the length of a mercury column one sq. mm. in section, whose resistance is 1 ohm.

Ans.—1·04 metre.

27. Find the ratio of the resistance of silver and platinum wires of the same dimensions.

Ans.—1 to 6·02.

28. Find the internal resistance of a cell containing dilute sulphuric acid (5 per cent. acid), the plates measuring 12 cm. by 8 cm., and being separated by 2 cm.

Ans.—·1 ohm nearly.

29. Find the resistance of an iron telegraph wire, 30 kilometres long, and whose sectional area is ·1051 sq. cm. (B. W. G., No. 9).

Ans.—280·5 ohms.

30. Four cells, each of E.M.F. 1·8 volt, and resistance 1·5 ohm, with a galvanometer of 3 ohms resistance, are fitted up in compound circuit with an external resistance of 23 ohms. Find the current strength.

Ans.—·225 ampère.

31. Compare the current with that obtained from one cell with the same external conditions.

Ans.—As 55 : 16.

32. Six cells, each of E.M.F. 1·07 volt, and resistance 3·6 ohms, with a galvanometer of ·4 ohm resistance, are fitted up in simple circuit with an external resistance of one ohm. Compare the current with that obtained from one cell with the same external conditions.

Ans.—As 5 to 2.

33. Five Bunsen cells, each of E.M.F. 1·8 volts, and internal resistance 1·2 ohms, are used in compound circuit with a resistance of 24 ohms: find the current in absolute measure.

Ans.—·03 in absolute electro-magnetic units.

34. Will it be better to arrange six Daniell cells in simple or compound circuit, the resistance of each cell being ·6 ohm, and the external resistance 2·4 ohms?

Ans.—Compound series.

35. Twenty-four cells, each of E.M.F. 1·6 volt, and of 2·4 ohms resistance, are arranged in four rows. If the external resistance be 9 ohms, find the current strength.

Ans.—1 ampère.

36. Calculate the best arrangement of 48 cells, each of internal resistance 1·5 ohms when the external resistance is 12 ohms.

Ans.—Either two rows or three rows.

37. Find the resistance in a divided circuit whose two branches offer resistances 6 ohms and 30 ohms respectively.

Ans.—5 ohms.

38. What resistance is offered by a divided circuit of three branches, in which there are resistances of 6, 8, and 24 ohms?

Ans.—3 ohms.

39. The plates of a cell whose E.M.F. is 1·9 volt, and whose resistance is 2·8 ohms, are joined by three wires whose resistances are 2, and 3, and 6 ohms respectively. Find the current in each branch.

Ans.—·25 ampère; ·16 ampère; ·083 ampère.

40. Find how many grams of water would be heated 1° C. by immersing in it a wire coil whose resistance is 7 ohms, and passing a current of ·3 ampère for five minutes, supposing all the heat communicated to the water.

Ans.—·45 grams.

41. Eight Daniell cells, of each of which the E.M.F. is 1 volt, and resistance 3·5 volts, are arranged in compound circuit, and the terminals joined by a wire of 35 ohms resistance, which is immersed in

a kilogram of water. Find the rise in temperature of the water after the current has passed for ten minutes, supposing no heat to escape.

Ans.—·08° C.

Chapters V. and VI.

42. A straight bar magnet is placed in the field of a straight wire traversed by a voltaic current. Explain the position which the magnet will take up. If the direction of the current be reversed, what change will take place in the magnet's position?

43. A vertical wire carrying a current is brought near to different parts of a magnet, suspended so as to move horizontally. Explain at what parts of the surface attraction or repulsion will be shown.

44. A vertical wire carries an upward current. In what direction would it be carried if free to move under the earth's magnetic field?

45. A horizontal wire carries a current from east to west. In what direction would it move under the action of the earth's magnetism?

46. A straight wire is pivoted at one end so as to move freely in a horizontal plane, and is traversed by a current which flows from the pivot. Find the direction in which it will move under the earth's magnetism.

47. A straight and thin bar magnet is held parallel to the surface of water on which is a De la Rive's floating battery. Describe the position which the floating battery would take up under the magnetic force.

48. If a straight wire carrying a current be placed over the water near the floating battery, what position will it take up?

49. Describe how a coil of wire, traversed by a current, would place itself if suspended between the poles of a horse-shoe magnet.

50. Show that a galvanometer could be constructed by means of a coil of wire traversed by the current suspended between the poles of a powerful horse-shoe magnet.

51. How would a coil of wire, traversed by a current, place itself if suspended within the core of another coil traversed by the same current?

52. A beaker is placed on one pole of an electro-magnet and filled with liquid, which is traversed by a current from the centre to the circumference. What motion would be observed in the liquid?

53. A wide beaker is placed on one pole of an electro-magnet of horse-shoe form, and filled with dilute acid. At the bottom of the acid is put a zinc plate, and near its surface a copper plate, from both of which insulated wires pass to outside. Show that on connecting these wires together the liquid will begin to move.

54. When a wire is dipped into a small mercury cup on the pole of a magnet, and the current passed through it, the mercury is often seen to be rapidly rotating. How do you explain this?

55. The two rails of an ordinary railway are insulated from each other, but connected with the two terminals of a powerful battery, so that the current passes through the rails to wheels and axles of the carriages placed upon the line. Show that if the current were strong enough, the carriages would move along the line under the magnetic field of the earth, the direction of motion depending on the direction of the battery current.

56. A vertical wire, forming part of a closed conductor, is moved rapidly from east to west: show the direction of the induced currents.

57. A horizontal wire, forming part of a closed circuit, is placed east and west, and carried towards the north. What will be the direction of the induced current?

58. A copper hoop in a vertical plane is rapidly rotated about a vertical diameter, and a magnet is suspended horizontally at its centre. Show that the induced currents in the hoop will cause the magnet to be deflected in the direction of the rotation.

59. A metal sheet, held vertically, is drawn between the poles of an electro-magnet, its upper and lower edges being pressed by fixed springs which are connected with an external galvanometer. Draw a diagram showing the direction of the current in the galvanometer.

60. A stream of liquid is flowing between the poles of an electromagnet. In what position would you place electrodes to test for an induced current in the liquid?

61. A soft iron horse-shoe coiled with wire has its extremities placed opposite the poles of a horse-shoe magnet. If the ends of the wire be connected with a galvanometer at a distance, what currents will be observed on drawing the horse-shoe away from the magnet and moving it towards the magnet again?

62. Show that the swing of a compass-needle will be "damped" by hanging in a metal box.

63. If insulated wire be coiled round a metal cylinder, show that induced currents will travel round the cylinder at every change of current in the wire. How would you prevent these currents without abandoning metal as the material of which the cylinder is made?

BOOK IV.

THERMO-ELECTRICITY.

236. Definition of Thermo-Electricity.—If two rods of different metals be soldered at their ends, and not in contact elsewhere, on bringing the junctions to different temperatures, a current of electricity flows round the circuit made by the two metals. To this current, and the phenomena which accompany it, is given the name of Thermo-Electricity.

237. Elementary Experiments.—The phenomenon, which was discovered in 1821 by Professor Seebeck of Berlin, is very easily shown by a strip of copper bent down at its

FIG. 237.

ends, and soldered to a bar of bismuth (Fig. 237), a magnet being pivoted so as to swing freely between the copper and bismuth. After placing the compound bar in the magnetic meridian, so that the needle remains parallel to it, we observe, on heating one junction with a spirit-lamp, that the needle is immediately deflected, the direction of the deflection proving that a current flows from the bismuth to the copper through the hot junction. If, instead of heating with a spirit-lamp, we cool this junction with ice, the magnet will be deflected in the opposite direction.

The apparatus is made more sensitive by being arranged as in Fig. 238, with a galvanometer of low resistance between the binding-screws which are attached to the copper. In this case the heat of the finger applied to one junction will cause a considerable deflection in the galvanometer.

FIG. 238.

238. The Thermopile.—To still further increase the sensitiveness, a number of couples are arranged in compound series (Fig. 239, *a*), and are folded together as in Fig. 239, *b*, to bring all the junctions of the same kind into a small area, generally in form a square. The instrument then forms the essential part of a thermopile (Fig. 240), whose terminals are joined in circuit with a delicate galvanometer of low re-

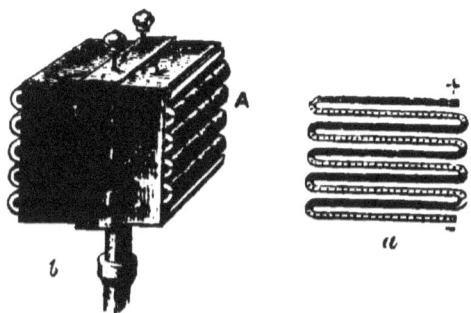

Fig. 239.

sistance. The cone of polished metal attached is useful in experiments on radiant heat to limit the area from which the radiations proceed on to the face of the thermopile. The

Fig. 240.

metals employed in the thermopile are usually bismuth and antimony, which of all the more common metals give the

2 A

highest E.M.F. at ordinary temperatures, though a couple of bismuth and tellurium would be of much higher power.

With a good thermopile a considerable deflection will be given to the galvanometer by holding the hand a yard from one face; otherwise a heated poker, or the blackened surface of a vessel containing hot water (Leslie's cube), may be employed. It was by help of the thermopile that Melloni and Tyndall carried out their researches on radiant heat, and that astronomers have been able to detect and measure the heat reaching us from the moon and the brighter fixed stars. This shows that it is in skilful hands infinitely the most delicate thermometer we possess.

239. Thermo-electric Power and Diagram.

—Seebeck thought that, with a given couple, the E.M.F. of the thermo-electric current was proportional to the difference of temperature. Such is only the case if the mean of the temperatures of the hot and cold junctions be constant. Thus, for each pair of metals we may determine at each temperature the E.M.F. in a circuit made of these metals, one junction being half a degree above and the other half a degree below the assigned temperature. This E.M.F. per degree of temperature at a given temperature is defined to be the thermo-electric power of that pair at that temperature.

Professor P. G. Tait, by measuring the E.M.F. of pairs of metals through the whole range of mercury thermometers, has shown that in each pair the change in thermo-electric power is proportional to the change in temperature. If, therefore, we construct a figure in which horizontal lines represent temperatures, and vertical lines the thermo-electric powers of a given couple, the extremities of the vertical lines would all lie on a straight line. Thus, in Fig. 241, if the base line represent any metal (say lead), the thermo-electric power of a lead-copper pair would be given by a line such as $P'P$, and of a lead-iron pair by such a line as $Q'Q$, the lead being positive to the iron through the part of the diagram where the iron line is above the base line, and negative where below it.

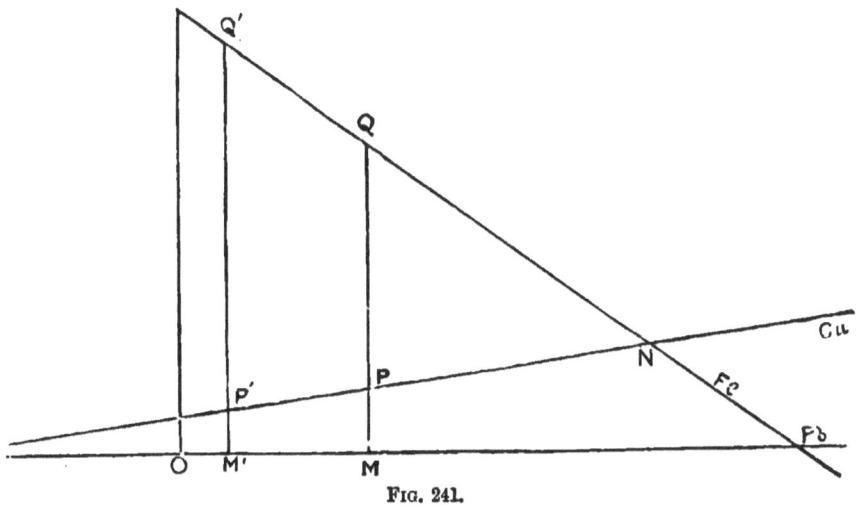

FIG. 241.

Moreover, it appears from experiment that if at a given temperature we observe the thermo-electric power of two metals $A - B$, and also that of a pair $C - B$, then their difference will always give us the thermo-electric power of the pair $A - C$. Consequently, if we draw one ordinate MPQ through the diagram for the temperature OM, so that PM represents on our assigned scale the thermo-electric power of Cu—Pb, and QM that of Fe—Pb, then QP will represent the thermo-electric power of Fe—Cu on the same scale.

Thus, taking as base line any metal (and there are theoretical reasons for choosing lead), each of the metals will be represented through ordinary temperatures by a straight line, and the thermo-electric power of any pair of metals can be at once taken from the diagram by drawing an ordinate through the assigned temperature, and measuring the distance between its section with the lines of the two metals. Such a diagram has actually been constructed by P. G. Tait, and Fig. 241 is a rough copy of the actual lead, copper, and iron lines in his thermo-electric diagram.

To find the E.M.F. of a given pair with junctions at the assigned temperature, we have only to find the thermo-electric power at the mean of the two temperatures, and multiply it by the range. Thus, if we require to find the E.M.F. of the Fe—Cu pair with junctions at temperatures denoted by M, M', the thermo-electric power at the mean temperature is $\frac{1}{2}(PQ + P'Q')$, and the E.M.F. is therefore $\frac{1}{2}(PQ + P'Q') \times (OM - OM')$. But by ordinary geometry this expresses the area of the trapeze $Q'Q\,PP'$. Since throughout the range copper is positive to iron, the direction of the current is from copper to iron, through the hot junction, or in the direction $P'PQQ'$.

It will be noticed in the diagram that the Fe and Cu lines intersect at a point N, whose temperature is about 284° C., and therefore well within the range of experiment.

At this point Fe and Cu are neutral to each other, below that temperature Cu being + to Fe, and above it − to Fe. The existence of such a point was demonstrated first by J. Cumming[1] soon after Seebeck's discovery. On arranging a

---

[1] Late Professor of Chemistry in the University of Cambridge. There is reason for believing that he independently discovered Thermo-electricity.

Fe-Cu couple brazed together at the junctions, and arranged as in Fig. 238, on heating one junction and leaving the other at the air temperature, the current in the galvanometer is seen to rise slowly to attain a maximum, when the temperature of the hot junctions is about 284°, and then slowly to sink again as the heating is continued.

This is quite in accordance with what the rule given above teaches us, since, if the hot junction were above, and the cool below the neutral temperature, the trapezium would degenerate into two triangles, of which that to the right must be subtracted from that to the left.

240. Electro-motive Force of Thermo-electric Currents.—On account of the extreme smallness of the E.M.F. in these currents, the most convenient unit is the microvolt or millionth part of a volt. The following table of thermo-electric values, or values of the thermo-electric power at temperature $t°$ C., was constructed by Professor Everett, from P. G. Tait's Thermo-electric diagram (*Trans. R.S.E.*, 1873). Bismuth and antimony, which are added to Professor Everett's list, have been calculated from Tait's data. It is assumed that each metal forms a couple with lead, and the signs + and − denote that the metal is respectively positive or negative to lead; when it is positive, the current passes from the assigned metal to lead through the hot junction. The range of temperature through which these values may be assumed is from −18° C. to 416° C., with the exceptions—zinc up to 373° C., and German silver, to 175° C. (The calculation of the values involves the assumption that the E.M.F. of a Grove cell is 1·97 volt.)

THERMO-ELECTRIC VALUES IN MICROVOLTS OF METALS AT $t°$ C. REFERRED TO LEAD.

Iron,	$-17·34 + ·0487\, t$
Steel,	$-11·39 + ·0328\, t$
Soft Platinum,	$+ ·61 + ·011\, t$
Hard Platinum,	$- 2·6 + ·0075\, t$
Alloy Platinum and Nickel,	$- 5·44 + ·011\, t$
Alloy Platinum, 95%/ Iridium, 5%	$- 6·22 + ·0055\, t$
Alloy Platinum, 85%/ Iridium, 15%	$- 5·77$
German Silver,	$+12·07 + ·0512\, t$
Zinc,	$- 2·34 - ·024\, t$
Cadmium,	$- 2·66 - ·0429\, t$
Silver,	$- 2·14 - ·015\, t$
Gold,	$- 2·83 - ·0102\, t$
Copper,	$- 1·36 - ·0095\, t$
Tin,	$+ ·43 - ·0055\, t$
Aluminium,	$·77 - ·0039\, t$
Palladium,	$6·25 + ·0359\, t$
Bismuth,	$62·84 + ·1084\, t$
Antimony,	$-35·03 - ·2246\, t$

Since the values vary greatly with the specimens of the metals employed, these values are only true in a general sense.

The above table enables us to solve many problems in the thermo-electric behaviour of pairs of metals. Thus the neutral point can be found by equating the thermo-electric values of the two metals concerned. The thermo-electric power at any temperature is given by simply subtracting the thermo-electric values and substituting the value for t.

The E.M.F. of a couple of two metals is found by taking their thermo-electric value at the mean of the temperatures of the hot and cold junctions, and multiplying by the range of temperature.

Example 1.—To find the neutral temperature of iron and zinc, we have from the table

$$-17\cdot 34 + \cdot 0487\, t = -2\cdot 34 - \cdot 024\, t.$$
$$\therefore \cdot 0727\, t = 15. \qquad \therefore t = 206° \text{ C.}$$

Example 2.—To find the thermo-electric value of an iron-zinc couple at temperature 100° C.

Thermo-electric value for iron-zinc

$$= (-17\cdot 34 + \cdot 0487\, t) - (-2\cdot 34 - \cdot 024\, t)$$
$$= -15 \quad + \cdot 0727\, t$$
$$= -7\cdot 73 \text{ microvolts, when } t = 100.$$

Example 3.—To find the E.M.F. of an iron-zinc couple when the junctions are at 15° C. and 185° C. respectively.

The mean of 15° C. and 185° is 100°, and thermo-electric value at 100° of iron-zinc $= 7\cdot 73$ by last example.

$$\therefore \text{E.M.F.} = 7\cdot 73 \times (185 - 15)$$
$$= 7\cdot 73 \times 170$$
$$= 1314 \text{ microvolts.}$$

241. Thermo-electric Diagrams for Higher Temperatures.

—P. G. Tait has pushed his investigations into the thermo-electric behaviour of metals to temperatures far above the range of a mercurial thermometer. He finds in several metals, especially iron and nickel, that the lines are by no means straight. Thus iron has two neutral points with lead, and it has certainly two and probably three neutral points with the platinum-iridium compound, whose line in the diagram is parallel to the lead line. In working problems, therefore, temperature outside the range named must not be considered as having any physical meaning.

242. Thermo-electric Currents in circuits of one Metal.

—Magnus has shown that if a circuit is formed of one metal homogeneous throughout, no unequal heating can produce thermo-electric currents. In the case of a single metal, when two parts are of different structure, as in hard and soft iron, a current is produced just as if they were two metals, on heating unequally the discontinuous portions. It seems that any cause which gives rise to molecular change in the wire may also give rise, on unequal heating, to currents of electricity. Thus if part of a wire be twisted, or hammered, or knotted, or magnetized, and heat applied on one side of the changed part, currents can usually be detected in the wire.

*243. The Peltier Effect.

—On the general principle of conservation of energy, it is clear that the thermo-electric current is developed at the expense of the heat at the hot junction—the tendency of the current, when no other work is done, being to neutralise the differences of temperature in the circuit, the hot junction being cooled, and *perhaps* the cold junction heated.

That this is actually the case was proved by Peltier, who showed that when a current from a voltaic element is passed round a bismuth-antimony couple, that junction in which the current goes from bismuth to antimony is cooled, and the opposite junction heated; that is to say, the current cools

Thermo-Electricity.

that junction which, when heated, gives a current in the direction of the battery current.

This is called the Peltier effect, and may be shown by two bars,—one of bismuth (AB, Fig. 242) and the other of antimony (CD), arranged in a cross, and soldered at the junction E. If the current from one or two elements be sent from

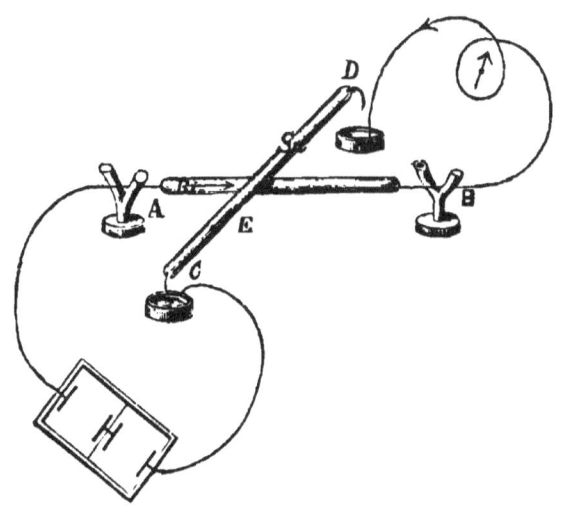

FIG. 242.

A to C, it cools the junction. This cooling is best shown by arranging the cross so that C, D are over mercury cups, and the cross rocking on two Y's at A and B, either C or D may dip into a cup, but not both at once. If a galvanometer be connected with B and the mercury cup at D, and after passing the current in direction AEC, the cross be rocked, there will be a current in the galvanometer in the direction DEB, thus proving a cooling at E.

*244. Theoretical Measure of the E.M.F. of a Thermo-electric Couple.—If a battery be included in any circuit of several metals it is theoretically easy to suppose that the battery current continues until the thermo-electric E.M.F. (caused by the heating and cooling of the junctions and other parts of the circuit, according to Peltier's law), balances the E.M.F. of the battery, when all current ceases. If we also suppose the current very weak and the resistance in the circuit inappreciable, the heat generated frictionally (Art. 169) will be very small, and we may treat the whole heat evolved as that due to the Peltier and similar effects. The energy given out by the battery has in this case been used up in heating and cooling the different parts of the circuit, and must therefore be equivalent to the total heat evolved, counting that absorbed negative. Now the energy given out from the battery is measured by $E\,I\,t$, when E is the E.M.F., I the current strength, and t the time. If I and t be each unity, the E.M.F. is the measure of the energy given out, and therefore equals the energy developed in the circuit per unit time by unit current. Thus if we allow unit current to pass round the circuit for unit time, the total heat evolved (counting that absorbed negative), according to Peltier's law, is equivalent to the E.M.F. of the thermo-electric circuit.

*245. **The Thomson Effect.**— Professor Cumming observed that at the temperature 284° C., at which the iron and copper are neutral to each other—that is, at the temperature represented by the point N on Fig. 241—the Peltier effect vanishes.

From this Sir W. Thomson argued that if the hot junction in an iron-copper couple be at 284° C., and the other at any lower temperature, no heat is absorbed at the hotter junction. We therefore have a thermo-electric current without any source of energy, unless heat is absorbed according to Peltier's law, but at other parts of the circuit than the junctions. This absorption can only be in the passage of the current from hot to cold, or from cold to hot, parts of the same metal. On experimenting with an unequally heated conductor of copper, it is found that the electric current, going from hotter to colder parts, transfers heat from the hotter to the colder parts; if the conductor were of iron, the transfer of heat would be from the colder to the hotter parts; heating and cooling being reversed with the direction of the current. Thus in a copper conductor the electric current tends to neutralise differences of temperature, but in an iron conductor it tends to exaggerate them. This electrical convection of heat, called the Thomson effect, has been proved by numerous experiments to exist in nearly all metals, but to vanish or become exceedingly small in lead and in certain alloys, whose lines on the diagram are parallel to the lead line.

It is the vanishing of the Thomson effect which gives the theoretical reason for choosing lead as the base line of the diagram.

246. Thermo-electric Batteries.—On account of the low resistance of thermo-electric couples, it has been proposed to construct batteries of numerous elements, arranged in compound series, to be used for telegraphy, electro-plating, and other purposes, but none of them have at present come into general use.

QUESTIONS ON BOOK IV.

1. Find the temperature of the neutral point of lead and soft platinum.
ANS. $-56°$ C.

2. Find the temperature of the neutral point of iron and copper.
ANS. $274°$ C.

3. Find the general thermo-electric value for a metal whose thermo-electric power at $0°$ C. is $-2·14$, and at temperature $50°$ C. is $-2·89$.
ANS. $-2·14 - ·015\,t$.

4. Find the E.M.F. of a soft platinum and iron pair, the temperatures of whose junctions are $15°$ C. and $175°$ C.
ANS. 2299 microvolts.

5. Find the number of bismuth-antimony pairs which will be required to give E.M.F. of 1 volt, the junctions being at temperatures $0°$ C. and $100°$ C.
ANS. 87.

6. Show that in a couple formed of two metals whose lines on the thermo-electric diagram are parallel to each other, the E.M.F. is directly proportional to the difference in temperature of the junctions.

7. Show that if in any couple the temperature of the hot junction is at the same distance above the neutral temperature that the cold junction is below it, no current will appear.

APPENDIX I.

ABSOLUTE UNITS IN C.G.S. SYSTEM.

247. Units and Measures.—The description of every physical quantity consists of a number, and a concrete thing of the same nature as that which is being described. Thus if we say a certain distance is 20 inches, the numerical part (twenty) expresses the ratio of the length to another length (the inch), the description presupposing a common understanding as to the nature of the inch. In this case the measure is twenty, and the unit an inch. If instead of the inch we wish to make the foot our unit, the measure is altered; in fact, 20 inches equals $\frac{5}{3}$ feet; or, again, equals $\frac{5}{9}$ yards. Thus we observe that the change of a unit changes all measures expressed in that unit, and the change in the measure is inversely proportional to the change in the unit.

248. Fundamental Units.—The fundamental units, from which all other units are derived, are those of length, mass, and time. There is great diversity in the units of these adopted in different countries, but the greatest care is taken by all civilised states to legalise one, and only one, unit with which all measures must be compared. Our own standard of length is the yard, and is defined by Act of Parliament as the distance between two transverse lines on two gold plugs in a bar of bronze deposited in the office of the Exchequer, the measure being taken when the bar is at 62° F.

The French standard of length is the metre, whose length

was made to equal, as nearly as possible, the ten-millionth part of the quadrantal arc of the earth in the longitude of Paris; but since such a measurement can only be made within tolerably wide errors of observation, the definition of the unit is the distance between the ends of a bar of platinum made by Borda, when the bar is at the temperature of melting ice. The subdivisions of the metre are the tenth or decimetre, the hundredth or centimetre, and the thousandth or millimetre. For all scientific purposes the French system of measure is used, owing largely to its being a decimal system. The unit of length we adopt is the centimetre. Its length, referred to British inches, is ·3937043, or rather more than one-third of an inch.

The British unit of mass is defined in the same way as the mass of a certain weight of platinum deposited in the office of the Exchequer, and denominated the Imperial Standard Pound Avoirdupois. The grain troy is defined as the seven-thousandth part of the pound avoirdupois.

The French standard is the mass of the Kilogramme des Archives, made of platinum by Borda, and representing as nearly as possible the mass of a cubic decimetre of distilled water at temperature 4° C.

The thousandth part of this, or the mass of a cubic centimetre of distilled water at 4° C., is chosen as the standard of mass, and called the gramme. This is found to contain 15·43234874 grains troy.

These are defined in their respective Acts of Parliament as standards of weight; but we see they are masses of metal, and their weights depend on the attractive force of the earth at the particular place where they are weighed, and their weight must change as they are carried either to places of different altitudes or different latitudes. If, however, any material body be balanced by an ordinary pair of scales *in vacuo* against the standard weight, it will also balance wherever the experiment be repeated, since the change of terrestrial gravitation will be equal on both the weight and its counterpoise. Thus it appears that in our ordinary commercial transactions, carried on by scales and weights, we are really dealing with masses, and not with weights, the so-called standards of weight being standards of mass.

The unit employed for time is always the second of our mean-time clocks. Since no clock-work can be made to go uniformly for ever, the standard unit of time cannot be defined as the second on a particular clock from which it can always be reproduced. The regulation of the clock depends on astronomical observations, and the constancy of the second hrough vast lapses of time assumes that the rotation of the earth is at a uniform rate, and also that the earth always takes the same time for its orbital revolution. It is by no means probable that either of these assumptions is true, though no doubt both are sensibly true during hundreds of years.

249. Mechanical Units.—Having established these three fundamental units—of length, the centimetre; of time, the second; and of mass, the gramme, we are able to express in terms of them every physical quantity whatever.

There are certain dynamical quantities which constantly recur in all physical science, whose nature and measurement we must briefly explain.

(1) *Velocity* is a property possessed by every moving particle at each instant of its motion. To define it we must know three things—the position of the particle in space, the direction of its motion, and its speed, or the rate with which it is moving. To represent the rate of motion we usually state the distance the particle would go supposing it to retain its present rate of motion for a certain time. Thus in speaking of the motion of a railway train we usually state it in *miles per hour*, meaning that if it continue moving for an hour at its present rate it will go so many miles in the

hour; not of course assuming that it has actually gone that distance in the hour, or will go that distance in the next hour. If we speak of the rate of a body falling under gravity, or of a cannon ball, we usually state it in feet per second.

It is very convenient for practical purposes to have many units of measurement, but for scientific purposes it is convenient to have only one, or at any rate to have units which may be with the least possible trouble converted into our assumed fundamental units. Thus we measure all velocities in centimetres per second, and we speak of a velocity of one centimetre per second as our unit velocity. Velocities can then be expressed by simple numbers—a velocity of 1000 meaning that the body is moving at the rate of 1000 centimetres per second.

(2) *Acceleration and Retardation.*—If the velocity of a particle is not uniform, it is at each instant either quickening or slackening its speed. To discover this we must observe the velocity at both ends of a certain interval, and find out whether it has changed during the interval, and if so, by how much. Thus acceleration is usually measured by the increase in velocity per second, not implying that the acceleration is uniform during a second, but only representing the amount by which the velocity would increase, supposing the increase to go on uniformly for one second. An acceleration of 1000 would then mean that the body would have a velocity of 1000 cm. per second greater at the end than at the beginning of a second during which the same acceleration was maintained. The unit of acceleration is therefore an acceleration of one cm. per second every second.

The best illustration of uniform acceleration is afforded by a body falling *in vacuo* near the surface of the earth. The acceleration of gravity at the level of the sea in the latitude of Paris is found to be 981, and will be sensibly the same at all altitudes which differ by only a few hundreds of yards or metres. This means that any particle falling toward the

Absolute Units in C.G.S. System.

earth increases its velocity by 981 cm. per second per second, and if it be projected upwards from the earth it will suffer retardation, or will lose velocity at exactly the same rate.

In England, feet and seconds have till recently been commonly used as units of length and time, and in terms of them the measure of gravitation at London is taken to be 32·2, denoting that the velocity of a falling body increases by 32·2 feet per second per second.

(3) *Force* is commonly defined as that which changes or tends to change a body's state of rest or motion. This comprises all such physical magnitudes as weights, pressure, tension, strains, etc. By the weight of a body we denote the pull exerted by the earth upon it, or by it upon the earth, for these two are equal and in contrary directions. We have noted that, if unopposed, the weight of any body whatever will alter its state of rest or motion in the vertical line by 981 units of velocity per second. Thus the change of motion caused by gravitation is independent of the mass of the body experimented on, but the pull of the earth, or the *Force* of gravitation, is not independent of mass. For all experience shows that if we suspend by a string a small mass, the string assumes a state of tension, which prevents gravitation from causing change of state; but if we suspend a larger mass the string can no longer bear the strain, and breaks, allowing gravity to produce its change of state in the body. We are thus led to see that the description of a force must express the mass of the body as well as the acceleration it will, if unopposed, produce in the body. Thus a *force* of 10 lbs. must mean a force which would produce in a mass of 10 lbs. the same acceleration as gravity, that is, an acceleration of 32·2 feet per second per second, and this is shown experimentally to be the same as would produce in a mass of 1 lb. an acceleration of 322 ($=32·2 \times 10$) feet per second per second, or in a mass of 322 lbs. an acceleration of 1 foot per second per second.

For scientific purposes we take our cm., gm. and second as fundamental units of reference, and define our unit force as the force which will produce in 1 gm. unit acceleration, or a velocity of 1 cm. per second per second. This unit of force we call a *dyne*,[1] and the weight of a gram in the latitude of Paris and at the level of the sea is 981 dynes.

(4) *Work.*—Work is said to be done whenever a mass is carried through space in opposition to a force. Thus Watt took as standard the work done in raising a pound against the attraction of the earth through 1 foot, and this he called a "foot-pound." It must be noticed that no work is done in moving a body at right angles to the force acting on it, as, for instance, in carrying a body horizontally, unless it be done against the resistance of the air or friction, since, could the body be started on a perfectly smooth and level surface *in vacuo*, it would move on for ever without the expenditure on it of any work whatever.

In the absolute system we use cm. – dynes instead of foot-pounds, the cm.–dyne being the work done in opposing through a centimetre the force of 1 dyne, or in carrying 1 gram through a centimetre in opposition to a force which unopposed would give it unit acceleration. This unit is commonly now called an erg.[2] To find the number of ergs in a foot-pound we notice that 1 lb. mass = 453·593 gm. mass, and 1 foot = 30·48 cm., and the acceleration of gravity = 981 units. Hence in carrying 1 lb. through a foot against earth's pull, we carry 453·593 grams through 30·48 cm. against 981 units of force, which is the same work as expended in carrying 453·593 × 30·48 × 981 grams through 1 cm. against unit force,—that is to say, 1 foot-pound equals 13,560,000 ergs nearly.

(5) *Energy, Kinetic and Potential.*—The power of doing work in an agent is called its energy, and the amount of energy is simply measured by the number of units of work it

---

[1] Greek, δύναμις = *force*.   [2] Greek, ἔργον = *work*.

is capable of doing. We may first have energy due to a body's motion. A bullet flying through the air, on striking against a block of wood, sinks into it till it is brought to rest. The energy of the bullet caused it to do work, in overcoming the resistance of the wood to disintegration, or against the molecular cohesion of the wood. Now it can be demonstrated mathematically that for every such case the amount of work done by the moving body before it is brought to rest equals half the product of the mass of the body into the square of its velocity. If different parts of the body are moving with different velocities, the total energy may be taken as the sum of the energy of each particle computed as explained above. This kind of energy, which a body has in virtue of its motion, is commonly called Kinetic Energy.

A body may, secondly, have energy, in virtue of position or of work having been expended upon it, which is retained in the body, and can be recovered at any future time. Thus when a stone is carried up to a height and placed on the edge of a cliff, work has been expended in carrying the stone, without any change in the stone, except in respect to position relatively to gravitation. A very slight touch may dislodge the stone, and it will, in falling down, acquire kinetic energy, which, when it reaches the level from which it was carried, will exactly equal that expended in raising the stone. In every form of catapult or bow used in archery, work is first done against molecular forces in compressing the spring or bending the bow; and on loosing the trigger or detent, a large share of this energy is concentrated on the arrow or other projectile, which thus acquires a high velocity. Were it mechanically possible to bring all parts of the machine except the projectile absolutely to rest at the instant when the projectile leaves it, the energy of the projectile would numerically equal the work done in compression. This kind of energy is often called Potential Energy.

The same general principles apply to other physical phenomena. Thus if work be expended in heating a body, the energy of the heat is numerically the same as the work expended in heating it. If work be done in making an electrical separation or an electric current, the energy of the separation or of the current is the same as the original work done. These are only illustrations of the great principle of conservation of energy, of which we find many applications in electrical and magnetic phenomena.

(6.) *Rate of Working.*—The rate at which an agent works is in practice expressed in horse power. The horse power was defined by Watt to be the rate of working of an agent which does 33,000 foot-pounds of work per minute. In conformity with our notation, we should naturally express the rate of working in ergs per second. To convert the horse power into ergs per second, we notice that the horse power is 550 foot-pounds per second, and the foot-pound is 13,560,000 ergs. Hence the horse power is $550 \times 13,560,000 = 7\cdot46 \times 10^9$ ergs per second.

APPENDIX II.

TABLE OF NATURAL SINES AND TANGENTS OF ANGLES FOR EACH DEGREE.

Degrees.	Sine.	Tangent.	Degrees.	Sine.	Tangent.	Degrees.	Sine.	Tangent.
1°	·018	·018	31°	·515	·601	61°	·875	1·804
2°	·035	·035	32°	·530	·625	62°	·883	1·881
3°	·052	·052	33°	·545	·649	63°	·891	1·963
4°	·070	·070	34°	·559	·675	64°	·899	2·050
5°	·087	·087	35°	·574	·700	65°	·906	2·145
6°	·105	·105	36°	·588	·727	66°	·914	2·246
7°	·122	·123	37°	·602	·754	67°	·921	2·356
8°	·139	·141	38°	·616	·781	68°	·927	2·475
9°	·156	·158	39°	·629	·810	69°	·934	2·605
10°	·174	·176	40°	·643	·839	70°	·940	2·748
11°	·191	·194	41°	·656	·869	71°	·946	2·904
12°	·208	·213	42°	·669	·900	72°	·951	3·078
13°	·225	·231	43°	·682	·933	73°	·956	3·271
14°	·242	·249	44°	·695	·966	74°	·961	3·487
15°	·259	·268	45°	·707	1·000	75°	·966	3·732
16°	·276	·287	46°	·719	1·036	76°	·970	4·011
17°	·292	·306	47°	·731	1·072	77°	·974	4·331
18°	·309	·325	48°	·743	1·111	78°	·978	4·705
19°	·326	·344	49°	·755	1·150	79°	·982	5·145
20°	·342	·364	50°	·766	1·192	80°	·985	5·671
21°	·358	·384	51°	·777	1·235	81°	·988	6·314
22°	·375	·404	52°	·788	1·280	82°	·990	7·115
23°	·391	·425	53°	·799	1·327	83°	·993	8·144
24°	·407	·445	54°	·809	1·376	84°	·995	9·514
25°	·423	·466	55°	·819	1·428	85°	·996	11·43
26°	·438	·488	56°	·829	1·483	86°	·998	14·30
27°	·454	·510	57°	·839	1·540	87°	·999	19·08
28°	·469	·532	58°	·848	1·600	88°	·999	28·64
29°	·485	·554	59°	·857	1·664	89°	·999	57·29
30°	·500	·577	60°	·866	1·732	90°	1·000	∞

Edinburgh University Press:
T. AND A. CONSTABLE, PRINTERS TO HER MAJESTY.

www.ingramcontent.com/pod-product-compliance
Lightning Source LLC
Chambersburg PA
CBHW020101020526
44112CB00032B/802